surveying the literary landscapes
of terry tempest williams

∾

surveying the literary landscapes of terry tempest williams

NEW CRITICAL ESSAYS

Edited by

Katherine R. Chandler

and Melissa A. Goldthwaite

THE UNIVERSITY OF UTAH PRESS

Salt Lake City

The Defiance House Man colophon is a registered trademark of The University of Utah Press. It is based upon a four-foot-tall Ancient Puebloan pictograph (late PIII) near Glen Canyon, Utah.

Printed on acid-free paper

08 07 06 05 04 03

5 4 3 2 1

LIBRARY OF CONGRESS CATALOGING-IN-PUBLICATION DATA

Surveying the literary landscapes of Terry Tempest Williams : new critical essays / edited by Katherine R. Chandler and Melissa A. Goldthwaite.

    p. cm.

Includes bibliographical references and index.

  ISBN 0-87480-770-0 (pbk. : alk. paper)

 1. Williams, Terry Tempest—Criticism and interpretation. 2. Women and literature—United States—History—20th century. 3. Environmentalism—United States. 4. Natural history—United States. 5. West (U.S.)—In literature. 6. Landscape in literature. 7. Deserts in literature. 8. Nature in literature. I. Chandler, Katherine R., 1949–   II. Goldthwaite, Melissa A., 1972–

  PS3573.I45575 Z88 2003

  289.3—dc22

2003016690

Lines from "Wild Geese," in *Dream Work*, copyright © 1986 by Mary Oliver, cited in the essay by Lisa Diedrich, used by permission of Grove/Atlantic, Inc., and the author.

Reproduction of pages from *Leap* by Terry Tempest Williams, copyright © 2000 by Terry Tempest Williams, in the essay by Bart H. Welling, used by permission of Pantheon Books, a division of Random House, Inc.

The lines from "Delta," copyright © 2002, 1989 by Adrienne Rich, from *The Fact of a Doorframe: Selected Poems, 1950–2001* by Adrienne Rich, in the essay by Katherine R. Chandler, used by permission of the author and W. W. Norton & Company, Inc.

CONTENTS

ACKNOWLEDGMENTS

Our collaboration on this project began when a friend, Jennifer Cognard-Black, recognized our common interests in literature and the environment and introduced us. She sat patiently at lunch while we enthusiastically discussed everything from the conferences we'd attended in common to the intricacies of Williams's prose. Both the idea for this book and our friendship began that September afternoon. We are grateful to Jennifer, our colleague and friend, for introducing us.

Flurries of e-mails, another conference, and many conversations later, we sent out a call for papers and began to receive abstracts and essays. Only then were we able to imagine the true shape of this collection. We thank the contributors whose work is featured here. Their ideas energize ours, and we have enjoyed the process of getting to know so many who share our scholarly interests.

We acknowledge the reviewers whose support for this project made its publication possible and whose detailed suggestions made it a stronger collection. We also thank Marcelyn Ritchie and those at The University of Utah Press who contributed to the design and production of this volume.

Our academic institutions have also supported our work. Saint Joseph's University provided Melissa a summer faculty research grant in 2002, when we were working closely with contributors on their early drafts, and St. Mary's College of Maryland provided Katherine a two-course teaching release in the spring of 2003, when we were preparing the final manuscript. These gifts of time have made our project possible. In addition, we thank our colleagues, friends, and Katherine's husband who, through writing groups and informal conversations, have helped ideas emerge and essays transform.

The person whose shared interest has been most significant and heartening to us is our editor at The University of Utah Press, Dawn Marano. She has had a hand in shaping this volume at every stage and is a writer and editor extraordinaire. We are deeply grateful to Dawn for her knowledge, experience, and guidance and for her belief in the importance of this book.

Finally, we thank Terry Tempest Williams—for her writing, her activism, her presence. Throughout the process of developing this book, we have talked with contributors about the complicated balance required in writing with "critical distance" about texts that they and we love, texts that have changed both our personal and our scholarly lives. We thank Terry for giving us her work, which makes our work—our teaching and scholarship—a meaningful joy.

KATHERINE R. CHANDLER

MELISSA A. GOLDTHWAITE

∾

Beginning Words

INTRODUCTION AND INVITATION

A story is never random. It must be framed with fierce attention, trust, and affection.
> —Terry Tempest Williams,
> *Pieces of White Shell: A Journey to Navajoland*

In the beginning, there were no words.
> —Terry Tempest Williams, *Desert Quartet*

This collection is a beginning. In this beginning, however, there is a need for words. Terry Tempest Williams's stories invite stories of another sort that engage with her prose in the interrelationship of the diverse neighbors who constitute a literary community. Williams's ideas interact as do elements in an ecosystem, but we do not yet fully understand the finer points within her system. Just as scientists are still discovering how fire can enable rather than disrupt forest growth, critics have yet to define all the relationships among the concepts in Williams's vision. Tensions and oppositions abound in her works, as they do in the natural world, yet conflicting ideas in Williams's texts do relate. The scope and capacity of her vision are yet to be determined, and as critics, we have set our sights on ferreting out how those contradictions contribute to a coherent vision. This volume, the first collection of critical essays on Williams's work, is committed to reaching toward a more comprehensive understanding of her body of writings.

We have chosen to publish only new essays in order to broaden the discussion. Critical attention has focused on *Refuge: An Unnatural History of Family and Place*. The place of *Refuge* in Williams's oeuvre is undeniably important, but her surrounding works also raise questions that we have long wanted to discuss. In the spirit of "opening," we see this volume as an initiator, extending the scope of analysis to other works and other questions and other answers to questions that still perplex.

Background: Williams's Life, Her Work, Her Words—So Far

Daughter of Diane Dixon Tempest and John Henry Tempest III, Terry was born on 8 September 1955 in Corona, California.[1] She has lived, though, nearly all her life in Utah, the place that defines her connection to family, to the land, and to her spiritual roots. Williams's connection to the natural world was established early and influenced largely by her paternal grandmother, Kathryn "Mimi" Blackett Tempest. Mimi gave Williams her first bird guide, *Peterson's Field Guide to Western Birds;* watched birds with her at Bear River; cataloged shells with her; and was the first to mention to her Rachel Carson's name. Williams recalls being seven or eight years old, watching goldfinches and towhees in her grandmother's garden, when Mimi said, "Imagine waking up to no birdsong" (1998, 28) and then mentioned Rachel Carson's *Silent Spring.* In several publications, Williams acknowledges Carson's work and spirit, how it reminds her to "question every law, person, and practice that denies justice toward nature" (28).

Williams's commitment to the natural world and her love for words were clear even before her first book was published. In college, she studied both science and English, earning a B.S. in English from the University of Utah in 1979 and her M.S. in environmental education in 1984, attending three of those summers, 1974–1976, the Teton Science School in Jackson Hole, Wyoming. The same year Williams received her bachelor's degree, she began work as curator of education at the Utah Museum of Natural History, a position she held until 1986 when she became naturalist-in-residence at the museum (1986–1996).

Williams spent much of her life working and living in or near Salt Lake City, but in 1998, she and her husband, Brooke Williams, moved from Emigration Canyon to Castle Valley, Utah, near Moab and Arches National Park. In "Ode to Slowness" from *Red,* she describes the difference between living in these two places: "The speed of my life in Salt Lake City was its own form of pathology" (2001, 142); in her desert home, however, she finds what she desires—time, space, and inspiration.

❧

Williams cowrote her first book, *The Secret Language of Snow* (1984), with Ted Major, founder of the Teton Science School. In this book for children, she uses science, story, and myth to explore varieties of snow illuminated by the vocabulary of the Inuit people of northwestern Alaska. Throughout, she asks many questions, invoking a sense of wonder, then provides scientific explanations, often rendered through metaphor and emphasized by activities and stories. Just as is evidenced by her later work, *The Secret Language of Snow* demonstrates Williams's interest in the relationships among language, culture, and human experience of the natural world.

Williams's second book, *Pieces of White Shell: A Journey to Navajoland* (1984), is, according to Williams, "a journey into one culture, Navajo, and back out again to [her] own, Mormon" (2). In writing this book, Williams was interested in how stories evoke a sense of place. The stories that compose *Pieces of White Shell* come from Williams's experience (teaching children on a Navajo reservation, family stories, and her work at the Utah Museum of Natural History), from mythology, and from books. She recognizes storytelling as a powerful form of education and shows herself to be both teacher and learner.

In *Between Cattails* (1985), we see hallmarks of Williams's writing: blurred genre (in this case, a scientific book written in verse for children), close attention to detail, and a belief in the power of story. Williams takes her reader on an imaginative, scientific, and lyrical walk through a particular ecosystem—a marsh. Through images and description, she introduces readers to the calls of red-winged blackbirds, the eyes of great blue heron, and the intricacies of a multitude of organisms living together.

In *Coyote's Canyon* (1989), readers are invited to see some of the places about which Williams writes, not only in imagination through her words but also through John Telford's stunning photographs. In "The Coyote Clan," the opening piece of this book, Williams points to southern Utah as "Coyote's Country . . . where nothing is as it appears" (16). The same trickster quality applies to Williams's prose; her writing takes on the same chameleon nature as the redrock canyons. That is, Williams writes story-essays in this volume—pieces that reside somewhere between nonfiction and myth.

In much of her work, Williams acknowledges what many writers of memoir and personal essays understand, that what is most personal is also universal. In her best-known, most critically acclaimed book, *Refuge: An Unnatural History of Family and Place* (1991), Williams chronicles her mother's diagnosis and eventual death from ovarian cancer as well as the rise of the Great Salt Lake and eventual flooding of the Bear River Migratory Bird

Refuge. In the face of the threat of loss, Williams writes, "I could not separate the Bird Refuge from my family. Devastation respects no boundaries. The landscape of my childhood and the landscape of my family, the two things I had always regarded as bedrock, were now subject to change" (40). *Refuge,* a meditation on loss and healing, is also about the process of coming to accept change and learning to question orthodoxy—both religious and political.

In her next book, *An Unspoken Hunger: Stories from the Field* (1994), Williams asks a central question that many nature writers confront: "Am I an activist or an artist?" (134). In *Brown Dog of the Yaak* (1999), Rick Bass asks essentially the same question, observing, "[Art and activism] shadow one another; they destroy one another: but they share the same inescapable, irreducible bedrock fuel—passion" (118). Williams's answer to her own question is that she is both artist and activist, yet she—like Bass—recognizes the tensions between the two. She seeks to reconcile the tensions with a commitment to stay home, to write and fight for the land she loves. The essays in *An Unspoken Hunger* are not all set in Utah—one takes place in the Serengeti Plains of Africa; another in Amarillo, Texas; one in Sitka, Alaska; one in New York City; another in Wyoming. Despite the various settings, though, Williams always makes reference to her home, the emotional and psychic lens through which she sees the rest of the world.

Dedicated to her husband, Brooke, *Desert Quartet: An Erotic Landscape* (1995) is a poetic meditation on the four primal elements: earth, water, fire, and air. A different form of *Desert Quartet* was published earlier as "Elements of Love," sans Mary Frank's artwork, in four issues of the *New England Review.* Like the pieces in *Coyote's Canyon,* the differing versions of the essay-stories in *Desert Quartet* demonstrate the fluid nature of genre in Williams's work. Both versions powerfully enact an erotics of place, showing Williams's deep physical and emotional love for the Colorado Plateau.

Leap (2000) was written out of Williams's experience of traveling in the landscape of Hieronymus Bosch's *El jardín de las delicias* for seven years. Stylistically innovative, stream-of-consciousness, almost obsessive, this book defies generic categorization perhaps even more completely than Williams's other texts. In it, she moves from painting to memory to diatribe to historical fact, forsaking clear transitions for the power of association. Just as the boundaries among genres are fluid for Williams, so are those between internal and external landscapes.

Though Williams's other books were dedicated to members of her family, she wrote *Red: Passion and Patience in the Desert* (2001) for "The Coyote Clan and America's Redrock Wilderness." Without the artwork, *Red* includes the full texts of both *Coyote's Canyon* and *Desert Quartet*, as well as an introduction—"Home Work"—that ties together the varied texts and brings the political situation that informs her writing to the forefront. This book also includes a section of newer essays (many previously published in literary journals) and a series of appendixes—America's Redrock Wilderness Act, a map of America's Redrock Wilderness, a citizen's proposal, and a list of supporting organizations—that provides further context and information for political action.

In this book, Williams asks, "How are we to find our way toward conversation?" (3). Her answer to this question is through story, but she doesn't stop there. She queries, "How do the stories we tell about ourselves in relationship to place shape our perceptions of place?" (4). In reflecting on the narratives she will tell, Williams considers how she might speak a language that opens minds rather than closes them, remaining credible as she speaks from a place of love on behalf of the land she loves.

Though the forms she chooses vary, Williams's body of work so far, written over two decades, is remarkably coherent, demonstrating the passion of her devotion to the land, people, language, and the questions that sustain her.

WILLIAMS'S WORK IN CONTEXT

Dramatic tensions are ubiquitous in Williams's work. Discussions about the ambiguous qualities of her ecofeminist position, for example, exemplify a complication that resurfaces in critical conversation about her writing. Cheryll Glotfelty previously set out the conflicting responses Williams exhibits regarding Western hierarchical dualistic constructs (1996, 162–66), and the debates over this issue continue—even into this volume. Several essays in this collection inform other existing debates about Williams's work, including her significant struggle with her Mormon faith, her widely misunderstood erotics of place, her politically charged beliefs and actions. However, we also include contributors who speak to issues not previously addressed in published criticism, since, evident in her work, there are other "canyons inside a divided heart" (Williams 1995, 44).

Williams's "divided heart" is a distinguishing quality of her writing. Among contemporary nature writers, we find few who manifest the intensity of struggle on as many fronts. Her crossing of multiple generic boundaries has drawn considerable critical attention and is one formal manifestation of Williams's attempts to bridge the canyons. As Lynn Ross-Bryant concludes in her 1997 examination of autobiographical features, however, for Williams

"[t]here can be no static or isolated or unified self, nor a resolution of opposing forces" (102). Patrick Murphy concurs, noting that contemporary
women nonfiction writers such as Williams "break with the pastoral utopian
tradition of constructing finished, static noplaces in which all struggles and
all contradictions are resolved" (2000, 93). Nevertheless, it seems almost contrary to Williams's wish that opposing forces reign in her writing, and such
struggles generate a number of this volume's essays.

Williams's style emphasizes the opposing pulls she feels toward silent,
sensory contact as well as toward conscientious, crafted narrative. "The open
expanse of sky," she writes, "makes me realize how necessary it is to live without words, to be satisfied without answers" (1995, 12). On occasions such as
these, Williams indicates that she privileges sensory interactions with the
natural world over even her own carefully constructed images, yet she sees
stories as ways to "empower us," "set us free," "heal us" (1994, 57). They provide a means by which she can both re-create and impart what has been
communicated to her through her senses, her "way of echoing experience"
(1984, 143).

Critics note that her idiosyncratic, at times exceptionally bare-bones, style
evokes the stark, exposed landscape of the sagebrush desert and slickrock
terrain with which she feels akin. In "To Be Taken," for example, she puts into
play techniques borrowed from poetry:

> Tortoise steps.
> Land-based. Land-locked.
> Land-based. Land-locked.
> Learning the slow art of revolutionary patience . . . (2001, 98)

When she re-creates the movement of the land tortoise, we see efforts to
bring the sensory into the world of signs. We see the reverse at work when
she describes other attempts to merge the two: "I am creating a narrative on
the forest floor out of found objects—pine needles, sticks, and branches,
pieces of bark, cones, stones, feathers, moss—it is a sentence written in the
native voice of the woods" (2000, 84). Although she claims that she does not
know "what it says," in this case Williams attempts to leap rather than bridge
the abyss separating the world of senses and the world of words. Her techniques, then, reward close attention, and several of our contributors have focused on formal features within Williams's style.

Williams saunters attentively with both body and mind—as does Henry
David Thoreau. Rarely, however, does the latter precede the former; her
senses lead her into reflective, imaginative modes: "Take off my shoes.

Unbraid my hair. Forget biological rules and constraints. Then could I see Pacific waves roll in, carrying pinecones from the sea? Or dream of fragile, fertile possibilities . . . ?" (1984, 39). She describes sauntering as a walking meditation and concludes, "What we know in a wild place is largely translated through the body" (2001, 186). Hearkening to the Thoreauvian commitment to living deliberately, Williams imbues each event with significance; even chance encounters are not, to Williams, chance: "I sauntered up Stone Creek. . . . An evening primrose bloomed. I knelt down and peeked inside yellow petals. The pistil and stamens resembled stars. My index finger brushed them, gently, and I inhaled pollen. No act seemed too extravagant in these extreme temperatures" (1994, 68–69). We can attribute this passionate attention, in part, to the sensitivity of her nature, in part to the depth of the spiritual bond she feels with the natural world. "Story is a sacred visualization," Williams asserts (1984, 143). That which is of the spirit resounds throughout her oeuvre, and our contributors explore her particular notions and trials of faith.

In her spirituality we also see a kinship with John Muir. Although Muir speaks in the more formal rhetoric of a grand flourisher, readers also discern the authenticity of his spiritual connection with the natural world. He writes: "If you are traveling . . . hide in the hills of the Hollow, lave in its waters . . . and your baptisms will make you a new creature indeed. . . . [Y]our soul [will] breathe deep and free in God's shoreless atmosphere of beauty and love" (1980, 87). Muir and Williams both attempt to bridge chasms via story and spirit, and indeed, this may be the way in which Williams is most successful. In her epiphanic moments, the sacred is manifested as existent. Like Muir, Williams views all as connected, and her "all" most assuredly contains a spiritual dimension. The wild is holy; the holy is wild, even when she writes of destruction and loss: "Cut the trees down. Believe the green stand is gone. Then walk among the stumps when the wind blows through and feel the phantom limbs bowing to what remains, what can never be destroyed" (2000, 88). Because Williams's art is infused with spiriting forces, it testifies of this union. "The choices an artist makes are the same choices a human being makes each day," observes Mariko Umeoka Taki, the artist Williams watches painting Bosch's triptych in the Prado—"[f]inally, they all become choices of spirituality" (2000, 157). Williams concurs, and nothing she views or does or writes is separate from what she understands as spiritual.

Herein lies another parallel to Muir, who viewed his stand in the world of politics in the framework of a higher calling. Williams speaks of "spiritual resistance" as "the ability to stand firm at the center of our convictions when

everything around us asks us to concede" (2001, 17). Williams embraces resistance, writing on many occasions something akin to what she states in
Red: "One can refuse to play the game" (2001, 94). Political activism's demands for public appearances interfere with the solitude she treasures, carv-
ing another of those canyons in her divided heart. Actions such as civil disobedience, having testified twice before Congress, and compiling *Testimony:
Writers of the West Speak on Behalf of Utah Wilderness,* which was delivered
to each member of the House, place her squarely in the Hetch-Hetchy tradition. Fighting for preservation of the natural world for spiritual reasons
drives her to accept if not bridge the canyon between politics and privacy,
another issue contributors address.

Although not a quality easily isolated in her writing, there is, nonetheless,
a tenacity, commitment, and grit similar to the toughness Williams respects
in Mary Austin, Rachel Carson, and Edward Abbey. She describes Austin as
"candid and direct," a woman "who was utterly focused on her vision, and
her vision was focused on the arid lands of the American West" (1997, x)—a
rather accurate description of herself. Of Carson, Williams highlights the
resoluteness, the steadfastness, and "the impact one woman can have" (1994,
137). Williams has written an encomium of sorts for each, noting how all
three mentors' dedication to the land drove their writing. "His words," she
says of Abbey, "tough as skin, are loyal to the earth, the earth that bore us and
sustains us, the only home we shall ever know" (1994, 76). Williams relies on
the "deep quiet of listening to the land, the river, the rocks" (2001, 17) to direct her reflection, as do the environmental thinkers and writers to whom
she turns as tutors. They are the primary philosophical sources underlying
her environmental vision, a focus for yet other essays in this collection.

Fierce attention, trust, and affection attend Williams's stories. A loyal ad-
vocate for the natural world, Williams reminds others of humans' participatory rather than acquisitive roles. In keeping with Williams's ecological philosophy, for this collection—which we characterize as "a beginning"—we
include analyses from a range of interests and disciplines. There is more to
be written on Williams; we have envisioned this anthology as adding pieces
to those already placed in a greater puzzle. Just as Williams's work is in-
progress, the critical understanding of her work is in-development, and we
look eagerly to the shapes taken as others engage the ideas presented in this
collection.

AN OVERVIEW OF
SURVEYING THE LITERARY LANDSCAPES OF TERRY TEMPEST WILLIAMS

The essays we have included allude to many of the themes and concerns taken up by others outside this volume, contributing to dialogues on the centrality of place in Williams's writing; the union of body and landscape; the productive tensions between personal experience and religious authority, water and desert, life and living; the significance of rhythm and sound; Williams's own compelling ethos and the ways she draws on the imagination of her readers; the passion, poetry, and politics of her prose. Although we have grouped the essays into three major categories—ecocriticism; craft and rhetoric; faith, ethics, and politics—to direct attention to associations among the pieces, many of these essays address more than one issue, and some merge multiple approaches, illustrating the many-natured character of Williams's writing.

We begin with Elizabeth Dodd's "Beyond the Blithe Air: Williams's Post-nuclear Transcendentalism." Her essay shows connections and divisions between Williams's work and the writing of nineteenth-century authors such as Thoreau and Emerson, explaining how Williams's contemporary aesthetics and political commitments lead to an adaptation of the American transcendentalist tradition, one that requires courage and action, not merely epiphanic appreciation.

In "Bombs in the Desert," Nathaniel Hart focuses on "All That Is Hidden," one essay from *An Unspoken Hunger,* detailing the urgency of specific present-day environmental issues in contrast to those in the past. Hart draws on Leo Marx's classic study *The Machine in the Garden* and discusses the ways the concept of the machine in the garden (focused on in nineteenth-century literature) is transformed by present-day nature writing such as Williams's essay, which is concerned not with locomotives but with jets and bombs. Hart considers the ways Williams's essay reads as a redemptive journey to the natural world, yet how it also confounds the expectations of such a narrative pattern since, instead of leaving the wildlife refuge cleansed and renewed, she leaves with a renewed sense of her own vulnerability and responsibility.

Like other contributors to this volume, both Nathaniel Hart and Elizabeth Dodd identify contemporary nature writers whose work demonstrates similarities to Williams's. What both Hart and Dodd offer readers is a new understanding of contemporary transcendentalism—a way of seeing past approaches revised by the exigency of our present-day aesthetic and environmental concerns.

Mary Newell, in "Embodied Mutuality: Reconnection to Environment and Self in *An Unspoken Hunger,*" uses feminist scientist Donna Haraway's concept of "situated knowledges" to explore Williams's process of relating to the range of environments represented in *An Unspoken Hunger.* She argues that Haraway's notion of "webs of connections" provides a model for establishing correspondence across difference. Newell traces visual and sensory experience throughout Williams's text, commenting on the ecological and ethical significance of perceptual engagement with the natural world. She argues that an embodied, relational approach to the environment helps guard against hierarchical binary oppositions where humans are dominant and nature is exploited.

The kind of relationship valued in Williams's work, as Sharon Reynolds observes, is one that is characterized by humility rather than dominance, reciprocity rather than transcendence, passion and eroticism rather than pornography. Through analysis of both the text and its accompanying artwork, Reynolds positions *Desert Quartet* in the tradition of American nature writing, arguing that Williams goes beyond the close contemplation of earlier nature writers, demonstrating both the risk and the pleasure of passionate interaction with place.

Jeannette Riley and Maureen Schirack deal further with the concept of Williams's erotics of place, what they define as "a sensual, spiritual way of knowing and interacting with the environment." As does Reynolds, Riley and Schirack discuss the ways this erotics of place plays out in a literary representation of an individual's interaction with the land (as demonstrated in *Desert Quartet*), yet they also move to an analysis of *Red,* working further to dismantle the nature-culture opposition. They point to the ways Williams extends the concept of an erotics of place to define interaction with not only landscape but also one's larger cultural community—all forms of life.

As we move to the craft and rhetoric grouping of essays, Masami Raker Yuki examines human responses to nature from a different perspective, arguing that an "inability to 'listen' is one of the most crucial problems in unsound human attitudes toward the environment." Her critical focus is on listening to and analyzing the soundscapes created in Williams's work. Yuki considers the linguistic and aural connection between Williams's words and the place in which she lives and writes, examining "how literary soundscapes echo soundscapes in the biophysical environment." Yuki demonstrates how William's use of sound, her poetic art, re-creates the interactions of beings in an ecosystem and develops readers' "sensitivity and imagination toward the environment."

Robert Miltner also pays attention to sound in his essay "In Cahoots with Poetry: Williams as Prose Poet in *An Unspoken Hunger* and *Desert Quartet.*" He does so from the perspective of a poet, giving equal attention to image, concision, and lyrical development. Miltner links Williams's work to a contemporary literary tradition, claiming Williams as a prose poet. Like Melissa Goldthwaite and Bart Welling, in essays that follow, Robert Miltner gives particular attention to Williams's use of style, commenting on her imagery, metaphors, symbols, alliteration, rhythm, and the other poetic features that add power and texture to her writing.

Considering the place of rhetoric in environmental discourse, two of our contributors recognize the need to define "rhetoric" and its provinces in more inclusive ways. Lisa Eastmond uses rhetorician and literary philosopher Kenneth Burke's theory of rhetoric as identification to analyze the connections among landscape, story, and identity. She explains the ways Williams persuasively uses a poetics of place in order to influence the politics of place, showing the interdependence of rhetoric, story, and the kinds of identification that can lead to political action on behalf of the land. In her analysis, Eastmond demonstrates the symbolic power of landscape, the ways it functions rhetorically in and through the stories Williams tells, creating a climate for political and environmental change.

Melissa Goldthwaite considers the usefulness of rhetorical theory for understanding what Williams is doing in her mixed-genre text *Leap*. Goldthwaite argues that rhetorical theory provides a constructive lens for understanding and explicating *Leap*, even as she claims *Leap* as a provocative text for expanding traditional notions of rhetoric through the theoretical lens of feminism. Like many of the other contributors, Goldthwaite considers the productive tensions in Williams's work, and she does so by examining both the conflicts and the connections between feminism and rhetoric, showing the ways Williams uses structures of threes, "unified triads," to transform faith, form, and rhetoric.

Toward the end of her essay, Goldthwaite explores the rhetorical canon of delivery in relation to Williams's performance of *Leap*. In a similar vein, Bart Welling, in "One Wild Word: *Leap* and the Art of Restoration," considers *Leap* a "highly self-conscious (logo)graphic performance," one that invites readers to "join in the dance of creative interpretation." Welling places *Leap* within the literary and cultural contexts of modernism and Mormonism, and, simultaneously, he takes account of his own position as a student of modernism and as a fifth-generation Mormon, providing a critical and engaged reading that enacts its own arguments concerning textual participation.

In our final grouping of essays—faith, ethics, and politics—Richard Hunt argues that Williams's concept of an erotics of place allows her to deal with another tension recognizable in environmental debates: the relationship between the physical needs of the body and the spiritual needs of the soul. In "Integrating Science and Faith: Williams and the Erotics of Place," Hunt shows the ways Williams dissolves the body-soul dilemma and the tension between science and faith by integrating the two and demonstrating the ways her faith is informed and transformed by direct, even scientific, experience with nature. Hunt considers the power of Williams's unlikely unions, her marriage of faith and science in her experience of the physical world.

In "Potsherds and Petroglyphs: Unearthing Latter-day Saint Sources for Williams's Environmental Vision," Katherine Chandler further develops the relationship between Williams's faith and writing, discussing the ways in which what others see as unlikely unions in Williams's writing (specifically her Latter-day Saint theology and passionate experience with nature) are not surprising if understood within the context of key doctrines from the Church of Jesus Christ of Latter-day Saints. Chandler explains the doctrinal foundations of Williams's environmental commitments, showing the connections, rather than divisions, between Williams's faith and experience of the natural world. Chandler's essay provides additional historical and religious context in which to consider both Williams's work and the essays of Hunt, Welling, and other contributors who reference Williams's religious background and beliefs.

Drawing on the Latter-day Saint concept of testimony, Lisa Diedrich explores two forms of witnessing—testimony from firsthand knowledge and bearing witness to the unseeable—in relation to Williams's work, arguing that both kinds of witnessing can result in personal and political transformations. Diedrich considers the necessary and difficult task that Williams has set out for herself in writing *Refuge:* telling the story of her mother's death from cancer as well as the story of the flooding of the Bear River Migratory Bird Refuge. Through listening to her mother and to the land, and struggling to incorporate other viewpoints and experiences into her own, Williams practices both forms of witnessing, paying close attention to her own experiences of loss and change, even as she looks outward. Diedrich shows Williams's movement from mourning to political action, a transformation Diedrich links to witnessing.

Tina Richardson also deals with the personal and political possibilities of testimony and witnessing in *Refuge.* She claims *Refuge* as breast cancer literature yet also shows how Williams's position as a nature writer allows her to go beyond traditional conventions of breast cancer literature to make a political statement that challenges the status quo, asking readers to pay attention to the corporeal consequences of environmental destruction.

Karl Zuelke also makes connections between *Refuge* and politics, extending the conversation into the philosophical realm by invoking the ideas of political philosopher Hannah Arendt. Zuelke argues that the natural world needs to be conceived as an entity that merits political recognition, a cultural reality that Williams has come to recognize. When nature is known to be aware and spiritual, Zuelke asserts, then it "merits membership identity in a political realm." Somewhat unexpectedly, it is through participation in the polis and bringing nature into that arena that Williams finds refuge.

Taken together, the essays in this collection cover the range of Williams's published writing to date and intersect with various conversations important to the multidisciplinary field of literature and the environment. Our hope is that these essays will answer some questions, even as they create others, becoming a small part of a much larger and longer conversation—a conversation that we invite others to enter.

Note

1. Much of the information in this section appears—in a different and expanded form—in the entry on Terry Tempest Williams written by Melissa A. Goldthwaite in *Dictionary of Literary Biography: American Nature Writers,* edited by J. Scott Bryson and Roger Thompson (Gale Group Publishing).

Works Cited

Bass, Rick. 1999. *Brown Dog of the Yaak: Essays on Art and Activism.* St. Paul: Milkweed Press.

Glotfelty, Cheryll. 1996. "Flooding the Boundaries of Form: Terry Tempest Williams's Ecofeminist *Unnatural History.*" In *Change in the American West: Exploring the Human Dimension,* edited by Stephen Tchudi, 158–67. Reno: University of Nevada Press.

Muir, John. 1980. *Wilderness Essays.* Salt Lake City: Peregrine Smith.

Murphy, Patrick D. 2000. *Farther Afield in the Study of Nature-Oriented Literature.* Charlottesville: University Press of Virginia.

Ross-Bryant, Lynn. 1997. "The Self in Nature: Four American Autobiographies." *Soundings* 80:83–104.

Williams, Terry Tempest. 1984. *Pieces of White Shell: A Journey to Navajoland.* Albuquerque: University of New Mexico Press.

———. 1985. *Between Cattails.* Illustrated by Peter Parnall. New York: Charles Scribner's Sons.

———. 1989. *Coyote's Canyon.* Salt Lake City: Peregrine-Smith.

———. 1991. *Refuge: An Unnatural History of Family and Place.* New York: Pantheon Books.

———. 1994. *An Unspoken Hunger: Stories from the Field.* New York: Pantheon Books.

———. 1995. *Desert Quartet: An Erotic Landscape.* New York: Pantheon Books.

———. 1997. Introduction to *The Land of Little Rain,* by Mary Austin. New York: Penguin.

———. 1998. "Rachel Carson." In *Legends,* edited by John Miller, 28. Novato, Calif.: New World Library.

———. 2000. *Leap.* New York: Pantheon Books.

———. 2001. *Red: Passion and Patience in the Desert.* New York: Pantheon Books.

Williams, Terry Tempest, and Ted Major. 1984. *The Secret Language of Snow.* San Francisco: Sierra Club.

ecocriticism

ELIZABETH DODD

☙

Beyond the Blithe Air

WILLIAMS'S POSTNUCLEAR TRANSCENDENTALISM

The "marriage of the ecological with the autobiographical" is how Brooke Libby describes *Refuge: An Unnatural History of Family and Place;* it exemplifies, she says, "what is the general though perhaps unstated aim of most nature writing: to write about the natural world and about oneself simultaneously, to look mutually outward and inward" (2000, 252). This is true, as well, of much of Terry Tempest Williams's other work, including most of the essays in *An Unspoken Hunger.* Thus far, however, *Refuge* remains her most significant book, at least in terms of critical attention. It is considered a hallmark of contemporary ecofeminist autobiography, although, as Cassandra Kircher notes, the book recapitulates some rather facile dichotomies, "embracing of dualisms" as she puts it (1998, 161), that suggest a less examined—certainly less nuanced—stance than some readers would prefer. Rather than continuing this focused discussion of how gender functions in Williams's environmentalism, however, I want to examine her contributions to what John Tallmadge calls the "complex Thoreauvian excursion" (1998, 197), and take note of what I believe is a salient adaptation of the American transcendentalist tradition. Reaching beyond issues of ecofeminist spirituality, the "nature" of essentialism, and related concerns, I want to examine specifically Williams's evocation of natural—and, in terrible contrast, unnatural—history. This is a path of inquiry that is obviously invited by the subtitle of *Refuge: An Unnatural History of Family and Place,* but it is also suggested by Williams's self-introduction to a group of literary scholars attending an academic conference at the University of Utah in 1994. Standing in a bus that would take several of us out to Great Salt Lake for a tour with Williams herself as our guide, she said, "Hi, I'm Terry"—and was greeted with a ripple of chuckling, since we certainly knew her name, as well as her work. "And as of right now, I am in Naturalist Mode," she finished, smiling.

I am not the first to compare Williams with Henry David Thoreau. While Tallmadge looks to "Walking," Libby is reminded of the "Spring" chapter in *Walden*. However, Libby goes on to say, "For Williams, then, the natural (abnormal, wild, disruptive, ambivalent, perhaps even cancerous) world is supremely creative, allowing new ideas, identities, narratives to develop, surface, and eventually subsist independently" (2000, 260). This last description is less helpful, since it assigns "disruptive, ambivalent," and "abnormal . . . perhaps even cancerous" aspects of being equivalent constituent placement in "the natural . . . world" of Thoreau's "wildness." Despite the book's symbolic structure, which explicitly equates Williams's mother with the lake and the cancer with the flood, the narrative contradicts and ultimately refutes that ecofeminist metaphor. Williams herself "wants" to hold on to this essentialist, gendered view; indeed, she finds it comforting and returns to similar tropes in later work.[1] But as is sometimes the case, *Refuge* is larger, wiser, and richer than its own author's explicit intentions. While the book repeatedly supports her early claim that, as a Mormon in the Great Basin, "one of the things you do know [is] history and genealogy" (1991, 13), by the end both Williams and reader alike find that "family and place" are not what she believed them to be. Tallmadge says, "Pain and grief cleanse her vision, destroying false hopes and illusions. It's an involuntary ascetic process that intensifies as the cancer and flooding progress" (1998, 204). Yet only after the cancer has run its course, after both her mother and her grandmother have died, does Williams come to full realization about her family and their legacy of place in the desert landscape. As transformative insight often does, it arrives in a flash when her father confirms that her recurring dream "of a flash of light in the desert" (1991, 282) is not a dream, but an actual event from her childhood. It is also the key to the book's great political and artistic triumph, what I will call its postnuclear transcendentalism.

FEAR AMONG THE FOREBEARS

"Standing on the bare ground,—my head bathed by the blithe air, and uplifted into infinite space,—all mean egotism vanishes. I become a transparent eyeball; I am nothing; I see all; the currents of the Universal Being circulate through me; I am part or particle of God" (1991, 8). This famous moment in Ralph Waldo Emerson's *Nature* represents a hallmark aspect of nineteenth-century transcendental literature: what Joel Porte calls the

Epiphanic Moment, combining nature and self into an overwhelming realization of awe, beauty, solitude, and sacredness. Just six sentences earlier, Emerson says, "I am glad to the brink of fear." If fear is a part of transcendental epiphany, it is achieved through joy. "In the woods we return to reason and faith" (1991, 8), says Emerson, pulling well back from the brink.

Henry David Thoreau ventured farther than the woodlots of Concord, into landscapes where fear played a more significant role, even to the point where reason and faith might quail. He writes, "Think of our life in nature,—daily to be shown matter, to come in contact with it,—rocks, trees, wind on our cheeks! the *solid* earth! the *actual* world! the *common sense! Contact! Contact! Who* are we? *Where* are we?" (1972, 71). The heights of Mount Ktaadn in *The Maine Woods* bring Thoreau to his literary knees, confronting in something of a panic the amazing juxtaposition of his own emotive and spiritual existence against all that physical presence of the world's being.

Nineteenth-century writers differ in their views of just how large a role fear plays in the epiphanic moment, yet for each the Emersonian formula pertains: fear, or its brink, is reached through joy, through contact with the beautiful, if awesome, eastern woodlands landscape. Transcendental epiphanies may lead to ontological questions, like Thoreau's, or to Emerson's "reason and faith"; either way, the New England transcendentalists arrive at a sense of community and oneness with both nature and humanity alike. This sense of community led variously to Alcott's failed experiment at Brook Farm, Thoreau's investigation of prior residents at Walden Pond, and reached its logical extension in the transcendentalists' vigorous opposition to slavery. Thus, "fear" comes from the very splendor of nature's beauty, and the richness of that gift (Emerson calls it all humankind's "dowry and estate" [1991, 17]) allows one the freedom of spirit and imagination to imagine the "not me" *as* "me," and so to engage in altruistic politics—as many transcendentalists did, to one degree or another, through abolitionism.

I want to emphasize the importance of nature's beauty—and bounty—to this view. We remember Emerson's insistence that nature was a "commodity" meant to "serve" humankind "as meekly as the ass on which the Saviour rode" (1991, 35); we recall the passion with which Thoreau extolled the particulars of Walden and the woods around, finally addressing the thou of the pond's pellucid waters, asking, "Walden, is it you?" (1997, 174). Aesthetics and morality both derive from a form of the sublime that *is* the beautiful, and the beautiful is powerful enough to prevent even Thoreau from recognizing the full implications the railroad holds for his beloved woods.

Unlike nineteenth-century transcendentalists, contemporary American nature writers have a keen sense of the systemic and psychic consequences culture has imposed upon the landscape and its ecosystems. Such writers, focusing on any geography, may catalog the ravages upon the landscape more than they do its prior beauty. Further, they are shaped by the major historical developments of the twentieth century, from modernism's personal and ontological malaise to postmodernism's (and physics's) discarding objective certainty, to the holocaust's stark rebuke of the nation-state and both political and ethical will. And the landscape of the arid American West has been particularly significant in shaping this contemporary work.

FEAR IN A HANDFUL OF DUST

Unlike the ubiquitous, bountiful "woods" of New England that led the Concord transcendentalists to focus on nature's beauty, the American West's landscape of extremes prompts writers such as Williams to focus on the awesome, even awe-ful sublime, nature's powerful otherness. These extremes include aridity and heat, vastness of space, mountainous heights, and even the visible history of previous inhabitants, such as the Anasazi and the Fremont, whose cultures ceased to flourish. Despite Williams's personification of Great Salt Lake, or the dunes around Fish Springs ("Sensuous curves—the small of a woman's back" [1991, 109]), the desert remains much more unknowable and dangerous, as in the salt flats near Crocodile Mountain where Williams develops heatstroke or Dark Canyon where she falls and splits open her face from forehead to jaw. Though she is with her husband and a few friends, she finds that self-reliance keeps very close company with mortality: she must receive medical help, but the car is hours away, over hot southeastern Utah's desert terrain, and "I was the only person who could carry me out," she realizes (1991, 243). "To enter wilderness," she muses, "is to court risk" (244). Unlike their New England forebears, contemporary western transcendentalists find that rock is often a far more telling aesthetic touchstone than tree; water is valued against its absence, not for degrees of comparative clarity.

One might see this kind of awareness as mere modernist angst—"after such knowledge, what forgiveness?" But we do not find Eliotic paralysis or Poundian condescension in *Refuge*. Williams is keenly aware of the great numbers of people who continue to be casualties of World War II and the cold war, yet she finds meaning and community in activism, group demonstration; this commitment again invites comparison with nineteenth-century transcendentalism. Many of the white, mostly male New Englanders placed their love of nature securely in the realm of altruistic humanism; never themselves threatened with enslavement, their social activism was intended to benefit others, while, full of optimism and appreciation of beauty, they viewed nature, in Emerson's words, as "emblematic . . . a metaphor of the human mind" (1991, 29). Williams ultimately "grounds" her activism in a love of the geographic sublime that is the American West, in combination with a recognition that her family's bodies and health have been put at much greater, "unnatural" risk.

FEAR AND LOATHING

Williams points out that her Mormon family members do not share many of the common "risk factors" for cancer: the women bear children in early adulthood (though this is not true for Williams herself), and they do not smoke or drink. From her father she learns that they are quite literally downwinders, people who lived in the path of radioactive fallout from nuclear testing in the Nevada deserts, places seen by others as "a blank spot on the map" (1991, 241). However, with her father's revelation that she and her parents were both witnesses to bomb testing, she sees swiftly and terribly how "family" and "place" have converged into this "unnatural" legacy of cell mutation and death. Her father tells her, "You were sitting on Diane's lap. She was pregnant. . . . Within a few minutes, a light ash was raining on the car" (283). Within a few sentences, Williams herself declares, "It was at this moment that I realized the deceit I had been living under" (283).

This portion of the book appears as an epilogue, "The Clan of One-Breasted Women," the only section of *Refuge* not to take its title from birds that appear within the narrative. Its tone and style are also different, as in the stark sarcasm with which she quotes government statements, preparing for the civil disobedience of the Nevada Test Site protest in which she participates in the book's last pages. Williams quotes the Atomic Energy Commission's (AEC) description of the lands north of the test site as "virtually uninhabited desert terrain" and then follows the language to its (il)logical extension: "[M]y family and the birds at Great Salt Lake were some of the 'virtual uninhabitants'" (287). The original phrase, with the grammatical subject "terrain," reduces the place to the linguistic equivalent of a document, a topographical map; my dictionary notes that *terrain* has especial reference to "military advantages." Everything else is auxiliary, adjectival; by restoring "uninhabited" to the noun form, Williams satirizes the bureaucratic decision not to value the communities living within the landscape.

Similarly, she quotes an AEC memo that describes a "low-use segment of the population" (283): this language is so curious that she doesn't need to further satirize it. What is actually being described is a "segment"—not place, not people. And the "low" rate of "use" is what is noteworthy: the place—or was it the people?—isn't efficient, isn't being put to good "use." Or, in the words of a 1950 government publication, *Armed Forces Talk,* to which Williams also refers, this land is "a damn good place to dump used razor blades."[2]

Throughout *Refuge,* Williams criticizes such purely utilitarian views of the land, along with the technologies that enact them, likening the various proposals for reducing the flood levels in Great Salt Lake to the various failed cancer treatments her mother undergoes. Despite her hesitation to overtly criticize her father for his pipe-laying business, she allows his own language to make the implication. Speaking of the elaborate plan to pump water from the lake into West Desert, "'I'd love to get this job,' he said, his eyes squinting from the sun. 'It would be exciting to be part of this project, even though I think the whole thing is ridiculous. . . . The lakeshore industry is hurting financially. The pumping project is a way to bail out the salt and mineral companies, Southern Pacific Railroad, and a political career as well'" (139). Even well-intentioned efforts to change the desert, to impose human notions of form, are fundamentally connected to a kind of militaristic violence. Thus, her mother's remark that the morphine drip dulling her pain in the final weeks of her life sounds "like helicopters coming over the rise" (219) recalls the dream from which her mother's phone call woke her at the book's opening, when Williams first learns the cancer has returned: "I was deep in dream. This particular episode found me hiding beneath my grandmother's bed as eight black helicopters flew toward the house. I knew we were in danger" (22). These implicit criticisms, initially made through imagery or juxtaposition, become explicit in the epilogue. Though Williams has been seeking meaning in silence, in landscape, in unlanguaged nature, for the book's conclusion she chooses language, from the pen and paper "tucked inside my left boot" as "weapons" (290) to her rejection of a form of silence. "The fear an inability to question authority" (286).

Grandmother Mimi offers Williams her nearest model of questioning authority, as well as her first experiences bird-watching. Williams draws on both in the chapter "Snowy Plovers," structuring the narrative so as to bring her reader sequentially to beauty through fear. Williams and a colleague conduct a census of breeding plovers—an endangered species—walking through a grueling desert landscape. For a moment, Williams sounds a bit Emersonian, declaring, "Snowy plovers are the scribes of the salt flats. Their tracks are cursive writing, cabalistic messages for the birdwatcher who cares enough to follow their eccentric wanderings" (259). But shortly thereafter, "I have a headache," she admits. "I fear I may be suffering from heatstroke and begin to worry about getting home" (260). Her fear is soon realized when, driving home alone, she pulls off the road to be sick and later blacks out altogether. In a following scene, discussing the cancer that runs in their family, her cousin Lynne says, "I'm scared for you and me" (263), and Williams agrees. At the chapter's end, Mimi sums up the narrative's search for beauty beyond the brink of fear: "How do you place a value on inspiration?" she asks. "How do you quantify the wildness of birds, when for the most part they lead secret and anonymous lives?" (265).

Even though, as Kircher points out, Williams "fails to examine the consumerism" exhibited by members of her family (1998, 168), the book ultimately differentiates its strain of nature writing from its New England transcendentalist predecessors through a rejection of Emerson's principle of commodity. Williams disavows the premise, still highly prevalent in American politics, that nature is "made to serve," offering "all its kingdoms to man as the raw material which he may mould into what is useful," though she might sadly agree that "[m]an is never weary of working it up" (35). Further, she distrusts technology (Emerson's "useful arts") as something very different from natural processes; the hubristic desire to change the very matter of this world is what is at issue. Despite her frequent anthropomorphism, or more accurately gynemorphism, her pursuit of beauty by way of fear rather than vice versa has led her to see nature as functioning without the individual will so key to human ingenuity.

It is an interesting irony that while nuclear testing and radioactive repercussions present a new, different kind of physical and psychological threat in the American imagination, atomic weapons technology can also be seen as the direct outgrowth of a long cultural mission central to Western societies. Jeff Smith argues that nuclear weapons are not something new and different, a product of scientific knowledge rather than cultural choice, but instead are the twentieth century's addition, albeit a more far-reaching one, to a tradition extending at least to the European Renaissance. They reflect an ongoing cultural desire for both technologies of efficiency and politics that eclipse the individual responsibility of leaders in a kind of personification of the state as a single entity, directly representative of a monolithic "people" and effacing the protests of individual citizens against the "majority will." As he says, "Violence is essentially the exercise of power over nature, and by transcending (in fact, authorizing) the natural order, the state gains the right to exercise this power at will. The state's prime prerogative, its monopoly of violence, is a corollary of its new position vis-à-vis nature" (1989, 85).

Williams would likely agree with this view, yet it took the explicit narrative revelation of her and her mother's exposure to radioactive fallout from "The Day We Bombed Utah" (1991, 283) to bring this recognition of the "state's monopoly of violence" into clear, environmentalist focus. This was, for Williams, a second bombshell that required reexamination of the meaning and order the preceding bulk of the book had so urgently sought. "[O]ne by one, I have watched the women in my family die common, heroic deaths. We sat in waiting rooms hoping for good news, but always receiving the bad" (285), she says grimly, sadly, angrily. And I believe that with the fuller understanding of the context for all this "bad news," some of the realizations made earlier in the book must be revised and reconsidered—that is, complicated and challenged. *Refuge,* then, rewards rereadings with wider, wiser perspective.

Consider, for example, this passage from early in the book, where Williams longs to "re-think cancer":

> We can surgically remove it. We can shrink it with radiation. We can poison it with drugs. Whatever we choose, though, we view the tumor as foreign, something outside ourselves. It is, however, our own creation. The creation we fear.
>
> The cancer process is not unlike the creative process. . . . I can hardly wait to tell Mother. (44)

The desire to embrace the cancer, to embrace one's own death as part of one's self, part of the whole of one's life—all these are real, vital constituents of *Refuge*'s vision. But through the viewpoint from "The Clan of One-Breasted Women," the claims of ownership sound either diabolically chilling or hollowly ironic. The quest to accept death as natural, to believe "[d]ying doesn't cause suffering. Resistance to dying does" (53), must alter course. "Death" may be natural, but these specific cases of terminal cancer are unnatural. The literal tumor, creation of the body, becomes again figurative, a figure of the bomb. The pronoun "we" transcends the individual, mortal women and becomes instead "we-the-people" in whose name the bombs were built and tested. Yet "we" are the victims, also.

PITY AND FEAR

Elsewhere, Williams discusses her reading of John Cobb. She writes, "[H]is theory is that . . . usually it is a point of disaster or deep pain that propels us from one era into the next. I would suggest that we are already in a disaster:

the deaths of other species, the loss of our forests. I think that we have for-gotten the option of restraint" (1996, 109). In this context, Williams does not specifically cite the disaster of radioactive fallout, but we can clearly apply this trope to *Refuge:* disaster—not just an individual, personal death, but widespread, unnatural, unrestrained, and deadly contamination—propels Williams into activism, and the book into a deeper, less easily categorical, re-consideration of its own tenets and conclusions. Thus, despite Kircher's in-sightful comment on the cyclic structure of the book (1998, 166), I believe that a more apt image than the actual circle would be the spiral familiar from countless rock-art sites throughout the Great Basin and desert Southwest re-gions; the curving path does turn and return on its course, but it travels also more deeply inward, changing course.

Thus far I have been addressing Williams specifically, but she is not alone in laying a course for postnuclear transcendentalism. Poet and essayist Reg Saner shares in this literary expedition. In "Technically Sweet," an essay from his collection *The Four-Cornered Falcon,* Saner retraces, and tries to imagine, J. Robert Oppenheimer's dual aesthetic loves for the arid New Mexican land-scape and the potential of nuclear fission. "The solace these people take in the beautiful Pajarito Plateau and its setting will help them make areas of the West, and our Earth's northern hemisphere, unnaturally radioactive for the next 24,000 years," he writes. "Yet they mean well. Hitler's *Wehrmacht* is no figment. Amid leftovers from the Stone Age, they mean to make the world's most intelligent bomb" (1993, 89). Saner visits Oppenheimer's home near Los Alamos and travels through the surrounding countryside, usually alone. In the dry, hot days of summer, he camps near the ancient Anasazi shrine the Stone Lions and drinks the small amount of rainwater that collects on his tent fly during the night. He realizes, "If research is to be believed, I've a touch of plutonium in my body right now. If research is to be believed, so has virtually everyone alive. We're a sort of alchemical experiment nobody intended" (84). That sense of being one among many also accompanies Saner as he rides his bicycle to a mass demonstration at Rocky Flats Nuclear Weapons Plant near his home in Colorado. Holding hands with both a friend and a stranger, he thinks, "I find that 12,000 people make an incom-parable silence, as if humankind's highest good could be right now" (92).

I find it ironic that a writer would feel, if only briefly, that "humankind's greatest good" must be a moment of the effacement of language, community without verbal communication. Surely, helplessness and rage lie behind that statement, though not the kind of stunned numbness that leads to apathy. Even more ironic is the sense of danger Saner articulates from his own sought-after *contact, contact,* with outdoor places.[3] The Thoreauvian desire for the "brink" of fear leads these writers, ultimately, beyond that nine-teenth-century brink of fear, as Williams says, into a new era. One of the strengths of their work, therefore, is its courage—a willingness to explore an important cultural direction that it may not be too late to follow: one that si-multaneously rejects postmodern cynicism, modernist despair, and roman-tic anthropocentrism.

Emerson's age certainly lived in close proximity to mortality and the grief and despair attendant on disease and death. But I believe there is, at a psy-chological and ethical level, a qualitative difference between despair from the death of one's child or sibling or spouse and that from the specter of large-scale annihilation, that is, nuclear fear. For postnuclear nature writers, the "not me," the potential sublimity of the natural world, does not hold the in-violate power of solace it did for Emerson and his contemporaries. He wrote, "In the presence of nature a wild delight runs through the man, in spite of real sorrows. . . . There I feel that nothing can befall me in life,—no disgrace, no calamity (leaving me my eyes), which nature cannot repair" (1991, 9–10). The postnuclear writer knows that nature itself is vulnerable, perhaps even beyond repair. Despite their recognition of the sea change (what Bill Mc-Kibben has called in his book by that title "the end of nature"), postnuclear transcendentalists are willing, in their lives and in their work, to live *as if* there is a future, all the while articulating how that future has been severed from the prenuclear past. Thus, their work offers an aesthetic of courage, of beauty well beyond the brink of fear.

Notes

1. She says explicitly in *Refuge,* "I want to see the lake as Woman, as myself, in her refusal to be tamed" (92).

2. Identified in prologue to *American Ground Zero: The Secret Nuclear War* (Gal-lagher 1993).

3. A similar irony is noted by some of the downwinders interviewed in Carole Gal-lagher's *American Ground Zero* (1993). They point out that working outdoors (ranch-ing and gardening especially) brought them into greater contact with fallout than they would have experienced as urban office workers; moreover, they raised much of their own meat, fruit, vegetables, and dairy products, all of which gave them increased doses of radiation.

Works Cited

Emerson, Ralph Waldo, and Henry David Thoreau. 1991. *Nature / Walking.* Edited by John Elder. Boston: Beacon Press.

Gallagher, Carole. 1993. *American Ground Zero: The Secret Nuclear War.* Cambridge: MIT University Press.

Kircher, Cassandra. 1998. "Rethinking Dichotomies in Terry Tempest Williams's *Refuge.*" In *Ecofeminist Literary Criticism: Theory, Interpretation, Pedagogy,* edited by Greta Gaard and Patrick D. Murphy, 158–71. Urbana and Chicago: University of Illinois Press.

Libby, Brooke. 2000. "Nature Writing as *Refuge:* Autobiography in the Natural World." In *Reading under the Sign of Nature: New Essays in Ecocriticism,* edited by John Tallmadge and Henry Harrington, 251–64. Salt Lake City: University of Utah Press.

McKibben, Bill. 1989. *The End of Nature.* New York: Random House.

Porte, Joel. 1966. *Emerson and Thoreau: Transcendentalists in Conflict.* Middletown, Conn.: Wesleyan University Press.

Saner, Reg. 1993. *The Four-Cornered Falcon: Essays on the Interior West and the Natural Scene.* Baltimore: Johns Hopkins University Press.

Smith, Jeff. 1989. *Unthinking the Unthinkable: Nuclear Weapons and Western Culture.* Bloomington: Indiana University Press.

Tallmadge, John. 1998. "Beyond the Excursion: Initiatory Themes in Annie Dillard and Terry Tempest Williams." In *Reading the Earth: New Directions in the Study of Literature and the Environment,* edited by Michael P. Branch, Rochelle Johnson, Daniel Patterson, and Scott Slovic, 197–207. Moscow: University of Idaho Press.

Thoreau, Henry David. 1972. *The Maine Woods.* Edited by Joseph J. Moldenhauer. Princeton: Princeton University Press.

———. 1997. *Walden.* Edited by Stephen Fender. Oxford: Oxford University Press.

Williams, Terry Tempest. 1991. *Refuge: An Unnatural History of Family and Place.* New York: Pantheon Books.

Williams, Terry Tempest, and Ona Siporin. 1996. "A Conversation." *Western American Literature* 31 (2):99–113.

NATHANIEL I. HART

❧

Bombs in the Desert

WILLIAMS'S "ALL THAT IS HIDDEN"

In his classic study of American literature and culture, *The Machine in the Garden*, Leo Marx identifies key passages in the works of Thoreau, Emerson, Hawthorne, even Henry James, illustrating how the steam locomotive is depicted as the envoy of industrialism rapidly encroaching on rural America. Typically, the steam locomotive or the railroad train appears as a "sudden, shocking intruder" (1964, 29) upon an otherwise peaceful rural setting, its shrieking whistle and clatter disrupting the pastoral tranquillity. Marx calls this recurring literary image "the machine in the garden" and a "metaphor of contradiction" (4), one that incorporates two competing but equally alluring myths about the nation's origins and destiny: America as the pastoral ideal or new Eden, its people embracing a simpler, natural life far removed from the oppressive, authoritarian regimes of the Old World, and America as the model of industrial progress, its people bringing civilization to the wilderness, subduing nature and harnessing its forces for material and economic benefits. Both myths promise plenitude, social equality, economic independence, and a release from human labor. Both are still alive in the American psyche, motivating personal behavior and political action, though it is obvious that industrialism has run roughshod over the pastoral ideal and the practical expression of it in the agrarian economy. Today farming or agriculture is itself industrialized, while the steam locomotive is no longer an alarming presence on the American scene.

But the successes of industrialism have brought a multitude of environmental crises. In a growing body of serious literature and art reflecting the urgency of these environmental issues, the pattern of the machine in the garden is dramatically transformed. The setting for the present clash of cultural values has moved from New England's cultivated gardens and hospitable countryside to the forbidding deserts of the American West, and the steam locomotive is superseded by the machinery of modern warfare, particularly military aircraft and their lethal payloads. The image of the steam locomotive in the garden has been replaced by a new metaphor of contradiction, bombs in the desert. This new metaphoric design is at the core of Terry Tempest Williams's essay "All That Is Hidden" (1994).

At first glance, the new pattern seems similar to that of the machine in the garden. Marx begins his study with an example from the notebooks of Nathaniel Hawthorne, a long passage in which Hawthorne, seated in the woods near Concord, records his precise observations of the natural world. For Hawthorne, the sounds of the village and of agricultural activities are not unnatural: a striking clock, a cow bell, the sharpening of scythes blend harmoniously with the forest sounds of birds, squirrels, insects, and rustling leaves. Only the whistle of the steam locomotive disrupts this harmony, "the long shriek, harsh, above all other harshness," Hawthorne writes (Marx 1964, 13). Here then is the emblem or "metaphoric design" that Marx finds scattered throughout nineteenth-century American writing, an Edenic scene violated by the shrieking locomotive—the machine in the garden, a metaphor of contradiction that represents the antithetical values of the simple agrarian economy and the onrushing force of industrialism.

Perhaps the best-known example of this image occurs in Thoreau's extended commentary on the railroad in *Walden*. For half an hour, Thoreau has been observing the flights of birds and passing animals while the "rattle of railroad cars," he tells us, thrums insistently behind his meditation like the drumming "beat of a partridge." Then Thoreau drops the image of the partridge for the more aggressive image of a rapacious hawk: "The whistle of the locomotive penetrates my woods summer and winter, sounding like the scream of a hawk sailing over some farmer's yard." The threat of plunder implicit in this image is then confirmed: "All the Indian huckleberry hills are stripped, all the cranberry meadows are raked into the city" (1971, 114–16).

A passage in Terry Tempest Williams's essay "All That Is Hidden" holds much in common with these selections from Hawthorne and Thoreau. Williams is describing her visit to a remote desert wildlife refuge, and at midpoint in the essay, its climax or turning point, she writes:

> It begins to rain, lightly. As far as we can see, the desert glistens. The Growlers, jagged black peaks, carry the eye range after range into Mexico; no national boundaries exist in the land's mind. The curvature of the earth bends the horizon in an arc of light. Virga: rain evaporating in midair, creating gray-

blue streamers that wave back and forth, never touching the ground. Who is witness to this full-bodied beauty? Who can withstand the recondite wisdom and sonorous silence of wildness?

All at once, a high-pitched whining shatters us, flashes over our shoulders, threatens to blow us off the ridge. Two jets scream by. Within seconds, one, two, three bombs drop. The explosions are deafening; the desert is in flame. (1994, 121–22)

Like Hawthorne and Thoreau, Williams experiences an interrupted reverie. Her lyrical description depicts a natural setting whose features blend harmoniously and whose beauty evokes delight and wonder. Artificial national boundaries evaporate in midair like the desert rain, the rain itself a source of beauty. Opposites are resolved: silence is sonorous; desert and rain, near and far, dark and light, earth and air are held in an equilibrium only to be shattered by the high-pitched whine of jet aircraft and their exploding bombs.

But if the design of this passage mirrors the pattern of the machine in the garden, the differences in detail are of singular importance. In our own age, the easily accessible, seemingly undefiled garden has more or less disappeared from the scene, but so too has the steam locomotive. In this contemporary representation, there is no garden such as Hawthorne or Thoreau knew it, but the Arizona desert, actually the Cabeza Prieta National Wildlife Refuge, and instead of the steam locomotive, a Fairchild A-10 Thunderbolt II military aircraft firing live ammunition into the desert earth, practicing air-to-surface missile attacks. For Hawthorne and Thoreau, the encroaching machine threatens a *way* of life, but for Williams, life itself is at stake.

That the desert signifies a repository of life rather than a barren wasteland is itself a remarkable shift in perspective. It is only in the twentieth century that writers, artists, naturalists, and photographers—people such as Mary Austin, Aldo Leopold, Joseph Wood Krutch, Edward Abbey, Wallace Stegner, Edward Weston, and Ansel Adams, and more recently Richard Misrach, Gary Nabhan, Gretel Ehrlich, and Williams—have cultivated an audience for the desert's sculptured beauty, its vast expanse of land and sky, the play of light, the shifting shades of color. They speak convincingly not only of the desert land but also of its remarkable flora and fauna as well as the genius of indigenous people who understand how to live in this spare setting. Having focused attention on the vitality of the desert, contemporary writers and artists have also exposed "all that is hidden" there that threatens life not only in the desert but globally as well—the Air Force bombing ranges, the nuclear test sites, the radioactive dispersals, the secret military research, the contaminated earth and water, irradiated humans and animals, the land itself pockmarked with craters, unexploded bombs, and the twisted metal of abandoned military targets. The paradox of the desert setting is caught in the haunting images of Richard Misrach's photographs—the remarkable combination of desert splendor and ravaged landscape, of vast beauty scarred by a military presence, ungainly tourists, commercial enterprise, failed experiments, abandoned buildings.[1]

In the metaphoric design Williams adopts, ironies abound. Although she is within a wildlife refuge established by the government, the wildlife and her own life are threatened by that government's own military aircraft. The nation, after all, is a political construct that owes its very existence to the appropriation of the wild, annexing and subduing it. Can it also be trusted with responsibility for preserving and protecting it? This particular wildlife refuge, Cabeza Prieta, lies near no densely populated city or commercial center or along well-traveled freeways; its very geography should be refuge enough, except that it is located within the Barry M. Goldwater Air Force Bombing Range. If the steam locomotive of Hawthorne's day was destructive of the natural environment, that consequence was incidental to its principal objectives of promoting commerce, public transportation, and economic growth; but the military aircraft that replaces the steam locomotive in this metaphoric design has destruction as its primary goal: "'These babies carry sixteen thousand pounds of mixed ordnance: bombs, rockets, missiles, laser-guided bombs, and bullets. They are specifically designed to destroy enemy tanks, and they do. Twenty-three hundred Iraqi vehicles were knocked out during Desert Storm.'" These are the words of the Air Force spokesman quoted in Williams's essay (121–22).

Desert Storm. The rain in the Cabeza Prieta Wildlife Refuge also turns into a desert storm: "We are now in a cloudburst," Williams writes, "the land, the mountains, and the aircraft disappearing in a shroud of dense clouds. Rolling thunder masks the engines and the explosions. Everything is hidden" (121). For the moment, nature's storm prevails over the man-made storm, and the image of the interrupted idyll is reversed: the alienating roar of invasive technology is effaced by the sounds of nature. Does nature's storm portend a still more violent apocalyptic response to the human desecration of the desert, or does its ephemeral nature suggest inevitable defeat?

Williams's narrative, brief as it is, seems to take the form of what Leo Marx calls the classic American fable, "a redemptive journey away from society in the direction of nature," beginning with a renunciation of one's own society (1964, 69). But Williams's essay reveals what John Elder has observed, how problematic this form becomes in the more desperate circumstances of our time (1996, 24). In the American fable as Marx describes it, particularly as it appears in nineteenth-century literature, the retreat to nature is followed by a return to and reintegration with society, but Elder points out limiting factors: "Retreat into the wilderness and cultural integration serve beneficial purposes when they represent smoothly revolving sides of a balanced process of health and wholeness. But when such terms grow rigidly antithetical, each focused on the other's destruction, the larger principle of complementary relation has been broken" (1996, 25). Williams's essay makes clear how out of balance the relationship between wilderness and culture is in the present age. The journey *toward* nature can no longer be a journey *away* from society if nature is found only in preserves where government is the gatekeeper. Instead, the journey leads to confrontations.

Williams's essay does begin with a renunciation. In her opening words, "I refuse to sign," she declares her unwillingness to enter into an agreement with her government that would absolve it of responsibility for harm that may come to her in the refuge–bombing range (115). The document warns of the possibility of injury or death from falling aircraft, live ammunition, missiles, unexploded ordnance, abandoned mine shafts, and other unmarked hazards. But Williams's refusal to sign does not enable her to elude the detritus of society scattered throughout the desert, threatening life and making a mockery of the very term *refuge*. Signing is no mere formality for Williams; she tells her husband, "'I want my government to be accountable'" (116), and she herself is keeping accounts. She has come to Cabeza Prieta, she says, to make her own unofficial count of desert bighorn sheep.

While searching for bighorns in the refuge, Williams recalls many ways that different cultures, both ancient and modern, have honored, mythologized, and appropriated the image of the ram. These details, including her personal associations with this animal, form a powerful shaping motif of the essay, revealing not just the human propensity for warfare but also the complex and ambiguous relationship between humans and animals, our love of them, to be sure, but also our eagerness to appropriate them to our own use. "In Celtic lore," she tells us, "the spiral horns of the ram are attributes of war gods. In Egyptian mythology, the ram is the personification of . . . the Sun God. . . . It is virility, the masculine generative force, the creative heat. In the Bible," she notes, "it is the sacrificial animal" (116–17). Williams recalls the last time she saw a bighorn. She was traveling in the Grand Canyon when she spied a young ram drinking from the Colorado River. "In the Grand Canyon, we were no threat," she says (119). But the word *threat* brings to mind her teenage high school experiences. The bighorn ram, associated with warfare and masculine virility, was her high school team's mascot, and Williams was president of the pep club. She recalls the football fight song, her organized promotion of the team, the ballyhoo. "In the desolation of the Cabeza," she writes, "I wonder how I have found my way from the pom-pom culture of Salt Lake City to this truly wild place" (119).

But, of course, very little has been left behind. She carries into the Cabeza Prieta, in her memory, the traditions of Western civilization as well as her own past, carries them along with the "two water bottles, sunblock, rain gear, a notebook and pencil, and a lunch of raisins, cream cheese, and crackers" and some lemon drops (117). "An individual can no more renounce his cultural heritage," John Elder notes, "than he can deny his genotype" (1996, 25). And in this "truly wild place" she also is confronted by the most stunning achievements of her own civilization, the culmination of centuries of human warfare honed to the technological marvel of high-speed precision aircraft. Like her nineteenth-century predecessors—just as Thoreau, for example, despite his hawk image, is fascinated by the power and promise of the steam locomotive—so Williams, even at the instant of her own victimization by these aircraft, cannot resist their lure: "The dark aircraft bank. I have seen them before, seabirds, parasitic jaegers that turn with the slightest dip of a wing. I am taken in by their beauty, their aerial finesse" (121). Just as Thoreau compares the whistle of the locomotive to the shriek of a hawk, so does Williams link the artificial to the natural, seeing not the hawk's threat but the beauty of birds in flight.

Seabirds. Parasitic Jaegers. The Fairchild A-10s are called "Warthogs." The F-16s are dubbed "Fighting Falcons." The F-15Es "Strike Eagles." What can one say about such language? Williams calls it "military ornithology" (1994, 123). What does this language suggest about American people and their culture? Paul Shepard maintains there are important qualities of personality and culture that are not "easily seen in the self or even in other people" but are "discoverable only as they inhere in other creatures" (1996, 51–52). Does this "military ornithology" reveal some intangible but essential trait of the American character? Or is it meant to mask it?

One might reasonably expect that because she is a woman, Williams would be absolved of responsibility for the virile, masculine assault on nature she experiences in the desert. Williams is well aware of the discourse on the feminization of nature and male exploitation of it. Gender differentiation is a theme that threads its way through her essay. She is traveling in the company of two men who, unlike her, willingly sign the "hold harmless" agreement of the government whose spokesperson also is male. Her husband, she tells us, "is irritated by my unwillingness to do what we have to do *to get into beautiful country*" (116; italics mine). Both men "tease" her about a dream she had the night before, a dream of searching for a one-eyed ram. "Sounds phallic to me," her husband says (116). In their trek through the refuge, the men take the lead and must wait for her to catch up. Later, she lingers behind deliberately. When alone, she sees what others do not. Once, a saguaro cactus in the shape of "the reverend Mother" beckons to her, and she finds "at her feet . . . an offering of gilded flicker feathers." Later, she comes upon ancient petroglyphs and recognizes among these drawings the one-eyed ram of her dream (118, 124).

But neither her gender nor her sensitivity nor her mysterious encounters absolve her from complicity in the transgressions of her species. Her own confessions convict her—writing "go-fight-win" letters to the athletes at school, marveling at the beauty, the "aerial finesse," of fighter aircraft. She too must take responsibility for what happens in the desert. "Instead of counting sheep, I am counting bombs," Williams writes (122). Earlier, she hopes the scene from atop Sheep Mountain will inspire her and her companions "to think like a ram," but it is the unrelenting sorties of military aircraft that reduce her to what she calls "an animal vulnerability" (119, 123). To the aircraft, she and the other creatures of the earth are not merely expendable, random targets: "No, it's worse than that—we do not exist," she says (123).

Although Williams's essay begins with a reproof of the government and is modeled on the form of the redemptive journey to the natural world, the experience described here is not cleansing, does not free Williams from distress or wrongdoing, does not release her from blame. She learns that though she renounces her government, she cannot escape identification with her nation, her culture, her species, and cannot dodge responsibility for their acts. She entered the refuge with the declaration, "I want my government to be accountable" (116), but through her desert experience she learns that others hold her accountable. In her journey, Williams moves persistently toward confronting and acknowledging her own culpability, an understanding expressed grimly in the closing sentences of the essay: "Tonight in the Cabeza Prieta, I feel the eyes of the desert bighorn. It is I who am being watched. It is I who am being counted" (124).

Williams's essay reveals a stark transformation of the metaphoric design that Leo Marx observed in nineteenth-century American literature. Today's writers encounter the sonic boom in the desert, the bombs in the refuge. It is tempting to say this is not so much a transformation of the earlier image of the machine in the garden but rather its unveiling, a revelation of the inherent tensions stripped bare. But this suggestion implies an inevitability to history that certainly Williams will not admit. In the collection of essays *An Unspoken Hunger,* "All That Is Hidden" is strategically placed near the end of the book and is immediately followed not by another essay but by the record of Williams's congressional testimony protesting the trashing of the Pacific yew whose bark has medicinal use for cancer patients. It's as if Williams's self-recognition in the desert motivates and empowers her subsequent political engagement. As she herself has said of *An Unspoken Hunger,* "I think those are essays that really talk about how a poetics of place translates to a politics of place" (Siporin 1996, 112).

Williams is not alone in exploring the meanings that accrue to this new metaphoric design, bombs in the desert. Her companion in the desert, Gary Nabhan, in his essay "Hummingbirds and Human Aggression," uses the occasion of another visit to Cabeza Prieta Wildlife Refuge to explore the nature and origins of human aggression. He is troubled by the war in Kuwait called Desert Storm: "I've fixed on a global issue through concentrating my attention on this desert microcosm" (1997, 112). In this essay, Nabhan probes his own Arab American family history. He describes the challenge of soldiers with automatic rifles who come upon his pickup truck there in the refuge. He studies the territoriality of hummingbirds, notes the distinction between innate aggression and adaptive behavior, recalls the peaceful behavioral patterns of O'odham people native to this place in contrast with intruders who horde and waste the scarce resources. He deplores the loss of human life in the Gulf War and describes in precise detail the environmental destruction inflicted on the desert that is an integral part of the planet's life-support system: "If there is something peculiar about us latter-day human beings," he writes, "it is our willingness to destroy a resource essential for everyone's survival" (127).

Like Nabhan and Williams, the writer Gretel Ehrlich, in her essay "The Fasting Heart," also seeks insight into the human experience by focusing on the desert microcosm. This concluding essay in her collection *Islands, the Universe, Home* takes the form of journal entries extending from February to late August. At the very center of Ehrlich's essay is an account of her visit to the White Sands Missile Range in New Mexico where she marvels at how the grama grass cactus, the buffalo gourd, the yucca plant, and a particular species of moth are adapted for survival in the desert environment. She is near Trinity Site, crawling over radioactive ground, but it is springtime and the desert is in bloom. She is studying its flora while overhead B-17 bombers roar toward a nearby bombing range and F-15s destroy simulated forests that the army has erected on the desert flats. She is intensely aware of the military presence as she ponders how the uncommon grama grass cactus survives "by giving up its best defense"—its spines are soft and elongated—and blending in with the grama grass among which it grows: "Then it occurs to me that this cactus's best defense is a peaceful one: not meting out pain but merely blending in" (1992, 178, 180). Although these grasses are grazed and the cactus eaten, the consequence is that the grazing animal, through its manure, distributes the ingested seeds for propagation. For Ehrlich, this desert scene mirrors with concentrated intensity the enigma of life and death, the recognition that enables her to move beyond spiritual aridity. Ehrlich's essay is deeply personal but not without warning for the world's superpower: "Here on the missile range," she writes, "death is thought to have the power to end things. But that truth is incomplete" (181).

From these essays of Williams, Nabhan, and Ehrlich, it becomes clear that environmentalists and the military have competing definitions of "desert." Is it a fragile, ecological environment with its own right of survival, or is it wasteland, empty space, inert matter? Is the desert's silence, solitude, and vastness to be a refuge from military aggression, a sanctuary where plant and animal life is protected and humans may seek solace and spiritual renewal, or is it a place to conceal the secrets of military experiments in annihilation? In addition to military secrets, are there secrets for survival concealed in the desert, its flora and fauna, the grama grass cactus and hummingbirds, for example, or the way of the O'odham people? Must the desert have any utility to justify its being? How much of it must be destroyed to save the nation? Williams has written that "the way in which we treat the world is a measure of our sensitivity." And she asks the salient question: "Can we really survive the worship of our own destructiveness?" (Whitt 2002, 85).

Evocative images of the military presence in the deserts of the West are a recurring pattern in contemporary American literature and art—the photographs of Richard Misrach, the essays of Gary Nabhan, Gretel Ehrlich, and many others including Terry Tempest Williams. Elaborated in fine detail, the images of overwhelming military power assaulting the desert environment prove to be a trenchant emblem or metaphoric design that fires the imagination of contemporary artists who invest it with a significance that cuts to the heart of the most urgent concerns of our age.

What then is the significance of the desert setting and the machinery of modern warfare in this writing? There is no easy answer and no satisfactory short answer, though shorthand terms are convenient. Today's soaring aircraft, exploding bombs, and military presence in the desert evoke such phrases as "the military-industrial complex," "global capitalism," and—even though the assault is in and on our own land—"U.S. hegemony." "The bombing," Rebecca Solnit suggests, "no longer requires an enemy . . . unless landscape itself as space and matter is the enemy" (1996, 50–51). But Williams carries this argument one step further. True, the land as well as its plants and animals is treated as an enemy, but even people like herself who act on behalf of the natural world and also are treated as an enemy are nevertheless complicit in the assault. The image of bombs in the desert reveals a nation at war with itself. If the desert is a refuge from worldly concerns, if it is the place of spiritual renewal, if patches of the desert are the last remaining wilderness in a land whose identity rests in the idea of wilderness, then what is at stake is the soul of the people and the very ground of the nation's being.

Note

1. Richard Misrach's photographic series "Desert Cantos" is superbly reproduced in Tucker 1996. Rebecca Solnit's essay in this same volume provides not only an insightful and moving cultural history of the desert but also a sensitive study of its aesthetics. In addition, I recommend Solnit's book *Savage Dreams: A Journey into the Hidden Wars of the American West* (1994). Of special interest is Misrach and Misrach, *Bravo 20: The Bombing of the American West* (1990), which, in addition to Richard Misrach's photographs, contains an account of military activities in Nevada written by Myriam Weisang Misrach. Readers will appreciate two other works to which I am indebted, John Beck's perceptive analysis of Misrach's photographs (2000) and the essay by Martin Padget, "Desert Wanderings" (2000), that incorporates into a scholarly article the narrative of his own treks in the American desert, including his experience with war planes and a missile launch.

Works Cited

Beck, John. 2000. "Blown Away: Wars Visible and Invisible in Richard Misrach's *Desert Cantos*." *European Journal of American Culture* 19 (3):156–66.

Ehrlich, Gretel. 1992. "The Fasting Heart." In *Islands, the Universe, Home*, 163–96. 1991. Reprint, New York: Penguin.

Elder, John. 1996. *Imagining the Earth: Poetry and the Vision of Nature*. 2d ed. Athens: University of Georgia Press.

Marx, Leo. 1964. *The Machine in the Garden: Technology and the Pastoral Ideal in America*. New York: Oxford University Press.

Misrach, Richard, and Myriam Weisang Misrach. 1990. *Bravo 20: The Bombing of the American West*. Baltimore: Johns Hopkins University Press.

Nabhan, Gary Paul. 1997. "Hummingbirds and Human Aggression." In *Cultures of Habitat*, 112–32. Washington, D.C.: Counterpoint.

Padget, Martin. 2000. "Desert Wanderings." *European Journal of American Culture* 19 (3):167–83.

Shepard, Paul, ed. 1996. *A Paul Shepard Reader: The Only World We've Got*. San Francisco: Sierra Club Books.

Siporan, Ona. 1996. "Terry Tempest Williams and Ona Siporin: A Conversation." *Western American Literature* 31 (2):99–113.

Solnit, Rebecca. 1994. *Savage Dreams: A Journey into the Hidden Wars of the American West*. San Francisco: Sierra Club Books.

———. 1996. "Scapeland." In *Crimes and Splendors: The Desert Cantos of Richard Misrach*, by Anne Wilkes Tucker, 37–58. Boston: Bulfinch/Little, Brown.

Thoreau, Henry David. 1971. *Walden*. Edited by J. Lyndon Shanley. Princeton: Princeton University Press.

Tucker, Ann Wilkes. 1996. *Crimes and Splendors: The Desert Cantos of Richard Misrach*. Boston: Bulfinch/Little, Brown.

Whitt, Jan. 2002. "'The Sorcery of Literature': Terry Tempest Williams and Her Stories of the West." *Journal of the West* 41 (1):83–89.

Williams, Terry Tempest. 1994. "All That Is Hidden." In *An Unspoken Hunger: Stories from the Field*, 115–24. New York: Pantheon Books. First published in *Sierra* (March–April 1993) and also anthologized in W. Scott Olsen and Scott Cairns, eds. 1996. *The Sacred Place: Witnessing the Holy in the Physical World*. Salt Lake City: University of Utah Press.

MARY NEWELL

❦

Embodied Mutuality

RECONNECTION TO ENVIRONMENT AND SELF IN
AN UNSPOKEN HUNGER

The only way to find a larger vision is to be somewhere in particular.
—Donna Haraway, "Situated Knowledges: The Science Question in Feminism and the Privilege of Partial Perspective"

Throughout *An Unspoken Hunger*, Terry Tempest Williams expresses a passionate plea for reconnection to the natural environment and to
a fuller sense of embodiment.[1] This action could not be a "return to nature"
in the sense of reentering a pure, original, or monolithic "Nature," both because humans are already biologically embedded in the natural world and
because we know this world only via human constructs.[2] Instead, the movement of reconnection is one of experiencing a wider spectrum of "the life we
so often refuse to see" in wild nature (Williams 1994, 57). My focus is on the
perceptual processes that support this reconnection, specifically vision and
kinesthesia, or bodily awareness.[3] I will explore them via an ecocritical model
grounded in "situated knowledges," defined by Donna Haraway as "partial,
locatable, critical knowledges sustaining the possibility of webs of connections" (1991, 191). Haraway has sketched a framework whereby situated acts
of vision could bypass dichotomous constructions and support moments of
relation. Williams describes moments that substantiate Haraway's paradigm
in environments as diverse as the African Serengeti and City Island, New
York.

The other perceptual modality through which I will explore Williams's
writing is kinesthesia, which is inherently embodied. Kinesthesia is the
largest sensory modality, comprising our perceptions of the environment
through touch and our perceptions of our own corporeality. Kinesthesia

plays an important role in Williams's narrative: it is the primary substrate of presence and self-construct, and the main medium for exchanges with wild nature. She recommends that women broaden their sense of self through incorporating from wild nature capacities that have been eclipsed in our "distractive and domesticated life" (1994, 57). I interpret these exchanges as a kinesthetic dialogue. Williams's movement toward intimacy with nature flirts with the boundaries of species and self. In *An Unspoken Hunger,* Terry Tempest Williams exemplifies embodied perceptual processes that support reconnection to a wider spectrum of life in environment and self.

RELATIONAL WEBS

The exploitation of the natural world, with no concern for sustainability, has been justified by dichotomous epistemologies in which mind, male, and human are valued while body, female, and nature become devalued "others." In dichotomous models, position is relative to an empowered center. Ecological approaches are, in contrast, relational; they view the natural world as an interlinked, mutually sustaining web of life, in which all animate forms have subjectivity and agency.[4]

The importance of a relational model for human-nature interaction is emphasized in Haraway's paradigm of situated knowledges.[5] Whereas dichotomies tend to be fixed, hierarchical and singularly referential, relational models are dynamic and generative of multiple interconnections. Located positions can interrelate in multiple ways, through what Haraway calls "webs of connection." As Haraway summarizes her model,

> The alternative to relativism is partial, locatable, critical knowledges sustaining the possibility of webs of connections, called solidarity in politics and shared conversations in epistemology. Relativism is a way of being nowhere while claiming to be everywhere equally. . . . But it is precisely in the politics and epistemology of partial perspectives that the possibility of sustained, rational objective inquiry rests. (1991, 191–92)

I will elaborate "locatable positions" in terms of perceptual processes.

SEEING TOGETHER

The "Hunger" of Williams's title is a hunger for direct connection to that which enlivens. In the one-paragraph title chapter, the narrator and another person share "one avocado between us." To enjoy the avocado, they divide and slice it. This dividing action does not divide them from each other; a mutual look sustains their connection: "We look at each other and smile, eating avocadoes with sharp silver blades, risking the blood of our tongues repeatedly" (79). This simple passage evokes possibilities for inclusion and mutuality in relation to embodiment and vision. The reciprocal gaze across a shared meal tacitly acknowledges mutuality: while enjoying the sensual pleasure, they are aware that the same bodies that experience pleasure are also vulnerable. Williams exemplifies embodied vision in more challenging contexts, where its action initiates an attunement with the environment.

Perceptual processes act across the human-environment boundary. They provide awareness of the environment but often structure that awareness into limited patterns. To reestablish a sense of connection with a living world would therefore require a change in the quality of perceptual acts. In the older scientific model that Haraway critiques, the observer is assumed to be an "impartial subject" viewing a passive, distanced object (1991, 188). Such a unidirectional, dichotomous action readily becomes hierarchical when agency, and therefore capacity to relate, is attributed only to the viewer. In contrast, situated viewing allows for multiple sites of agency, and, therefore, for a variety of relational interactions. I would claim, in agreement with Haraway, that moments of nondichotomous vision are acts of relation.

The visual system is not a transparent receiver of impressions like a camera lens but is an interpretive system in which new information is associated with former perceptions. As indicated by Haraway, this interpretive process allows looking in new ways: "All eyes, including our own, are active perceptual systems, building in translations and specific ways of seeing. All these pictures of the world should not be allegories of infinite mobility and interchangeability, but of elaborate specificity and difference *and the loving care people might take to learn how to see faithfully from another's point of view*" (1991, 190; italics mine). Haraway is proposing that we look for the potential within the concrete and specific rather than in the abstract "unlimited possibilities" agenda of pure social-constructionist positions. She associates "elaborate specificity" with a process of learning that includes "loving care." "Elaborate" implies a nonautomatic action, performed with attentiveness. Such a quality of looking invites reciprocal exchange between those with differing viewpoints and characteristics. Rather than reinscribing the hierarchy inherent in the dichotomous model of vision, it supports finding relation across "difference."

Because vision is an interpretive process, the meaning derived from visual perception reflects the focus and intention of the observer. I suggest that to see ecologically is to intentionally look for patterns of relationship, or nodes of mutuality. Williams's embodied visual practices, illustrated below, include seeing with "beginner's eyes," seeing in parallel with another, and seeing reciprocally. Williams's attentiveness in seeing from another's point of view both in the African Serengeti and in the Bronx exhibits her "loving care" for the environment. Overall, her ecological values are evident in her perceptual focus.

Recounting her experience in the unfamiliar landscape of the Serengeti Plains of Africa, Williams writes, "For a naturalist, traveling into unfamiliar territory is like turning a kaleidoscope ninety degrees. . . . You enter a new landscape in search of the order you know to be there" (1994, 3). Linking "kaleidoscope" with "order" suggests the same reality viewed from a number of different subject positions. She says she looked with "beginner's eyes," a phrase that connotes a willingness to let the patterns appear, rather than imposing categories from one's prior experience. Williams's natural world, in correspondence with ecological principles, is never a passive background. For instance, she figures the sky as a "taut bow," implying a system of energy that can change its state (3). Further, she is not a distanced observer who dominates a view, but a participant in dialogue with an ecosystem.

Williams evokes an embodied relation to her material by including herself in her description. The Serengeti, Williams claims, is "one of the last refuges on earth where great herds of animals and their predators can wander at will. I chose to wander in the northern appendage of these plains" (4). By repeating the word *wander,* Williams establishes a bodily parallel between humans and other animals, through their movements. I will refer to such parallel activities, capacities, or vulnerabilities as "nodes of mutuality." They would correspond to intersections in Haraway's "webs of connections." Williams creates an embodied context by presenting her perceptions as they unfold rather than merely stating facts extracted from her experience.

Williams learns to attune her vision to the ecosystem by seeing in parallel with her Masai guide, Samuel. In the Serengeti, she suggests, the Masai are close enough to the earth that "they know the songs of grasses and the script of snakes."[6] Williams intones, "The umbilical cord between man and earth has not been severed here" (4). Although her Masai guide, Samuel, has modified his traditional lifestyle, he "has not abandoned his native intelligence. Samuel felt the presence of animals long before he saw them. I watched him pull animals out of hiding with his eyes. I saw him penetrate stillness with his senses" (4–5). The dynamic and active quality of his perception has little resemblance to a snapshot. He is not recording; he is anticipating through his awareness of the life forms of the area. Williams mentions a similar ability to anticipate in her "homeland," the Great Basin. Such sensory attunement to an ecosystem, the knowledge one learns in the process of attentively inhabiting a locality, is probably the original situated knowledge, and certainly a significant one. It establishes reciprocity between humans and wild nature, or between the act of looking and what is seen.

Williams recounts her process of learning to comprehend the new terrain: "When traveling in a new country, it is a gift to have a guide. They know the nuances of the world they live in. Samuel smells the rain the night before it falls. . . . I trust his instincts and borrow them until I uncover my own. But there is danger here. One can become lazy in the reliance on a guide. The burden of a newcomer is to pay attention" (5). Williams learns actively by borrowing Samuel's skills, not just passively relying on them. She understands the need to focus her own awareness, "to pay attention." In this sense, contact with the wild brings her awareness into sharper focus. The "danger" might be physical; it could also be the danger of not fully understanding the environment, and so failing to find a relation to it. She is grateful to have a guide who dispenses information slowly, allowing her the "pleasure of discovery" (6). The gradual process of "discovery" allows a range of impressions to be incorporated, so that the learning is embodied rather than merely conceptual.

Williams's attentiveness reveals relationships already potential but previously unnoticed. She writes, "[A]s my eyes become acquainted with lion, I begin to distinguish fur from grass" (6). The emergence of pattern from the background also implies their interconnectedness. The lions are at home in the grasses, which hide them. When the lion becomes aware of her look, though, "the lion's eyes change" (6). This shared gaze does not reflect mutual enjoyment, like the reciprocal gaze across the avocado. Rather, the lion's awareness of being seen by a human charges the atmosphere with a taut awareness. For a moment, she is afraid. This encounter is a more obviously dangerous moment than eating an avocado, yet the desire for, and risk of, encounter is shared in both experiences. In the fixed dichotomies of the "impartial observer" scientist and the natural object, one has a safe epistemological stance. To go beyond the unidirectional subject-object viewing, to go toward encounter with another agent, is to risk a situation one cannot control. To be situated is to admit partiality, and so, vulnerability. "Location is about vulnerability; location resists the politics of closure, finality" (Haraway 1991, 196). It is also, though, an opportunity for new understanding. As Haraway explains, "[W]e . . . seek partiality . . . for the sake of the connections and unexpected openings situated knowledges make possible. The only way to find a larger vision is to be somewhere in particular" (196). In this instance, the larger vision is the paradoxical experience of interspecies difference *and* mutuality.

Williams shows no sentimental inclination to collapse the categorical distance between lion and human. The autonomy of each is retained in the moment of relation. Soon, though, the situation becomes a familiar one of prey and the sequence of predators that "clean the kill." For Williams, the memory that "we too are predators" is a "precious possession" (8). In this act of recognition, predatory activity becomes a node of mutuality, connecting the varying life forms, without erasing other differences.

To see a new landscape with "beginner's eyes" is less challenging for Williams than to see natural vitality in the built environment of City Island, Bronx. She finds "the juxtaposition of concrete and wetlands . . . unsettling" (42). Williams is challenged to find a hopeful view in the face of environmental pollution. The City Island site "smelled of sewage. Our wetlands are becoming urban wastelands." Her view is expanded, though, by sidestepping to see from the position of her Bronx associate Lee Milner. While Williams saw the "gnarled oysters with abnormal growths on their shells," covered with black oil slick as "moribund," Lee saw them as "systems of regeneration. She walked toward us with a bucket of killifish, some hermit crabs, one ghost shrimp" (43). In ending this list with one lone "ghost" shrimp, Williams's more doubtful attitude toward the Bronx environment shadows her associate's hopeful one: "ghost" resonates ominously, as if it were a predictor of fate for the whole area. Nevertheless, Williams's Bronx example shows that even in a degraded ecology, one can find the embodied qualities of attentiveness and reciprocity. Her colleague attests that "these open lands hold my sanity," while most of the tenants of Co-op City "don't see the marsh at all" (42). Lee's ecological commitment allows her to be nourished by views that others ignore. Again, ecological or nondichotomous vision derives from choice and focus.

Williams dialogues between her view and Lee's until they are more convergent. Her fears in the "sinister" location are offset by the "implacable focus" of a heron that her associate points out when Williams had not seen "anything but my own fears fly by with a few gulls." This ironic statement underscores the subjectivity of vision. Seeing the heron made her feel "more at home" (44), not only because she recognized him and could fit his food-gathering activities into a known pattern, but also because she found a parallel between the bird's focus and her associate's "stalwartness" in retaining a positive attitude toward her local ecology. Human-nature reciprocity is implied: for her friend, the songs of the red-winged blackbirds "keep her attentive in a city that has little memory of wildness" (48). Attentiveness becomes an enlivening node of interspecies mutuality.

By demonstrating her processes of coming into relation with new or challenging environments, Williams allows the reader to follow her processes of embodied perception. Meaning arises out of embodied interactions in context. Through "looking with" rather than "looking at," through sharing a reciprocal gaze or attentively "looking like" the birds do, Williams finds nodes of mutuality across dissimilar contexts. Williams illustrates, as parallel qualities between humans and other animals, the facts that both wander, both participate in the food chain, both can display an enlivening attentiveness, and both are vulnerable. These experiences of connection allow feelings of mutuality toward other species that share our reliance on the ecosystem.

GROUND RULES: SITUATED AND EMBODIED

The human-ecosystem relationship falls into Haraway's category of an "unhomogeneous relationship" (1991, 3). On one hand, humans have faculties not found in the rest of nature—for instance, written language. On the other hand, the earth could presumably survive without humans, but humans are not in a similar privileged position. Williams figures this basic dependence on the earth in a Masai story of a child grasping a handful of grass as a gesture of humility: "The child remembers where the source of his power lies" (12). Ecocriticism differs from many critical approaches because it references the earth we live on, a ground that exceeds human constructions. To be situated in an ecocritical approach, therefore, always means to be located in terms of place. Within the ecosystem as a whole, each individual is situated in a local context, composed of interacting biological, geographical, historical, and sociopolitical aspects. Within that context, each is situated in her or his own body, with all its many-layered specificity. The movement away from universal claims and distanced, privileged views is also a movement toward embodiment, toward inhabiting one's own space.

Embodiment references a post-Cartesian body-mind that is not only socially constructed, but also biologically constituted. Feminists have often eschewed biological arguments because they have been used to justify the marginalization of women. Thus, to claim that women are closer to nature leaves the field open for saying that women are more primitive, and therefore unsuitable for enterprises open to men. Newer biological models, however, accord with feminism in providing for dynamic change. Lynda Birke describes such a model: "Our bodies are constantly being made and remade; bones, muscles, connective tissue—all are constantly in flux. . . . Such a view insists on seeing organisms and their biology as transformative" (2000, 151). While these processes are constrained by organic limits, as noted by Birke, these are species-wide or interspecies limits, not gendered ones, and therefore cannot be applied to denigrate women. Instead, they can be the basis for experiences of mutuality. Many of the nodes of mutuality mentioned by Williams are biologically based.

Embodiment functions not only as the container of life processes, but also as the locus of ongoing human-environment interactions. According to contemporary life sciences, the nervous system completes its development by means of dynamic interactions with the environment.[7] The particular emphasis of ecological approaches is the attribution of agency to nonhuman aspects of nature. Patrick Murphy coins the word *interanimation* to describe "the ways in which humans and other entities develop, change, and learn through mutually influencing each other day to day" (2000, 99). We interact with our local environment by means of perceptual and movement processes and the related conceptual processes. The ongoing stream of sensory impulses to the brain orients us to the local environment in present time. The brain responds to this input by sending signals to the muscles, so that appropriate action can be taken. I propose that situated perceptual activities offer a spectrum of knowledge important in reconnecting us to our natural environment. I have exemplified this above with vision and will now discuss the contributions of kinesthesia to processes of reconnection.

Embodiment is the locus of experiences related to inhabiting a particular body; kinesthesia is the sense through which its inhabitant knows that body. Kinesthesia, which encompasses touch and all forms of surface-to-surface contact, develops as one matures in an environment; it is therefore the sensory system through which we can experience our embeddedness in the natural world. In more culturally mediated contexts, the kinesthetic aspects of our experience tend to be subordinated in favor of verbal-conceptual modes. However, kinesthesia underlies all embodied experience, and is essential in attuning with the environment. Kinesthesia creates and references maps in the brain that relate the body's geometry to that of the environment. These maps allow us to attune to the environment and to interact reciprocally. Williams's acts of embodied vision discussed above are interconnected with kinesthesia. She also mentions tactile means of becoming familiar with new environments: "In remote and unfamiliar territory, I must learn to read the landscape inch by inch. The grasses become Braille as I run my fingers through them" (1994, 10). Williams's choice of the word *Braille* accentuates the primacy of touch in the experience. The phrase "inch by inch" further evokes a process of touching or moving through an environment that must be experienced bodily, and gradually. A multilayered meaning accrues through such embodied practices.

In the Bronx, the two naturalists demonstrate an understanding that is kinesthetic, concrete, and not just conceptual. Their mutual familiarity with birds is evidenced by their capacity to imitate the bird movements: "Both of us could re-create their steady wingbeats with our hands as they moved though crepuscular hours." Their knowledge becomes a shared gestural language. Lee Milner also gestured to demonstrate ecological features analogically: she would "run her fingers" across the map, indicating all the features of the ecosystem. "She would gesture with her body the way light shifts, exposing herons, bitterns, and owls" (40). Her gestures demonstrate embodied ecological knowledge.

As well as promoting a renewed relationship to the environment, kinesthesia brings one into a fuller contact with one's own embodied presence. Williams uses "presence" to connote full awareness of embodiment, or full self-inhabitation. For instance, she claims that both she and Samuel are "fully present" as they enter the savannah of the Serengeti (5). Such self-inhabitation seems to be the basic preparation for the quality of focus Williams brings to the environments she visits. Focus in turn allows nondichotomous perceptual experience. Birds, as well as humans, are said to exhibit presence (64). As a feature that is shared with other species, presence can be a component of mutuality. Williams's description of swimming at Stone Creek shows the linkage between kinesthesia and presence: "I shed my clothing like snakeskin. I swam beneath the waterfall, felt its pelting massage on my back, stood up behind it, turned and touched the moss, the ferns, the slippery rock wall. No place else to be" (69). This sequential description of linked action and sensation creates for the reader both the quality of the waterfall and the narrator's corporal sense of contact with it. The *s* alliteration invokes sinuous movement. "Pelting massage" and the references to moving and touching are more kinesthetic than visual. The narrator's nakedness relates to the hunger of the title, a hunger for less culturally mediated experience; shedding clothing allows her to bring the entire surface of her body in contact with the element of water. Touching is bidirectional: you touch something "outside" yourself, yet the impulses from the touch define your own boundary as well. The contact with the waterfall is felt simultaneously with the contours of the body. The usage of "to be" rather than "to do" in the final phrase affirms how such direct, embodied contact with place intensifies her sense of presence.

Undomesticating the Feminine: Wild Dialogues

Williams exemplifies moments of recognizing shared features, which I have called nodes of mutuality. These nodes can support more sustained interactions with wild nature. Haraway proposes that an exchange with the environment would be in the form of a "situated conversation" (1991, 200). The term *conversation* implies a desirable reciprocity between agents in dynamic, nonhierarchical exchange. However, its implication of a verbal locus of exchange may be misleading. I suggest that a large part of our capacity for experiencing "interanimation" is kinesthetic, which is a nonverbal register. Williams speaks of two forms of nonverbal vocalizations. She mentions echo and response, which imply moments of reciprocal dialogue, rather than extended conversations. Second, she reports on Georgia O'Keeffe and herself howling, which could be considered a brief dialogue. Their howling seems, in different instances, a natural response to the surroundings, a feeling of rapport with other animals, and a ritual attempt at reconnecting with wild nature. Williams also writes of embracing and dancing, which are kinesthetic forms of encounter. These vignettes indicate how kinesthesia can support interactions with nonhuman species that have analogous sensory and movement faculties, but do not share our speech.

The hunger for direct, embodied contact is largely "unspoken," then, because it is experienced through nonverbal sensory faculties. Williams frequently writes of engagement with the land as erotics, which implies a physical, sensual contact: "There is no defense against an open heart and a supple body in dialogue with wilderness. Internal strength is an absorption of the external landscape. We are informed by beauty, raw and sensual. Through an erotics of place our sensitivity becomes our sensibility" (1994, 86). This passage alludes to a kinesthetic encounter, not a verbal conversation; it is the heart and body that are "in dialogue with wilderness." "Absorption" is a sensorial process; one is "informed" not of concepts, but of new, "raw and sensual" impressions. The final sentence implies that by allowing the new impressions to be absorbed, the sensory feeds thought, which becomes more grounded in embodiment. The passage as a whole conveys the reinvigorating effects of opening toward new perceptions of wild nature.

Kinesthesia is also crucial in our relationship with our own embodiment. The same brain maps that relate body to environment maintain a sense of embodied self that is the basis for attitudes toward one's body and its capabilities. Through its role in creating and maintaining these maps, kinesthesia forms the elusive construct commonly called "body image," which I refer to as self-construct. Like vision, this process is culturally modulated; one evaluates one's capabilities in comparison to others or to cultural norms. Constrictions in self-construct might interfere with full presence. Williams urges women to reconfigure their self-constructs through contact with wild nature.

In the chapter "Undressing the Bear," Williams proposes an expansion of self-construct through reclaiming elements of "wildness." Wild nature is represented by bears, both actual bears and bears inscribed in myths, stories, and a novel. She is not proposing an idealized rapport with an idyllic nature, but an imaginative expansion of self-definition. "When in the presence of the natural order," says Williams, "we remember the potentiality of life, which has been overgrown by civilization" (8). Widening one's self-definition moves in the direction of developing this potentiality. Bears have some analogous features to humans, all of which are nonverbal. The bear-women exchanges could be considered a kinesthetic dialogue with "wildness." Because Williams frames this dialogue as an address to women, it is a call to undomesticate women.

Williams grounds her bear collage in concrete experience by beginning and ending the chapter with stories of actual encounters with bears. The chapter begins with a story of a hunter who suddenly realized that the bear he had just shot, and was skinning, was "not a bear. It was a woman" (52). At this moment, the hunter saw the bear in its subjectivity, not as the object of his hunt. This story presents the bear as a concrete subject, and also establishes the chapter's theme of women-bear interplay. Then Williams mentions a near encounter, an echo: "Standing naked in the sand, I noticed bear tracks. Bending down, I gently placed my right hand inside the fresh paw print" (56). This language is kinesthetic: it shows the movement and not just its result. Her nakedness connotes both vulnerability and availability to kinesthetic experience. The hand in the fresh paw print connotes both proximity and distance between their bodies and their species. They don't quite meet, yet are close; the hand fits within the paw, and is structurally analogous, but does not match it. As well as the hint of mutuality, one is left with a resonance of paradox. Toward the chapter's end, a graphic depiction of a real bear devouring her prey reinserts the naturalistic context of the food chain.

Williams briefly mentions Marian Engel's novel, *Bear*, which "portrays a woman and a bear in an erotics of place. It doesn't matter whether the bear is seen as male or female. The relationship between the two is sensual, wild" (56). In this comment, "wild" is an experiential quality, not an attribute exclusive to women. The pairing of "sensual" and "wild" suggests an extension of the boundaries of self-definition. For Williams, the various bear contacts bring a surge of life beyond what is contained in the "distracted and domesticated life" of everyday human communities (57).

Williams does not treat the bear interludes as an encounter with "other" so much as a reclaiming of a wider spectrum of human potential. The encounter with the bear opens one to aspects of self that embody similar energies, energies that have been culturally subordinated. Williams writes, "Why should we give up the dream of embracing the bear? For me, it has everything to do with undressing, exposing, and embracing the Feminine" (51). The action of "undressing" implies, first, that one has already abandoned any pretense at being a distanced, "impartial observer." Further, it evokes a less mediated contact with wild nature, in which one does not immediately impose one's concepts on what is encountered. As in the waterfall episode, "undressing" is an invitation to kinesthetic intimacy; it exposes the whole sensory boundary, in order to allow intense contact. By substituting "the feminine" for "the bear" in this parallel construction, Williams implies interspecies mutuality; she expands the field of associations around the "feminine" to refer to a wider scope of living beings and capacities. She explains:

> I see the Feminine defined as a reconnection to the Self, *a commitment to the wildness within*—our instincts, our capacity to create and destroy; our *hunger for connection* as well as sovereignty, interdependence and independence, at once. We are taught not to trust our experience.
>
> The Feminine teaches us experience is our way back home, the psychic bridge that spans rational and intuitive waters. To embrace the Feminine is to embrace paradox. (53; italics mine)

To capitalize the "feminine" and to mention "the" self is, of course, dangerous in feminist and postmodern circles. I for one would want to affirm multiple versions of the feminine and reify none of them. In this case, though, the "Feminine" is not simply associated with "wildness," but rather with a "*commitment* to the wildness within." Williams is proposing not a reification of features, but an intentional choice to recognize a larger spectrum of potentiality within embodied experience. As with the view of the environment, the view "within" can be expanded to allow a richer "experience." "Wildness" is a state where one can feel closer to the natural world, because one is more in touch, kinesthetically, with the parts of oneself that developed in concert with the environment. Then, "home" becomes a site enriched by wildness and by multiple intelligences: "experience" bridges the "rational and intuitive waters." This is not an abandonment of culture for nature, but rather the expansion of a self-definition that was unnecessarily constricted.

In the last sentence of the above quotation, Williams associates paradox not with the female gender per se but with the expansion of self-definition she proposes for women. Haraway speaks of paradox as a basic element of embodiment, not a gendered attribute. The "view from a body, always a complex, contradictory, structuring and structured body," she claims, is in contrast to "the view from above, from nowhere, from simplicity" (1991, 195). Williams's uncle proposed a similar view: we can "hold opposing views in our mind at once," he observed, so that happiness and sadness "live in the same house" (Williams 1994, 31). The use of "house," a frequent metaphor for body, grounds this observation in embodiment. It implies that an expansion of presence allows paradoxes to be contained within the same embodied form. Williams's figure of embracing the bear suggests a similar inclusion of qualities that might logically be considered contradictions, but that can be contained in a more expanded state of presence.

The examples of paradox in the Williams quotation demonstrate an acceptance of human complexity: as predators, we "destroy," but we can also "create." The ambivalence that many people feel toward the natural world is expressed by the tension between desire for "sovereignty" and "hunger for connection." In Western culture, humans have claimed a privileged position in relation to the rest of the natural world to the extent that we have forgotten our biological embeddedness in natural processes. "Interdependence and independence" are complementary, if paradoxical, modes of being in the world: the self-construct can provide integrity as an individual, yet allow for ecological interdependence; boundaries can be porous and flexible enough that one can experience cohabitation of the planet. By adding "at once," Williams indicates not just a larger repertoire of sequential states, but an expanded state that could encompass a greater range of potentialities. In another passage, Williams urges women to reclaim the right to a full range of qualities, from "nurturing" to "fierce," from "wicked" to "sublime" (59). To "embrace paradox," Williams suggests, would be to allow for multiple, sometimes contradictory, experiences contained within an embodied perspective.

Although this passage is addressed to women, the dialogue with "wildness" that Williams proposes is not necessarily a gendered action; Williams's traveling companions such as Edward Abbey certainly respected the wild.

Perhaps reclaiming wildness is particularly important for women because of their historical double bind: on the one hand, women have been more often confined to domesticity, and on the other, they have been accused of being unruly or volatile. Williams contrasts "wildness" to a "domesticated" life circumscribed by standard female gender expectations. The phrase "We are taught not to trust our experience" implicitly references the denigration of forms of knowing other than the strictly rational, forms that have been pushed to the devalued "body-intuition-volatile-woman" pole as opposed to the "mind-rationality–self-control–male" one. To "embrace paradox" would be to reject such constricted designations and to insist on a full range of potential, as Williams suggests.

In the same chapter, Williams narrates an experience in which her sensory boundaries expanded to encompass the whole environment: "In these moments, I felt innocent and wild, privy to secrets and gifts exchanged only in nature. I was the tree, split open by change. I was the flood, bursting through grief. I was the rainbow at night, dancing in darkness. Hands on the earth, I closed my eyes and remembered where the source of my power lies. My connection to the natural world is my connection to self—erotic, mysterious, and whole" (56). This seeing is nondichotomous: there is no background-foreground or subject-object split. "The wildness within" (53) and the wildness all around are not experienced as separate. Expressions such as "gifts exchanged" imply an agency in nature. The contact reverberates back toward herself: in touching the earth, she is aware both of the earth and of her own "power." As mentioned above, the act of touching reveals one's own boundaries, as well as the characteristics of what is touched; it can therefore augment presence as well as provide a sense of reciprocity with the immediate environment. Therefore, she experiences both an expanded perception and a movement of return to a sense of embodied presence.

For many, such boundary-crossing, transformative moments would initiate a conceptual leap toward the sublime, or transcendence. Instead, Williams keeps her focus firmly embodied, and accentuates the sensual aspects of contact. Developing from such moments of less mediated contact are the more intense, impassioned relations that Williams calls "an erotics of place" (56). Williams explicitly reverses the usual conception of an intimate contact as private by associating these erotics with "spending time outside" (86). She implies that we have left vital aspects of ourselves out in the wild, and need to recover them in order to be "whole." She portrays reconnection as a choice that demands appropriate action: "If we choose to follow the bear, we will be saved from a distractive and domesticated life. . . . We must journey out, so that we might journey in" (58). A "distractive" life would lack the edge of attentive focus that can be called forth by encounters with wild nature. The opening is both outward and inward, but in that order: outward to wilder nature, and outside of delimiting concepts and habits of response. It is a gesture of inclusion of instinctive and sensorial capacities that have been eclipsed within the human species by adherence to cultural norms. Further, it is a call both to widen our awareness and to attend. We can touch our own "wildness," Williams implies, when we shed limits to perception that are not biologically constrained but are culturally imposed.

A final parallel Williams describes is that between the bear's seasonal rhythms and her own attempts at balancing public and private life: "We are at home in the deserts and mountains, as well as in our dens" (58). To be "at home" in natural settings is based on kinesthetic awareness: one discovers nodes of mutuality that remind one of one's biological embeddedness. At the same time, one has one's own "den," where, in Williams's case, she engages in her human activity of writing. Her ecological commitment links the two locations.

Through repeating but augmenting her bear-woman dialogue, Williams creates a rhythm of recurrence that suggests both ongoing activity and the seasonality of rhythms in the natural world: "By allowing ourselves to undress, expose, and embrace the Feminine, we commit our vulnerabilities not to fear but to courage—the courage that allows us to write on behalf of the earth, on behalf of ourselves" (59). The engagement with wildness that accompanies a state of expanded self-construct can transform personal feeling into ecological commitment.

EMBODIED AFFECT, ETHICAL COMMITMENT

The vulnerability Williams felt when encountering a lion in the Serengeti involved the risk of danger to herself. The vulnerability she feels in response to the endangered wild life she values but may not be able to protect is a basic challenge of deep commitment: "it is a vulnerable enterprise to feel deeply and I may not survive my affections" (63). Yet turning away from environmental problems in order not to suffer the anguish of loss will result both in "more isolation" and in "greater ecological disease" (65). As Williams explains, "A man or a woman whose mind reins in the heart when the body sings desperately for connection can only expect more isolation and greater ecological disease. Our lack of intimacy with each other is in direct proportion to our lack of intimacy with the land. We have taken our love inside and abandoned the wild" (64–65). "Inside" connotes a collapsed presence, rather than one expanded to experience mutuality. Desensitization to one's surroundings, suggests Williams, will result both in degraded ecologies and in less capacity to relate to others. She writes, "We are a tribe of fractured individuals who can now only celebrate remnants of wildness. One red-tailed hawk. Two great blue herons. . . . Wildlands' and wildlives' oppression lies in our desire to control and our desire to control has robbed us of feeling" (65).

The mention of "desire to control" refers both to domestication and to dichotomies. It is the opposite of opening to a relation, which could extend to "a politics rooted in empathy in which we extend our notion of community, as Aldo Leopold has urged, to include all life forms" (87). Such a position would be grounded in moments of experiencing mutuality, expanded presence, and vision.[8]

Recollection of the most basic interspecies mutuality, our common reliance on the continuance and fertility of the ecosystem, can forge a strong sense of ecological accountability. In a moment of experiencing mutuality, one feels implicated in preserving the conditions that allow life to prosper. Such a feeling of responsibility corresponds with Haraway's paradigm of situated knowledges. In Haraway's terms, "Feminist objectivity is about limited location and situated knowledge, not about transcendence and splitting of subject and object. In this way *we might become answerable for what we learn how to see*" (1991, 190). The theoretical bridge from the perception of mutuality to the feeling of accountability—being "answerable" for the life forms to which one feels a relation—is not detailed by Haraway or Williams. One explanation has been provided by the paleoanthropologist Maxine Sheets-Johnstone, who theorizes how becoming aware of biological vulnerability, especially mortality, leads to empathic connections with other humans.[9] Sheets-Johnstone derives an ethic of mutuality from the embodied experience of intersubjectivity. One realizes that what happens to the other could happen to oneself. This in turn generates empathy. I suggest that this model can be extended to other life forms, with whom we share biological vulnerability. Vulnerability becomes a node of mutuality with broad application. Further, the extension of such situated-knowledge practices as those described above will promote a feeling of accountability; when one is included in the same expanded, nondichotomous view with other life forms, one will tend to accord them full consideration. The fundamental ecological commitment to the interconnectedness of all life forms is, therefore, grounded in relational acts of perception.

HOME GROUND

My focus has been on human-environment interactions. I will briefly mention some chapters of *An Unspoken Hunger* that refer to human-to-human interactions and indicate Williams's political engagement on behalf of the environment.

Having proposed departing from domestication to incorporate wildness, Williams later proposes staying home as a radical act. One is reminded of Wendell Berry's sense of the basic good of occupying one's own ground. Williams proposes a unique metaphor that draws "wildness" into the social arena without domesticating it. She proposes that each woman should carry a deck of "wild cards," "cards that could not only portend the future but create it" (134). The cards could be used to support, protest, or resist political actions. This metaphor suggests that women could make a political difference through actions that exceed yet penetrate institutional boundaries. The inclusion of wildness in daily life would then be a resistance to the "distracted" states that make one inattentive to ecological imperatives. In terms of environmental vigilance, Williams recommends "standing our ground in the places we love. This is the wild card we hold, and if we choose to adopt a Home Stand act, nothing will escape our green eyes" (136). She envisions this as a "community of vigilance and care toward the lands we inhabit" (135). The expression "vigilance and care" reinforces the association of attentiveness with responsibility toward the ecosystem. Staying home would allow one to witness cyclical events in the local ecosystem and "chart the changes," which she fears will include loss of species (134).

Throughout the text, the joys of intimate contact with the natural world are in counterpoint to the ongoing threats to the environment from pollution, land appropriation, and nuclear testing. For instance, Williams narrates an incident in her family history to personalize her report on the increase of cancer resulting from nuclear testing. Such episodes demonstrate how our treatment of the environment affects us, even if we turn away. The sense of reliability of familiar wild places is in tension with the thinning and pollution of ecosystems that Williams notes throughout the text. This tension intensifies Williams's call to awareness. Reconnecting to the environment also implicates us in caring for its continuance. Williams expresses the affective paradox of caring for an ecology that is in delicate balance:

> I have felt the . . . pain we hold when we remember what we are connected to
> and the delicacy of our relations. It is this tenderness born out of a connection
> to place that fuels my writing. Writing becomes an act of compassion toward

life, *the life we so often refuse to see* because if we look too closely or feel too deeply, there may be no end of our suffering. But words empower us, move us beyond our suffering. (57; italics mine)

The suffering from acknowledging the vulnerability of all life forms is partly mitigated, for Williams, by offering her experiences as testimony.

In the book's epigraph, Williams quotes Clarice Lispector: "'what human beings want more than anything else is to become human beings.'" One way to be fully human is to choose to see and sense in ways that create relation rather than hierarchy, and to write from such an embodied perspective. A language informed by embodied experience, rich with sensory and affective content, offers nodes of human-to-human contact that can reflect both our "connection to place" and the "delicacy of our relations" with the many life forms that cohabit the ecosystem. This is Williams's gift to her readers, a gift that places a demand to respond.

Williams's evocations encourage readers to choose similar embodied practices. Such practices encourage an experience of mutuality: an acknowledgment of shared activities and capacities, and a shared reliance on sources of subsistence. Williams has exemplified Haraway's statement that one must be situated in order to have a larger view. A situated position allows one to retain connection with one's own embodiment and, at the same time, experience the resonance of larger ecological "webs of connections." I have suggested that kinesthetic awareness is a key contributor to experiences of reconnection both to wild nature and to self. It can help us to become aware of our embeddedness in the natural world, and, through experiences of reciprocity, to feel more responsible toward the rest of nature. Terry Tempest Williams exemplifies embodied acts of perception that encourage ecological accountability. Her insistence on situated, relational practices contests the habit of regarding nature as a resource that can be exploited without consequences. She reminds us of the vitality of wild nature, and of our implication in its survival.

Notes

1. Several critics have noted Williams's joint interest in relating to the natural world and to self or, in Brooke Libby's words, to both "narrativity and subjectivity" (2000, 252).

2. My use of the word *environment* will assume that the social and natural are intertwined, in varying degrees, in all human interactions. See Bono 1997, 184.

3. Although vision and kinesthesia are experientially linked, I will discuss them separately for purposes of analysis.

4. Bartsch, DiPalma, and Sells (2001) clarify the distinction between "relative" and "relational." An "other" is always defined relative to an authorized center; no amount of rearrangement within such a structure—for example, power inversions—will salvage it from being hierarchical and dichotomous.

5. Haraway's relational model corresponds with those of ecofeminist theorists such as Val Plumwood (1993) and Patrick Murphy (2000).

6. The Masai are a nomadic people who inhabit the Mara section of the Serengeti.

7. For a review of dynamic interactional models, see Bono 1997 or Varela, Thompson, and Rosch 1991.

8. I have chosen *mutuality* rather than *empathy* because the latter word is not unanimously understood to imply a nonhierarchical view.

9. For a review article, see Stocker 2001.

Works Cited

Allister, Mark. 2001. "An Unnatural History Made Natural." In *Refiguring the Map of Sorrow: Nature Writing and Autobiography,* 58–80. Charlottesville: University Press of Virginia.

Bartsch, Ingrid, Carolyn DiPalma, and Laura Sells. 2001. "Witnessing the Postmodern Jeremiad: (Mis)Understanding Donna Haraway's Method of Inquiry." *Configurations* 9 (1):127–64.

Birke, Lynda. 2000. *Feminism and the Biological Body.* New Brunswick: Rutgers University Press.

Bono, James. 1997. "Introduction: Does the Body Matter?" *Configurations* 5 (2): 177–87.

Cuomo, Chris. 1998. *Feminism and Ecological Communities: An Ethic of Flourishing.* New York: Routledge.

Haraway, Donna J. 1991. "Situated Knowledges: The Science Question in Feminism and the Privilege of Partial Perspective." In *Simians, Cyborgs, and Women: The Reinvention of Nature,* 183–202. New York: Routledge.

———. 1994. "A Game of Cat's Cradle: Science Studies, Feminist Theory, Cultural Studies." *Configurations* 2 (1):59–71.

Libby, Brooke. 2000. "Nature Writing as Refuge: Autobiography in the Natural World." In *Reading under the Sign of Nature: New Essays in Ecocriticism,* edited by John Tallmadge and Henry Harrington, 251–64. Salt Lake City: University of Utah Press.

Lock, Margaret. 1997. "Decentering the Natural Body: Making Difference Matter." *Configurations* 5 (2):267–92.

Murphy, Patrick. 2000. *Farther Afield in the Study of Nature-Oriented Literature.* Charlottesville: University Press of Virginia.

Plumwood, Val. 1993. *Feminism and the Mastery of Nature.* New York: Routledge.

Sheets-Johnstone, Maxine. 1994. *The Roots of Power: Animate Form and Gendered Bodies.* Chicago: Open Court.

Stein, Rachel. 1997. *Shifting the Ground: American Women Writers' Revisions of Nature, Gender, and Race.* Charlottesville: University Press of Virginia.

Stocker, Susan. 2001. "Problems of Embodiment and Problematic Embodiment." *Hypatia* 16 (3):30–55.

Tallmadge, John, and Henry Harrington, eds. 2000. *Reading under the Sign of Nature: New Essays in Ecocriticism.* Salt Lake City: University of Utah Press.

Varela, Francisco, Evan Thompson, and Eleanor Rosch. 1991. *The Embodied Mind: Cognitive Science and Human Experience.* Cambridge: MIT Press.

Williams, Terry Tempest. 1994. *An Unspoken Hunger: Stories from the Field.* New York: Pantheon Books.

SHARON A. REYNOLDS

∾

Beyond Mere Embrace in
Desert Quartet: An Erotic Landscape

Terry Tempest Williams makes a practice of reshaping the meta-phors representing our personal connections to the American West's expan-sive landscape, often challenging persistent fantasies of the land as plentiful virgin territory ready to be ravished by corporate America and casual day hikers alike. In her *Desert Quartet* (1995), the provocative subtitle, *An Erotic Landscape*, suggests that Utah's canyon country will be the subject of an in-timate survey—one that goes beyond the close, contemplative observations of earlier nature writers of the Southwest like Mary Austin and Aldo Leopold and environmental writer Edward Abbey. As one might expect from Williams, whose ecofeminist approach is particular to her writings, the tra-ditional metaphor "land-as-woman," specifically, "Mother, Mistress, and Vir-gin," shifts dramatically under her reflective scrutiny. Although Williams is not the first to reorient these long-standing images, she contributes yet an-other voice aimed toward restructuring our relationship to the western land-scape. In *Desert Quartet*, the vision she offers in an impassioned narrative voice comes across as both mystical and palpable.

In that regard, much has changed in the twenty-eight years since Annette Kolodny observed that our national literary history is "bound by the [mas-culine] vocabulary of a feminine landscape and the psychological patterns of regression and violation that [such a vocabulary] implies" (1975, 146). Williams therefore joins a host of voices, belonging to both women and men, that see the landscape as a place in which to find a sense of humility, not dominance; to find reciprocity, not transcendence. I'm not suggesting that a new hybrid version of nature writing overrides the literary value of the ex-plorers and observers from our past. Rather, visionaries like Williams arise out of a solid tradition of close observation and direct experience of the landscape. As Thomas Lyon maintains in *This Incomperable Lande,* whatever the artistic form, "the fundamental goal of [nature writing] is to turn our attention outward to the activity of nature" (1989, 7). Williams's writing falls within the more specific form Lyon calls the "nature experience," where "we are placed behind the writer's eyes here, looking out on this interesting and vital world and moving through it with the protagonist" (6).

In this light, what then makes Williams's writing differ from any other observer of the Southwest, such as Abbey, for instance? Where Abbey's relationship with the desert can vacillate between contemplative and confrontational, Williams's "vision" resituates the familiar yet terrifying desert landscape into a communal and intimately reciprocal context. Her writing may be more closely aligned with that of American Indian writers whose relationship with the land can be just as intimate as Williams's. However, at the risk of oversimplifying American Indian literary traditions, the record of their experience with the world is not expressed as a relationship but rather as a unity with the landscape and often includes ritual connections with spirit figures representing the sun, wind, mountains, and other aspects of the landscape. On the other hand, Williams's narrator demonstrates no enculturated sense of what Paula Gunn Allen calls "conscious harmony with the universe" (1996, 249). Instead, her narrator must first engage the land directly. Consequently, rather than merely describing the landscape from behind the writer's eyes, she instead places readers behind her heart so that our own reading of her passionate relationship to the desert borders on the experiential (Williams 1995, 5).

To share in this experience of the desert is, however, not without risks. Williams says of her southern Utah homeland, "To walk in this country is always a leap of faith" (1995, 7). With only the hand-stacked cairns to guide her, she strides off on an uncertain path. Similarly, she asks her readers for a leap of faith. In the earliest portion of the text, she names landmarks associated with Utah's canyon lands such as Druid Arch, Chesler Park, Elephant Canyon, and Cedar Mesa. However, as she proceeds, the references to specific places disappear, signaling that she has relinquished not only the claiming power of names but also the orienting familiarity of identifiable landmarks. Here, the narrative path becomes uncharted as well. Indeed, to plunge into the emotional depths of this small volume that combines lyrical prose, imaginative poetic narrative, and factual observation is a leap of faith.

In this regard, because of her lived experience in the desert, Williams's mixed narrative represents both the concrete and the imaginative—reality and metaphor. Though she claims in an interview with Ona Siporin (1996) that the narrator in *Desert Quartet* is fictional, the distinction between author and narrator blurs like the refracted light hovering above desert sand. If one is familiar with her work, it takes a leap of faith to accept that her narrator might be fictional. Consequently, in writing this experience, Williams may indeed be creating metaphor, but it is apparent she is also in the metaphor itself.

Throughout, Williams herself, not some fictional narrator, seems to anticipate her most avid readers' familiarity with both her subject and her prose. Yet this time her voice has an edge and an inconsistency that mirror the incautious behavior of her narrator. The emotional stakes seem higher, as if she needs to regain her readers' attention with increasingly provocative language and frighteningly passionate expression. Here Williams meets nature straight on rather than limiting herself to the reflective contemplation of its consequences as she did in *Refuge* (1991). Furthermore, the erratic and impulsive direction of the work is launched without the usual prefatory guidance, her erotic journey beginning with the first of the four elements, earth, followed in short order by water, fire, and air. Accordingly, just as the narrator must take the desert elements on their own terms, so must the reader take this narrative account with all its metaphorical leaps on its own terms.

For example, in the "Earth" section, she links the heat and the red color of the sandstone to human passion. If one considers Eros as the personification of earthly or purely sexual love, then linking the term *erotic* in her subtitle to the harsh desert sandstone may seem gratuitously provocative at first. In yet another interview in early 2000, Williams herself acknowledges the potential for such a facile conclusion. However, she states that her intention in *Desert Quartet* is to steer clear of her culture's definition of the erotic as pornographic and exploitative. Instead, she explores "what it might mean . . . to write out of the body, not out of the head" (Lynch 2000, 4). In *Desert Quartet*, her narrator observes, "There are always logical explanations for the loss of one's mind in the desert" (10). She is, however, less concerned with explanation than she is with results. In her experience, when the mind goes, raw emotion remains, and like the earth, the body becomes fractured by internal stresses. She asks, "Isn't that what passion is—bodies broken open through change?" (11). She questions our failure to form a "relationship of reciprocity" with the land, and further asks, "Why is it for most of us the vision of the erotic comes as . . . a moment of exotic proportion and not in a stable condition?" (14). Nevertheless, she answers her own question early on when she proclaims, "What I fear and desire most in this world is passion. I fear it because it promises to be spontaneous, out of my control, unnamed, beyond my reasonable self" (5). Her fear of being out of control and facing the unknown reveals how much of the culture of Manifest Destiny remains behind. Taming unknown territory is paramount. In this case, she faces the territory of the heart. Yet her desire for an intimate connection with the landscape pushes her to trust not only the anonymously constructed cairns that guide the traveler but also her own desire.

In the few mainly descriptive passages in *Desert Quartet,* the account is spare, providing a mere glance at the landscape's particulars. Indeed, Williams easily turns her focus to the unseen, commenting that the creatures' "shuffling in the dry leaf litter reminds me of all I do not see" (13). There are echoes here of Mary Austin who was attentive to "the rumor of tumult" (1997, 55), often relying on traces left behind in leaning grass and in small movements of air over lupine as evidence of the desert's vitality. In her introduction to a 1997 edition of *The Land of Little Rain,* Williams herself confirms, "Mary Austin haunts me" (ix). Williams too is drawn to the trace evidence of the landscape's ever changing face, declaring, "What has been opened, removed, eroded away, is as compelling to me as what remains" (1995, 15). Williams's inward-seeking quest is driven by the changeable desert. In her perspective are also echoes of American Indian thought, which Paula Gunn Allen describes as having "an enduring sense of the fluidity and malleability, or creative flux, of things" (1996, 255). Yet she remains grounded in the physical world where every touch is seemingly a "search for the pulse in the rocks" (Williams 1995, 8) beneath the shifting face of the earth.

While Williams's quest in "Earth" is for an opening to the passion within, in "Water" she redefines the erotic in a land where water is scarce. In this, she echoes Robinson Jeffers's declaration that humankind must learn to kiss and feel the earth again, to let life run down to the roots and become calm and full of ocean (paraphrased in Oelschlaeger 1991, 352). When one interviewer wonders, shortly after *Desert Quartet*'s publication, how the desolation and barrenness of the desert landscape could inspire such reverence and poetry, Williams confesses, "When confronted with big weather, big country, . . . there is a sense of humility that rises out of the landscape" (London 1995, 3). Along with the big weather and big country, however, comes scarcity, especially of water. Focusing on short-lived desert streams and shallow pools that "inevitably dry up," she suggests that "our capacity to love . . . is endless if we believe in water" (Williams 1995, 28). She seems to imply that the very scarcity of water draws us closer to the landscape. But how can this connection occur even as she states outright, "Desire begins in wetness"? (28). When she argues we gain intimacy and constancy through merging with water and recognizing that we are water, this plays as a circular argument in the dry desert. Yet the circular interplay is precisely what is at stake. Unless we develop an intensely close relationship with the desert, we cannot find water and, by extension, ourselves.

For most of the water chapter, the narrator's only companion is the desiccated carcass of a frog that she strings on a leather thong, wearing it not as a talisman but rather as a "heart beating" (30). The heartbeat draws her to a creek in the Havasu dawn, and then later tugs her deep into labyrinthine passages of a desert pool. These acts suggest both the baptismal renewal and the transformational communion that Vera Norwood and Janice Monk observe in *The Desert Is No Lady* when they assert that women's search for renewal in the landscape is based on reciprocity, on personal vulnerability, rather than on heroic dominance (1997, 234), thereby supporting Williams's visionary process.

For example, in a moment reminiscent of Edward Abbey's famous and near-fatal decision to dive into a succession of Havasu Canyon's stagnant pools, Williams's narrator approaches a cliff overlooking a pool. She surrenders to the temptation, "My fear of heights is overcome by my desire to merge. I dive into the water, deeper and deeper" (28–29). In more typical circumstances, fear is born when we let our preconceptions and past experiences drive our encounters with the unknown. However, Williams's desire allows her to be fully in the moment, embracing fear and allowing her to merge with the unknown. Norwood and Monk offer further confirmation of this capacity when they observe that rather than seeking to impose preconceptions on the landscape, women artists of the Southwest "strive to let the subject reveal itself" (1997, 233). The *Desert Quartet* narrator demonstrates this capacity when she moves through the milky depths of the pool, the current guiding her into the center of the underwater maze. Transformed by her acceptance that "I dissolve. I am water" (23), she moves outside her physical fears and into the murky world of emotions where she indeed merges with, rather than immerses in, the element water.

Whereas the details from Williams's venture center on merging rather than escape, Abbey's reckless foray into murky Havasu pools becomes a test for survival. Only with self-described "skill and tenacity" does he manage to claw his way out of the "dark, hard-edged canyon walls" (1968, 204). When he is again on his way, he bellows *Ode to Joy,* Beethoven's paean to personal victory. In contrast to Williams, Abbey pulls up short in giving himself over to the landscape. By comparison, Williams's immersion seems truer and borders on a variation of autoerotic asphyxia as she dives, struggles to hold her breath through the limestone passage, surfaces, dives again, and feels a scream surfacing within her as she ascends through the water yet again (30). Whether the experience is real or metaphorical, as she surrenders to the water, she is in the moment. Unlike Abbey whose peril and joy occur sequentially, Williams's moment is charged with peril and exhilaration simultaneously, giving an indication of the enormity of her commitment to having a relationship with the land. However, this underwater moment does not signal a denouement in the traditional sense of storytelling. Arguably, though, this encounter with the natural world is the most intense episode in the text because the danger is so immediate. Here our narrator faces the possibility of being trapped underwater, forcing a reflexive passionate response where intellect has no opportunity to get in the way.

"Fire" presents other challenges altogether, and there are two aspects of this chapter that are strikingly different from the others. First, whereas the elements earth, water, and air are encountered in situ, fire must be ignited and stirred by the narrator in order to be experienced. Whereas in the others she destroys nothing, in this section she deliberately shreds juniper into kindling. This manipulation suggests the difficulty in having a freely reciprocal relationship with the desert. At the same time, the narrator's actions speak to the interdependence between humans and the landscape. Just as the narrator must be willing to risk the self, the desert must also be made to give up something in order for fire to occur.

As the fire takes hold, the mood initially is one that might be set by someone starting a fire in the hearth. The narrator muses, "It feels good to be in the desert again. Home—where I can pause, remain silent" (35). However, the significance of the handmade fire is not apparent until later when she states she is "pleased that the fire is growing in the desert, in me, so that I can dream, remember, how it is that I have come to love" (37). Here, the second feature that differentiates this chapter from the others emerges. She unfolds her longing not for the warmth of a simple hearth fire, but rather for the consuming flames of physical love. The domestic image of the rising, curling, coiling smoke is exposed instead as a serpentlike phallus. The language of the imagery becomes more masculine: Flames "engulf" a triangle of kindling (37). "The fire is aroused" (39). "The fire explodes" (41). The narrator allows herself to be "ravished" (41). Eventually, she acknowledges that, as with a lover's passion, the fire will be spent: "The blue-eyed coals I gaze into will disappear. Ashes. Ashes. Death is the natural conclusion of love" (43). The prognosis becomes terrifyingly grim.

Is "cracking up" in desert space as unavoidable as Jean Baudrillard suggests in his treatise on the American landscape (1988, 10)? As noted earlier, even Williams herself acknowledges that the possibility of losing one's mind in the desert is a natural state, not an aberration. If "love is as transitory as fire," when do longing and the need "to step outside" of one's self to achieve love become sacrifice (44, 46)? Though no one could express views further from Williams's sense of relationship to the desert landscape than Baudrillard, he does point out, "Fire, heat, light: all the elements of sacrifice are here" (1988, 66). Indeed, the masculine imagery Williams chooses seems to suggest that she has sacrificed the feminist trajectory of her previous work. Or is it possible she has instead co-opted the masculine to highlight the risk in seeking a relationship with the desert? In that case, such a shift to the masculine would emphasize that regardless of the imagery, masculine or feminine, in the desert everything is at risk.

How can Williams reconcile the images of sacrifice and death with her desire to have an ongoing relationship with the desert? With near-hallucinatory agility, she turns to images of ritual to "remember the body as sacrament" (46). Transferring the flame to the white candles she has carried with her, she transforms the fire to religious form, becoming its curator and preserving it because "it is our nature to be aroused—not once, but again and again" (44). As Patricia Clark Smith and Paula Gunn Allen observe in their essay, "Earthly Relations, Carnal Knowledge," "Ritual is the means by which people, spirits, rocks, animals, and other beings enter into conversation with each other" (1997, 177). In this way, Williams's narrator prolongs her communion with the earth. However, the trappings of ritual also keep her narrator grounded in a recognizable world. Thus, turning to ritual enables her to be in a familiar place while repeatedly surrendering herself to the landscape in an act of both sacrament and fulfillment.

Though none of the chapters are lengthy, the relative brevity of the section "Air" reflects the accessibility of air. There is no need for desire to take hold in order to "reclaim the sweet and simple ecstasy of breathing" (54). It is simply inherent in our relationship with air. However, air is the most mystical element of all. It can't be seen, and as the narrator also observes, "There is nothing to taste. There is nothing to smell" (53). Evidence of air's existence can be found only when it is moving (or absent), and the narrator searches for such proof in a column of wind "wafting, rushing up from the center of Earth" (52). When its force pushes her away, she says, "I strain to see what it is, who it is" (53). As the chapter develops, the language becomes quieter and the tonal edges softer, natural consequences of the weathering effect of wind.

The risks evident in earlier chapters have dissipated into reflection: "My body softens as I make my wish to follow my breath. It settles on the backs of swallowtails. We are carried effortlessly through the labyrinth of labial canyons" (54). Though the landscape-as-body imagery remains, the chapter emerges as the most sensual because it is the least overtly and insistently sexual. Rather than opening her legs to the "fast finger" of rushing waters or the heated ravishment of fire, she allows the landscape to embrace her quietly on its unseen current.

In unfolding her narrator's relationship with air, Williams's memory surely calls upon the spirit of Mary Austin who also understood the great voice that the earth had in air: "Passing the wide mouths of cañons, one gets the effect of whatever is doing in them" (1997, 55). Like Austin, Williams's narrator recognizes the futility of shaping a communion with the earth's voice and turns her attention to her own quiet breathing. She discovers in that moment "the dreamtime of the desert, the beginning of poetry" (54). Only when she lets go of the pursuit and listens to the earth on its own terms does its voice become clear. Listening to earth poems becomes a transcendent version of lovemaking, leading to a denouement told through the earth's voice—a voice that offers a communion with the world that moves beyond forcible shaping of its articulations and beyond mere physical lovemaking.

The illustrations that accompany the textual images in *Desert Quartet* also transcend conventional representations of the landscape and our relationship with it. In that regard, artist Mary Frank's paintings and drawings offer a visual counterpart to Williams's unprecedented communion with the natural world. Frank is also an environmental activist, so her collaboration is sensitive to Williams's themes. At first reaction, Frank's contribution seems ill suited to the solo narrator in the text given the abundance of people populating the gutters and edges of the pages. However, both writer and artist explicitly identify the human body as landscape in the acknowledgments at the conclusion of the narrative. So, why not the reverse—landscape as body? In many of the drawings, the desert is transformed into human figures, often two or more engaged in erotic embrace (36, 56, 64–65). In other drawings, landscape seems to morph into a human shape or vice versa (9, 22–23, 31, 32). And that is precisely the point: where reciprocity is the goal, it is impossible to tell in which direction transformation moves.

The cover artwork's quirky coloration—fish swim in an orange sky; birds fly in gray water—signals a world where expectations have shifted. Inside, the "Earth" chapter begins with a painting depicting blue sky and ice-blue peaks crashing wavelike against brown cliffs. The human figure in this piece is the green blue of deep water. Contrarily, in the frontispiece for the "Water" chapter, earthlike brown and orange hues subsume the watery blues and blue-greens of a desert pool holding two figures also depicted in earth tones. The figure in the chapter "Air" represents another contrast. Though encapsulated in an aura of yellow, lavender, and pink, the figure itself is dark, matching the blue-black background that dominates the painting. The overall impression of "air" then is heavy and dark. Contextually, the reversals can seem oddly natural. The desert is, after all, the opposite of the Garden of Eden. In the harsh landscape, natural abundance and innocence turn inside out. Unlike the lush forests and fertile agricultural lands that often dominate our literary psyches, the desert offers little to cultivate. Yet, cultivate she does when Williams surrenders her corporeal fears and embraces her desire to make love with the landscape—with earth, water, air. In this world that is the reverse of everything Manifest Destiny promises, desire is about all one can cultivate.

Though it is not the final chapter, I mention the artwork depicting fire last because it is notably different from that of the other sections. The painting's colors are predictable sweeps of hot red and dense black that consume the entire page including a lone human figure that is startlingly male. The landscape is fully obscured by flame and smoke. In this regard, the painting seems intentionally unsettling, and unlike the paintings that precede the other chapters, it most clearly foreshadows the masculine imagery of that chapter's narrative. Despite the predictable coloring and the clear foreshadowing, the impact of the painting is no less intensely emotional than that of the other images. The sum of Frank's work in this volume, therefore, suggests that not only can the desert be nothing like our expectations, but it can also be everything we might expect of such a harsh and unforgiving landscape.

Taken together, Williams's narrative and Frank's images elevate the imagination while undermining our preconceptions of what it means to love the land. Even without the artwork, the narrator's inner thoughts and dangerous behavior suggest a measure of emotional instability and overshadow the brief glimpses of nature's ordinary goings-on. The insistent reckless communion with the landscape is terrifying yet artful. Williams takes the "landscape-as-character" literary strategy a step beyond mere metaphor by making the case that not only is human sexuality correspondent with the natural processes of the desert, but one can also connect directly with those processes by making love to the elements. However, although one can metaphorically imbue the

desert with skin and flesh, heartbeat and womb, and lips and breath, the reality of the landscape's indifference to human emotion stalks the edges of
this romantic fantasy.

Despite the mention of a few place-names early on, the loosely connected
fantasies outweigh a concrete sense of place, keeping the emphasis on the
power of her emotions. However, for those acquainted with Williams's body
of work, *Desert Quartet* is not an only child. It is surrounded by a rich family of literary works in various genres, including letters, fiction, nonfictional
stories, folklore, philosophical introspection, environmental essays, and
memoir. Subsequently reprinted in *Red* (2001), along with other familiar selections by Williams such as "Coyote's Canyon," "Testimony," and "A Letter to
Deb Clow," among others, *Desert Quartet* joins a community of thought-
provoking reflections. As a result, the very qualities that make it resonate poetically—the free-associative self-reflection and generalized description of
place—strengthen the whole. The prose style is a reflection of what
Wordsworth termed in another context the spontaneous overflow of powerful feelings. Because much of the community building has been done in her
other works, *Desert Quartet* has the freedom to be ethereal and can therefore
take its place as a kind of poetic shaman. Consequently, her writings lend
credence to the observation that the nature essay in the last decade of the
twentieth century is a remarkably diverse and elastic literary form (Murray
1995, 17). As her work continues to evolve through living in and observing
the natural processes of the environment, Williams makes a connection with
the self and, in the case of *Desert Quartet*, extends that connection to the
study of human emotion and sexuality.

Works Cited

Abbey, Edward. 1968. *Desert Solitaire*. New York: Touchstone.
Allen, Paula Gunn. 1996. "The Sacred Hoop: A Contemporary Perspective." In *The
    Ecocriticism Reader*, edited by Cheryll Glotfelty and Harold Fromm, 241–63.
    Athens: University of Georgia Press.
Austin, Mary. 1997. *The Land of Little Rain*. New York: Penguin.
Baudrillard, Jean. 1988. *America*. Translated by Chris Turner. London: Verso.
Kolodny, Annette. 1975. *The Lay of the Land: Metaphor As Experience and History in
    American Life and Letters*. Chapel Hill: University of North Carolina Press.
London, Scott. 1995. "The Politics of Place: An Interview with Terry Tempest
    Williams." In *Insight and Outlook Radio Series*. Available on-line at http://www.
    scottlondon.com/insight/scripts/ttw.html.
Lynch, Tom. 2000. "Talking to Terry Tempest Williams." Available on-line at http://
    web.nmsu.edu/~swlit.ttwinterview.html.

Lyon, Thomas J., ed. 1989. *This Incomperable Lande: A Book of American Nature Writing*. Boston: Houghton.

Murray, John. 1995. *The Sierra Club Nature-Writing Handbook*. San Francisco: Sierra Club Books.

Norwood, Vera, and Janice Monk, eds. 1997. *The Desert Is No Lady: Southwestern Landscapes in Women's Writing and Art*. Tucson: University of Arizona Press.

Oelschlaeger, Max. 1991. *The Idea of Wilderness*. New Haven: Yale University Press.

Siporin, Ona. 1996. "Terry Tempest Williams and Ona Siporin: A Conversation." *Western American Literature* 31:99–114.

Smith, Patricia Clark, and Paula Gunn Allen. 1997. "Earthly Relations, Carnal Knowledge." In *The Desert Is No Lady: Southwestern Landscapes in Women's Writing and Art,* edited by Vera Norwood and Janice Monk, 174–96. Tucson: University of Arizona Press.

Williams, Terry Tempest. 1991. *Refuge: An Unnatural History of Family and Place*. New York: Pantheon Books.

———. 1995. *Desert Quartet: An Erotic Landscape*. New York: Pantheon Books.

———. 2001. *Red: Passion and Patience in the Desert*. New York: Pantheon Books.

JEANNETTE E. RILEY AND MAUREEN K. SCHIRACK

ᕫ

Deconstructing the Language of Opposition

LOCATING WILLIAMS'S EROTICS OF PLACE

> Wildness reminds us what it means to be human, what we are connected
> to rather than what we are separate from.
> —Terry Tempest Williams, *Red:*
> *Passion and Patience in the Desert*

In *Red: Passion and Patience in the Desert* (2001), Terry Tempest
Williams documents her continually evolving concern with our relationship
to wilderness. The collection of writings combines reprintings of *Coyote's
Canyon* (1989) and *Desert Quartet* (1995) with new essays examining
Williams's belief in our spiritual need for wilderness and the wild. Throughout her writings, Williams explains her personal relationship with the land,
a relationship that depends upon an individual's ability to merge with the
natural world. This connection situates Williams in a unique position—that
of a person who refuses to see herself as separate from the land. The integral
connection of human and nature creates, for Williams, an "erotics of
place"—a sensual, spiritual way of knowing and interacting with the environment.

In order to better understand what Williams means by an "erotics of
place," as well as what role such a concept plays in an individual's and community's existence, we first need to consider the roots of Williams's notion of
the erotic and how it may illuminate the relationship between nature and
culture. Second, to contextualize the nature-culture relationship, we use
ecofeminist readings to underscore the importance of dismantling such oppositions. Then, we focus on Williams's *Desert Quartet* in order to delve into
her introduction of the resensualization of the relationship between an individual and the landscape. Last, we examine *Red: Passion and Patience in the*

Desert, which we believe extends Williams's message from *Desert Quartet.* This inquiry leads to our exploration of Williams's empowering argument that diffusing the nature-culture, land-woman dichotomies creates a transformative source of knowing the world, one's self, and one's community. As she rewrites traditional divisions between land and people, Williams suggests that engaging a new understanding and reconceptualization of our connection with nature proves our need for wilderness and exposes the ability of wilderness to inform, sustain, and transform identity and location in the world. Championing the need for interconnection and interdependence, Williams pushes her readers to embrace wilderness in order to locate a physical, sensual relationship with nature—an erotics of place.

DEFINING AN "EROTICS OF PLACE"

"The Erotic Landscape" provides a starting point for understanding Williams's erotics of place.[1] The essay opens with a description of Judy Dater's photograph *Self-Portrait with Petroglyphs:* "There is an image of a woman in the desert, her back arched as her hands lift her body up from black rocks. Naked. She spreads her legs over a boulder etched by the Ancient Ones; a line of white lightning zigzags from her mons pubis. She is perfectly in place, engaged, ecstatic, and wild." For Williams, the photograph depicts a woman immersed in the natural world, standing in "relation to everything around us, above us, below us, earth, sky, bones, blood, flesh." The woman finds herself surrounded by sky and earth, while also being fully aware of herself as a human being. Moreover, the picture implies that the woman and nature are engaging in a mutual sexual act as the lightning appears to simultaneously emerge from and enter her body. This intimate connection with nature and the woman's location, Williams suggests, enables a person to "see the world whole, even holy" (2001, 104). Juxtaposed against this nature-laden erotic imagery, Williams's shift in locations to the Det Erotiske Museum in Copenhagen jars as she confronts twelve video screens showing a range of pornographic images from 1929 to 1990. The natural and culturally mediated erotic dichotomy leads Williams to question our assumptions about the erotic and why "it is so often aligned with the pornographic, the limited view of the voyeur watching the act of intercourse without any interest in the relationship itself" (105).

Significantly, Williams's questioning is not without a precursor—most notably, Audre Lorde's well-known essay "Uses of the Erotic: The Erotic as Power" (1978), to which Williams herself refers. Like Lorde, Williams views the erotic as "a resource within each of us that lies in a deeply female and spiritual plane"—in other words, as a site of power for women (Lorde 1984, 53). Drawing upon Lorde's belief that the erotic is an "assertion of the life-force of women; of that creative energy empowered, the knowledge and use of which we are now reclaiming in our language, our history, our dancing, our living, our work, our lives" (55), Williams challenges Western culture's suppression and vilification of the erotic. Recognizing our fear of the power the erotic holds, especially for women, Williams contends that we have allowed the vilification to continue unchecked as we remain separate from the erotic, outsiders watching rather than engaging in the source of connection and creativity Lorde believes the erotic provides.

Williams extends her comments regarding the erotic by discussing the linking of eroticism and sexuality found in pornography. Too often, Williams asserts, we have "turned away from the exploration and consideration of the erotic as a source of power and information, confusing it with its opposite, the pornographic. But pornography is a direct denial of the power of the erotic, for it represents the suppression of true feeling. Pornography emphasizes sensation without feeling" (108). Williams equates our relationship with the erotic to our separation from the land. This separation results from our position as voyeurs of nature, which allows us to maintain a distinct division between culture and nature. Williams finds that the "world we frequently surrender to defies our participation in nature and seduces us into believing that our only place in the wild is as spectator, onlooker." Such a seduction creates "a society of individuals who only observe a landscape from behind the lens of a camera or the window of an automobile without entering in," an action that "is perhaps no different from the person who obtains sexual gratification from looking at the sexual play of others" (106). More important, Williams wonders if this role of observer represents a fear of feeling, a fear that causes us to "annihilate symbolically and physically that which is beautiful and tender, anything that dares us to consider our creative selves" (108).

As we annihilate, Williams finds that "the erotic world is silenced, reduced to a collection of objects we can curate and control, be it a vase, a woman, or wilderness" (108). However, Williams, like Lorde, believes in the power of the erotic to effect change—a belief she explains in describing our relationship to the environment and equating the erotic with the "wild" in nature—an erotics of place. For Williams, in order to reclaim our connection to the erotic and to the wild, we need to reconceptualize our expressions of both, as well as reposition ourselves in relation to both. Arguing for a "context for eros," Williams asserts we need to "take our love outdoors where reciprocity replaces voyeurism, respect replaces indulgence. We can choose to photograph a tree or we can sit in its arms, where we are participating in wild nature, even our own" (111). In joining culture and nature together, we will become active members of the wild. Such membership can take place only when we dispel voyeurism and the separation that exists between culture and nature, people and wilderness. Williams's context for eros reveals the belief that we need to love the earth if we are to be a part of it. Further, allowing ourselves to develop the capacity to feel, give, and connect with what we see and experience in wilderness enables us to experience an erotics of place—"to exist in relation to everything around us, above us, below us" (104). Ultimately, Williams's erotics of place requires the dismantling of the nature-culture dichotomy that governs us.

ECOTHEORIZING THE NATURE-CULTURE RELATIONSHIP

Understanding the socially constructed divisions that exist in the world around us is crucial in uncovering the destructive forces that constantly erode the physical, mental, spiritual, and emotional framework of our lives.[2] As many feminist scholars have discussed, within our Western culture various divisions exist that stem from the hierarchical posturing of a patriarchal society, with the most prevalent divisions being the male-female, mind-body, and nature-culture dichotomies. Val Plumwood argues that these pairs are "characterized by radical exclusion, distancing and opposition between [the] orders" (1993, 48). It is this socially constructed, dichotomous mind-set that underlies a pernicious ideology that has formed our ideas, assumptions, and views of the natural world. As a result of this ingrained oppositional ideology that favors the "masculine" identity within dichotomous pairs, the inferior "feminine" identity has been marginalized and controlled.

Ecofeminism seeks to reevaluate these divisions. Because of the destructive nature of dichotomies, Plumwood states explicitly that our culture must "challenge the dualised conception of human identity and develop an alternative culture which fully recognizes *human* identity as continuous with, not alien from, nature" (36). Historically, the nature-culture division manifests itself as most problematic for women. Nature's exploitation by a patriarchal culture has been based on the premise of reasoned oppositions that have placed culture, a body that is equated with rationality, against nature, a body that is equated with irrationality. As a result, the nonhuman realm of our ecosystem has been both conferred and aligned with an inherent inferiority and seen to be beyond control.

In turn, women's traditional alignment with nature—based upon women's traditional connection with irrationality and emotion—has placed them in a position of inferiority and otherness. However, as many ecofeminists have indicated, simply wresting women from this relationship serves to fragment their existence even more by denying their very nature. For instance, in "Healing the Wounds: Feminism, Ecology, and Nature/Culture Dualism," Ynestra King argues that a "feminist project should be freeing nature from men, rather than freeing women from nature" (1990, 118). According to King, a firm connection with nature should be women's source of strength in identifying and celebrating a sustaining connectedness. The role of ecofeminist critics should be to deconstruct the myths and metaphors that perpetuate images of weakness and passivity, an action that will in turn loosen the reins of hierarchical posturing.

Catrin Gersdorf's "Ecocritical Uses of the Erotic" explains this issue further. According to Gersdorf, "The West's cultural tradition to symbolically align 'nature' and 'woman,' and the subsequent hegemonist argument that woman has to be controlled and domesticated in much the same way as wild nature needs to be controlled and restrained," has been the foundation of the dichotomous ideology that degrades and destroys both nature and culture. As a result, Gersdorf wonders, "What images, what metaphors can be employed for a project that was launched to rethink the nature/culture relationship?" (2000, 175). In response to her musings, she argues that it is not the metaphors of nature as Mother Earth or the landscape embodied with female images that perpetuates the nature-culture split, but rather the prevalent metaphors of weakness and domination. Revaluing the nature-culture relationship depends not only upon dismantling the destructive philosophy that subjugates both women and nature, but also upon the removal of the hierarchical construction and the creation of new ways to imagine the interconnectedness of the relationship.

For Gersdorf, revaluing the women-nature association requires a new language of metaphors that reconceptualize "the relationship between humans and . . . nature." We need to find metaphors that transcend the boundaries separating humans from the land, as well as metaphors that replace current images of subjugation and mastery of the landscape. Replacing these images with images of passion and knowing wilderness offers the possibility of moving culture and nature into balance and wholeness. If we are to transcend the maelstrom of dichotomous thinking, we must move "from an economy of power to an ecology of intimacy"—a physical, palpable relationship with wildness (178).

DESERT QUARTET:
THE EMERGENCES OF AN INDIVIDUAL EROTICS OF PLACE

With *Desert Quartet,* Williams engages Gersdorf's "ecology of intimacy" and establishes her concept of an erotics of place. Williams originally created the four essays that compose *Desert Quartet* for the *New England Review* when she was the journal's essayist-at-large. At the time, as Williams reveals in a 1997 interview with Mary Hussmann, she was interested in exploring "the use of language in its purest sense, to use the word 'erotic' to intensify, to expand our view of Eros, to literally be in relationship on the page" (Bartkevicius and Hussmann 1997, 3). This desire is clarified further in a 1996 interview with Ona Siporin. There, Williams explains that she hoped to discover what "it might mean to write out of the body and to create a narrative where it was of the flesh, and even ask the question, 'what might it mean to make love to the land?' Not in an expletive manner, but in a manner of reciprocity. That's a very different question" (111). Williams's belief in an erotics of place, a location where the individual can merge and act in relationship with the land, drives her desire to understand what we can give to wilderness. How might we make love to and with the land? Creating this relationship between the land and self holds great possibility for Williams for many reasons; as she explains: "When we're in relation, whether it is with a human being, with an animal, or with the desert, I think there is an exchange of the erotic impulse. We are engaged, we are vulnerable, we are both giving and receiving, we are fully present in that moment, and we are able to heighten our capacity for passion which I think is the full range of emotion, both the joy and sorrow one feels when in wild country" (Bartkevicius and Hussmann 1997, 3–4). *Desert Quartet* expresses Williams's belief in the need to engage fully with social and natural communities. Such engagement, which ecofeminism and Williams argue may result from a revision of the metaphors we use to speak about the nature-culture relationship, fosters personal empowerment. This empowerment, in turn, enables the individual to bridge the gap between culture and wilderness—reaching out toward the capacity to fully experience life through each of the five senses.

More important, this bridging of culture and wilderness accomplished through a vital reconnection with the land, which Williams calls "Eros," encourages a more intimate connection with the land. This intimate connection can not only reconfigure an individual's conception of self, but also help people accept difference. For Williams, "our lack of intimacy with the land has initiated a lack of intimacy with each other." In an effort to cross this divide, Williams asks: "How do we keep things fluid, not fixed, so we can begin to explore both our body and the body of the earth?" Such an exploration, asserts Williams, could lead to "[n]o separation. Eros: nature, even our own." In turn, then, this lack of separation, which results from an ability to "speak about Eros in a particular landscape," opens to an acknowledgment of "our capacity to love Other," which relies upon a dissolution of boundaries, an understanding of difference, and a recognition of the need for difference (Bartkevicius and Hussmann 1997, 4). According to Williams, wilderness offers us metaphors for not only better understanding individual identities, but also comprehending ourselves in relation to others—human and animal —rather than in opposition to the natural and social ecosystems in which we exist. As such, Williams's exploration of an erotics of place in *Desert Quartet* argues for wilderness and for connection with wilderness rather than separation.

Throughout each essay in *Desert Quartet,* the narrator uses her senses of sight, smell, sound, taste, and touch in order to appreciate fully the tactile nature of existence. Seemingly, Williams purposefully begins *Desert Quartet* with the earth, grounding the essay's narrator and readers in the land. The narrator, walking barefoot over the sandstone of canyon land in southern Utah, moves quickly in her efforts to reach Druid Arch. Realizing that "no compass can orient" her, the narrator relies solely on her capacity to love "the terrifying distances before" her (5). As Gersdorf points out, the essay and the narrator have "remove[d] science and technology from their position of epistemological authority and assign[ed] that authority to the narrator's body. Instruments of navigation such as compass and map are insufficient means of orientation on the 'path to intimacy' [*sic,* DQ 7] with the land" (2000, 183). Rather than using scientific means to guide her journey, means that would separate her from and assert her imagined control over the landscape, the narrator turns to her body and her body's reactions to the desert heat, topography, and light. The physical becomes information, thus blurring the dichotomy between nature and culture, nature and woman.

Significantly, in making this decision, the narrator tells us: "What I fear and desire most in this world is passion. I fear it because it promises to be spontaneous, out of my control, unnamed, beyond my reasonable self. I desire it because passion has color, like the landscape before me. It is not pale. It is not neutral" (5). Immediately, the narrator articulates contradictions —her fear of passion's spontaneity and ability to move beyond her "reasonable self" versus her desire for color, for an emotion that reaches the landscape she walks upon and that refuses neutrality. As the essay continues, the narrator fuses these contradictions, recognizing their merged power. Specifically, as the narrator enters a trail, she imagines she is walking inside an animal, with the walls of sandstone holding her. Stopping, the narrator relishes the silence, giving herself over to the land: "I relax. I surrender. I close my eyes. The arousal of my breath rises in me like music, like love, as the possessive muscles between my legs tighten and release. I come to the rock in a moment of stillness, giving and receiving, where there is no partition between my body and the body of Earth" (10). In giving up control over human separation from nature, the narrator here allows herself to join with the land; in essence, she allows the boundaries between nature and culture to dissolve so that she can become a part of the landscape. In turn, "[t]he movement of the human body through the landscape, and the physical, sensual contact with the land perceived as a body capable of giving and receiving love, become prerequisites of knowledge" (Gersdorf 2000, 183).

Unsurprisingly, the narrator discovers that "[n]othing has prepared me for this insistence on being, the pure artistry of shape and form standing quietly, magnificently in the canyons of Utah." Touching the skin of her face, the narrator wonders "what it means to be human and why, at this particular moment, rock seems more accessible and yielding than [her] own species" (15–16). Here, the ability of landscape to accept and yield to change emerges. As the narrator points out, the desert canyon fluctuates naturally due to the transformative energies of wind, water, and sun. Druid Arch, "inorganic matter," is not as static as it might appear. The canyon's fluidity challenges our notion of rock and canyon as set entities. At the same time, the yielding nature of the canyon land suggests the need for a similar yielding on the part of human nature. Rather than attempting to control nature, Williams suggests we might benefit more from joining nature, learning to move fluidly with the influences around us.

The changeability of nature established, *Desert Quartet* moves on to "Water," where the narrator experiences the feeling of free fall, floating untethered in nature, allowing herself to yield to the landscape. Entering the Rio Colorado, the narrator becomes one with the river. The current of the water carries her forcefully downstream toward a cliff. As her "fear of heights is overcome by [her] desire to merge," the narrator dives into the cavern beneath the water's surface. The narrator purposefully offers up control of her body and her path to water. In doing so, she engages in a baptism that celebrates her connection to nature, her place as part of wilderness, understanding that "[w]e can always return to our place of origin. Water. Water music. We are baptized by immersion, nothing less can replenish or restore our capacity to love. It is endless if we believe in water" (28). She dissolves the separation between culture and nature, reveling in the connection she discovers, for the connection reminds her of the wildness inside herself. Such recognition reveals the value of passion to foster intimacy, thereby allowing a joining with what is outside and other than us.

The third essay in *Desert Quartet* explores the transitory nature of fire, its ability to smolder and then flare into flames, while also apprising how fire and humans reciprocally control one another. Thus, "Fire" moves the narrator and readers into a situation of balance as control is held equally by both culture and nature. The narrator, after making a fire in the desert, contemplates the flames, knowing that she "sit[s] inches away from something that tomorrow will not exist. The blue-eyed coals [she] gaze[s] into will disappear. Ashes. Ashes. Death is the natural conclusion of love." The fire's transitory nature emerges as a metaphor for the narrator's love and concern for wilderness. Understanding that all things she loves change or fade away, the narrator chooses instead to focus on life. As she stares at the fire, she acknowledges its existence and her willingness to remain near it: "But tonight it remains alive and I know in the shock of my heart that love is as transitory as fire. The warmth I feel, the flow of my body and the force of my own interior heat, is enough to keep me here" (43–44). The sharing of heat between the narrator and the fire grounds her, a grounding that provides sustenance when she realizes that this "wildness cannot be protected or preserved. There is little forgiveness here. Experience is the talisman I hold for courage. It is the desert that persuades me toward love, to step outside and defy custom one more time" (46). Regardless of obstacles, the narrator chooses to fight for wilderness.

As she "turn[s] toward the flames," "Fire" merges into "Air," the concluding essay of *Desert Quartet* (48). After starting with earth, a firm grounding in the landscape, and moving to water with its experience of free fall, then to fire and its transitory existence, the narrator explores air—the breathing of air, the feeling of air, the power of air, the very existence of air in all things. As such, the narrator joins our necessity for air to live with the necessity for our connection to and protection of wilderness, of wildness. The need to conserve, protect, and experience nature reveals itself through the narrator's complete engagement with her surroundings. She places her hands against staircase walls, kneels at the mouth of spaces between rocks, focuses on the act of breathing as the natural environs shift and breathe around her: "Inhale. Exhale. Inhale. Exhale. . . . On my back, I reclaim the sweet and simple ecstasy of breathing" (53–54). This reclamation occurs as the narrator has learned to lower her defenses, to cross the boundaries between herself and nature. As she concludes:

> Listen.
> Below us.
> Above us.
> Inside us.
> Come.
> This is all there is. (58)

One with wilderness, the narrator has rediscovered herself and her interconnection with social and natural ecosystems.

The narrator's rediscovery is better understood in light of Williams's comments on the transience of the American West. Williams believes the American West and the inhabitants of the West are currently undergoing tremendous changes, "questioning assumptions on every level. Public lands—whether it's the appropriation of water rights—what does that mean? What does that mean in terms of wildernesses, large wildernesses, what does that mean in terms of wildness within our own communities, what does that mean in terms of development, second, third, fourth homes in the American West?" (Siporin 1996, 107). These questions, which reveal uncertainties and oppositions, represent opportunity for Williams, for out of "chaos and out of a [seeming] polarity, when we hear, when we read in the papers, of environmentalists versus ranchers, developers versus conservationists, rural communities versus urban communities—it's all a shorthand to say that we are in flux, that we are rethinking who we are and where we live and how we want to be" (108). And rethinking who we are, (re)examining the nature-culture relationship, is very much a part of this flux.

Furthermore, if we make a correlation between the narrator and Williams herself, *Desert Quartet* effectively merges the divide between author and text, a strategy that disrupts the idea of the text or author as an independent authority. This disruption metaphorically challenges the separation between an individual and nature, introducing in turn Williams's personal (re)consideration of who she is and the importance of complete immersion with the environment. As the narrator resituates herself, confronting her fears of passion and otherness, she not only diffuses the traditional distance between texts and authors, but also eliminates the dichotomous split between nature and the individual that prevents us from knowing ourselves and our place —from knowing that "this is all there is" (58). Interestingly, *Desert Quartet* originally employed different narrative strategies: "Earth" used first-person narrative; "Fire" used the second-person narrative, "she"; "Water" used "he"; and "Air" used a plural narrative voice of "we." In her interview with Hussmann, Williams explains that she wanted to "explore each one of these sensibilities beginning with the personal, moving through the feminine and masculine and then ending with the collective" (Bartkevicius and Hussmann 1997, 5). Williams's editor asked her to rewrite the essays using only a first-person narrative. At first, Williams resisted, fearing the connection readers would make between the text and herself as the author. She also wanted to protect the "issues of masculine and feminine, singular and plural" (5–6).

In attempting the revisions, Williams reports that she discovered that the masculine voice no longer worked. The story became more complex as she found herself "div[ing] deeper into the water where the bloodwork of the writer occurs." In doing so, Williams understood that the writer has no protection from being connected to the text. Although our culture tends to criticize such a connection as "solipsistic, self centered, and indulgent," Williams argues that the "'I' becomes a universal 'I.'" Even more significant, Williams believes removing the mask of the pronouns led the essays to become less literal and more suggestive, an action that "opened up the text to the subtleties of the desert itself" (6). And, indeed, *Desert Quartet*, in its first-person voice, reveals the desert in all its intricacies. At the same time, the text engages the reader's imagination. Not only is Williams the "I" of the text, but the "I" also becomes the reader's voice—a universal "I" that can be adopted by either gender and encourages active participation in exploring one's erotics of place.

As a result, *Desert Quartet* teaches that dissolution of the boundaries between an individual and culture can be attained through understanding one's personal erotics of place. The narrator of the essays engages in a passionate relationship with the land, allowing herself to feel and make love with the landscape. Such engagement powerfully merges the individual with nature; in doing so, the narrator learns to revalue existence and recognizes the inherence of wilderness to her sense and understanding of self. Furthermore, as Gersdorf suggests, in *Desert Quartet* "the desert provides a whole archive of images which inform a language of sensual love and passion—be it for another human being, for an idea, or for the land—without drawing on metaphors of hierarchical gender relations, yet insisting on the metaphoric potential of the sensuous, lustful body" (2000, 14). In other words, the essays refuse to revert to the traditional hierarchy that privileges nature over culture, men over women; instead, the essays express the potential of the desert and one's body to teach interconnection and interdependence—a necessary state of being if wilderness areas are to survive. Moreover, Williams depicts the environment as a source of power and creativity if the traditional dichotomous relationship between humans and nature is bridged and individuals choose interdependence over domination and fear of a loss of control. The potential of merging nature and culture, the power that results from such an action, results from Williams's erotics of place—a sensual, personal relationship with landscape.

Red: Passion and Patience in the Desert: Extending the Vision

Williams continues to develop her erotics of place and the metaphoric possibilities of the desert in *Red*. Keenly aware of the metaphorical healing capacity of nature in the wildness of Utah, Williams sees "a metaphor of unlimited possibilities" (75). As well as concentrating on a future of possibilities, Williams reconceptualizes some old metaphors, too, specifically the woman-nature one. Rather than perpetuating the image of nurturing Earth Mother as inferior, she revalorizes the image, steering us from the fecundity-female metaphor that has been an exploitative tool of the woman-nature alignment into a different paradigm of nature giving birth to wholeness and imagination. Serving as an example, she expresses her own wholeness and creative power with her alignment with nature. The wildness becomes her "time to breathe, to dream, to dare, to play, to pray" (146). This creative power focuses on the relationship of wildness to identity.

American poet Gary Snyder explains the relationship in "Language Goes Two Ways": "Wildness can be said to be the essential nature of nature. As reflected in consciousness, it can be seen as a kind of open awareness—full of imagination but also the source of alert survival intelligence. The workings of the human mind at its very richest reflect this self-organizing wildness. So language does not impose order on a chaotic universe, but reflects its own wildness back" (2000, 1). Language, Snyder suggests, acts as our own body of wilderness. Through language, we can find our own wildness, while also understanding the wildness of nature. Williams demonstrates such an understanding through her reflections on her mystical consciousness of wildness. These reflections create a language in *Red* that draws the reader into a new awareness of the landscape. Moreover, as Williams's numinous imagination reflects her relationship with wildness, it also emerges as a healing force that mends the split between nature and culture. Williams draws upon language and the relational metaphors of the landscape to outline a plan for healing.

Due to the cultural construction of language, Williams carefully chooses her words of landscape chipping away "in a desert of cultural fear" (103). With its dichotomous roots, language needs to transcend gender. Williams's experiences and language push her into a "larger moment with the world" (Snyder 2000, 4) as she draws upon the landscape and the stories of indigenous people, recognizing that "healing must begin within our communities, within ourselves, regarding our relationship to the Earth, Wild Earth" (Williams 2001, 71). A Wild Earth that reveals a language that can be heard only through a respectful, physical encounter with it. A Wild Earth language that enables us to evolve—"to see the world whole"—into a balanced relationship absent of dichotomy (104).

In *Red*, Williams deconstructs the nature-culture dichotomy through her valuing of landscape—the very wildness that gives her balance. She recognizes that the split, whether it presents itself between nature-culture, political-spiritual, or even within ourselves, damages us all. Williams proves unity, wholeness, and balance cannot exist within a culture that embraces dichotomy through "the language of red," which emerges as a passionate, sensual way of expressing her stories of the landscape—stories embedded in the landscape and intricately entwined into slickrock and sandstone. Williams reflects that "[t]he relationship between language and landscape is a marriage of sound and form, an oral geography, a sensual topography, what draws us to a place and keeps us there" (136). Her love of wildness, as well as her unique understanding, gives "a positive value to what was previously despised and excluded—the feminine and the natural" (Plumwood 1993, 30). Through her writing, she reveals to us the discernible layers of difference that form a cohesive whole with "equilibrated grace" (Williams 2001, 137). In other words, Williams celebrates difference. Her language reveals itself as "indigenous to the heart" (140), and her organic stories of valuing memory, landscape, and tradition become the artifact—the foundation and seeds of our own growth and "the great map to our own evolution" (188).

Williams further argues that the current Western vision of the world leads to fragmentation and division. For Williams, to be "whole" and "complete" means understanding "what we are connected to rather than what we are separate from" (75). Williams's grasp of the interconnectedness of nature and culture is supported by the comments of Pulitzer Prize–winning scientist Edward O. Wilson: "The more closely we identify ourselves with the rest of life, the more quickly we will be able to discover the sources of human sensibility and acquire the knowledge on which an enduring ethic, a sense of preferred direction, can be built" (quoted in Williams 2001, 75). Acquiring knowledge based on the concrete foundation of wilderness anchors Williams's vision, an act that she believes will enable us to see the "world beyond the dualities of black and white" (134). In the wildness of Utah, the landscape—its history, its flora and fauna—becomes Williams's prism reflecting a spectrum of colors: "The desert before me is red is rose is pink is scarlet is magenta is salmon" (136). Her colorful views of nature depict a world painted with something other than a palette of binary oppositions. Wildness in Utah refracts into not only a landscape of red, but also an entire rainbow, rich in diversity, which illuminates what it means to be human. Through Williams's language of seeing nature, she moves our "human-centered point of view into an Earth-centered one"—a view that actively works to dismantle the divisions that color the world (162).

As Williams works to deconstruct dichotomous modes of thinking, she poignantly writes of the destruction that results from such thinking. Recounting the rape of a woman from Green River, Utah, Williams writes of what is lost, what we lose in the total marginalization and effacement of the other. The woman from Green River lost her voice—"unable to cry for help . . . violated and raw" (79). Stephanie Lahar, in "Roots: Rejoining Natural and Social History," argues that such losses prove that "[e]xploitation is a one-way, nonreciprocal relationship" (1993, 94). The muteness of the landscape in Utah is also the effect of a raping caused by society's insensitive, oppressive domination of the land. Williams argues that the landscape must be released, must be respected, must be listened to if we are to understand what it means to be human. Only through respect and passion for all that surrounds us, a valuing of difference and an understanding of others, can we as a culture learn to be human—to care deeply for all that is human and nonhuman. This relationship sustains, supports, and nurtures as it dissolves fear of difference and enables us to relinquish our desire to hold power over others.

In valuing her relationship with the landscape, Williams carefully observes and listens to the intricacies of wilderness. Writing about what she hears, Williams makes us aware of the beauty of silence. The metaphorical language of Williams's Utah landscape is silence; for her, nature's silence is indeed language, and her writing gives voice to that silence with the "hubris of language" (113). She wants "to translate this landscape of red into a language of heat that quickens the heart and gives courage to silence, a silence that is heard" (138). She writes "out of silence" in a way that gives voice to "honor beauty" but even more to transcend divisions (113, 112). In order to transcend divisions or boundaries, our culture must both observe and listen to what surrounds us. We are not separate or alone; instead, we exist as part of a bigger whole—an intricate ecosystem that begs for our attention.

Williams's writing brings us into this realm of awareness through her experiences with nature. Raia Prokhovnik believes that "[l]anguage is never simply a neutral instrument for naming. Language is saturated with value so that we respond to language with both reason and emotion." Prokhovnik further suggests that "[l]anguage is also metaphorical, generating proliferating chains of association" (1999, 87). Williams's language of red emerges as a critical step toward dismantling the previous negative association of the woman-culture relationship and as a bridge to a new vision. Such work is not easy or safe; as Williams admits, "words are always a gamble, words are splinters of cut glass" (114). Words, with their power to cut into and re-create ideas and beliefs, threaten long-held foundations and relationships. However, understanding that words can also be mystical and metaphoric, Williams's language continues to push beyond the existence of fragmentation in an effort to break new ground.

Nature is the creative force and community of interrelationships that reveal a way to bind our lives together. Williams takes us through this process of witnessing community and our "passionate participation" with it (19). One must not only witness from a distance the relationship, but also take a dynamic part in engaging with it. This action is an important first step because, as Ynestra King suggests, "the socialization of the organic is the bridge between nature and culture" (1990, 130). King's "socialization" is active participation with the nonhuman realm of nature, which relies upon the necessity of recognizing the intrinsic values and qualities of all that is natural. As a culture, she argues, we must recognize difference while participating fully in making nature an integral part of our lives. This is the bridge—the way "to heal a divided world" (131). Through such an intimate relationship with wilderness, we can learn both to respect and reconceptualize the relationship between the human and nonhuman world.

Williams, with *Red,* pushes her reader to see the human and nonhuman world whole instead of a mutually exclusive, oppositional pair. She firmly imbeds herself within nature, believing that "our sense of community and compassionate intelligence must be extended to all life-forms" (76). This connection and relational thinking is what Prokhovnik argues will help to overcome the hierarchical posturing that exists within dichotomy, for it is the "connection between the pair . . . which recognizes interconnection and interdependence" (1999, 46). Replacing a dichotomous-divisional consciousness with an intimate connection with other is the bridge. Williams's writing celebrates interconnection and interdependence as she writes about the "relationship between language and landscape" that she sees as a "sensual topography, what draws us to a place and keeps us there" (136). The relationship with nature defines who we are. The current trend of our Western culture to control and destroy wilderness extirpates a critical part of our being. Wilderness, like humanity, results from a relationship of many forces and elements acting upon it—all necessary to create wholeness. Within the landscape, Williams finds solace and metaphorical assurance even in the "oppositional relationship [between] element and form" (153). Writing of wind and rock—of the push and pull in nature that creates beauty—Williams suggests we can learn from the ability of wilderness to thrive despite oppositions and contradictions. Rather than attempting to eliminate cultural differences and discord, *Red* argues that the push and pull of relationships offer balance and wholeness.

These opposing perceptions in nature reflect Williams's own "collision of ideas, forces that shape, sculpt and define thought" (153). The push and pull in nature are an erosional, time-consuming process. The idea that balance and wholeness of spirit will eventually reveal themselves depends upon our respect for and preservation of primal wilderness. In asking, "How can we cut ourselves off from the very source of our creation?" (75), Williams confirms that it is not only the "kinship with nature" and the connection with wilderness that she values. She also values the symbiotic relationship—a relationship not predicated on economic value and essentialism but a relationship grounded in intimacy and mysticism, a symbiotic relationship in which living together provides an existence that is shared not controlled, valued not valuable. She writes that the land "possess[es] spiritual values that cannot be measured in economic terms"—"humility . . . reverence . . . faith." These beliefs impel Williams to invite us to (re)think and (re)value the continually changing geology of the wilderness—to appreciate the unique, natural form of hoodoo and metate.[3] And, more important, she pleads with those who have the authority to "exercis[e] restraint in the name of what lands should be developed and what lands should be preserved" (70).

Before the development or destruction of more wilderness, Williams suggests we need to learn to know the land intimately—both spiritually and physically—to understand its importance. This new knowledge, in Williams's eyes, will create the "great map to our own evolution" (188). To recognize where Western culture has been and what we are a part of gives us the consciousness to understand the interconnectedness and interdependence of all forms of life. That we share a past makes us part of a community that we can embrace as we realize what it means to be whole and balanced.

Our connection to wilderness will show us our connection to community—
to our place within the world. Our connection to wilderness will teach us "to
be more conscious with our lives"—to respect the past, the present, and the
future of our Earth, which nurtures and sustains us (143). We need to celebrate our place, for as Williams tells us, it is where "[w]e can dance; even in
this erosional landscape, we can dance" (163).

"THE SLOW ART OF REVOLUTIONARY PATIENCE": AN ECOCENTRIC VISION

Williams acknowledges that creating an individual and communal erotics of
place will take time and effort. She exemplifies this point when discussing
her frustration with her family's insensitivity to understanding the fragility
of the ecosystem of the Utah desert tortoise. The Williams family business,
which began with Williams's great-grandfather, is construction. As a result,
the Tempest Company confronts on a daily basis environmental issues that
affect and, on occasion, halt their work. The Utah desert tortoise, Williams
explains, stopped the Tempest Company from laying fiber-optic cable for
eighteen months. Environmental groups argued that the tortoise was in danger of being displaced, and the courts ruled in favor of the tortoise. Thus,
within her family, Williams confronts the struggle for ecological change and
protection. Her experiences, however, help her understand "the slow art of
revolutionary patience" (84). In learning from the desert tortoise and her
family's angry reactions, Williams understands the need to persist in her
writings to value and encourage others to value what is wild in nature. In
doing so, she continually works to loosen anthropocentric views gripping
our culture. This ecocentric vision works to dissolve the nature-culture dichotomy by reconnecting people to wilderness, which in turn will reconnect
people with their own humanity and place within their communities.

Williams's efforts remind us of Rachel Blau DuPlessis's seminal essay "For
the Etruscans" (1985). In discussing academic discourse and her experiences
with a writing workshop for women, DuPlessis questions our adherence to
fixed definitions, set structures, and hierarchical relationships. Instead of
favoring "either-or" relationships, DuPlessis argues for a "both/and vision"
that "is the end of the either-or, dichotomized universe, proposing monism
. . . in opposition to dualism, a dualism pernicious because it valorizes one
side above another" (276). In *Red,* Williams illustrates the value of a
"both/and vision" through her elucidation of an individual and communal
erotics of place. This erotics of place fosters an intimate relationship with
wilderness, encouraging individuals to refuse dichotomies that privilege one

side over another. If we learn to embrace Williams's ideas regarding an erotics of place—if we discover our own individual intimate relationship with wilderness—we might in turn realize the benefits of relationships that value all that is human and nonhuman. This communal way of relating to wilderness will develop respect for difference as well as responsibility for that which is other than us, which in turn will transform and enrich our worlds.

Notes

1. "The Erotic Landscape" is the seventh essay in the section "Red" found in *Red: Passion and Patience in the Desert.*

2. Ecofeminists tend to use the word *dualism* or *dichotomy* when defining cultural divisions. Ecofeminist interpreters Val Plumwood and Raia Prokhovnik explore the division but disagree about nomenclature. A writer's choice arises from each word's cultural connotation. For example, Plumwood argues that the word *dichotomy* has been traditionally defined as a division of two distinct entities without positing a hierarchical and oppressive construction for one of the pair. She therefore prefers the term *dualism* and defines it as "the construction of a devalued and sharply demarcated sphere of otherness" that "results from a certain kind of denied dependency on a subordinated other" (1993, 41). Plumwood argues that there is a hierarchical construction inherent within dualistic thinking, complicated by a dualistic ideology so ingrained in culture that equality between members of the distinctive pair in the relationship is "literally unthinkable" (47).

In *Rational Woman: A Feminist Critique of Dichotomy,* Prokhovnik acknowledges Plumwood's reasoning for using the term *dualism;* however, Prokhovnik argues for the use of the term *dichotomy,* carefully explaining why: "The four features [of dichotomy] are an opposition between the two identities, a hierarchical ordering of the pair, the idea that between them this pair sum up and define a whole, and the notion of transcendence" (1999, 23). Prokhovnik's parameters of dichotomy suggest that in addition to the dualistic construction of hierarchy and the inferiority label placed on "other" within the pair, superiority has been conferred on and defined by "not being the other kind" (30). For feminists, deconstructing dichotomous thinking that insidiously devalues difference makes an egalitarian existence possible. From our perspective, it seems apparent that both terms can be used interchangeably as long as it is understood that the terms agree in describing the hierarchical, oppositional ideologies that continue to denigrate and oppress others, which in turn results in an imbalance and inequality within the relationship. For the purposes of this essay, we have chosen to use the term *dichotomy.*

3. Hoodoo are rock columns formed by erosion found in the western United States. Metate are concave indentations in rock also formed by erosion.

Works Cited

Bartkevicius, Jocelyn, and Mary Hussmann. 1997. "A Conversation with Terry Tempest Williams." *Iowa Review* 27:1–23.

DuPlessis, Rachel Blau. 1985. "For the Etruscans." In *New Feminist Criticism: Essays on Women, Literature, Theory,* edited by Elaine Showalter, 271–91. New York: Pantheon Books.

Gersdorf, Catrin. 2000. "Ecocritical Uses of the Erotic." In *New Essays in Ecofeminist Literary Criticism,* edited by Glynis Carr, 175–91. Lewisburg, Pa.: Bucknell University Press.

King, Ynestra. 1990. "Healing the Wounds: Feminism, Ecology, and Nature/Culture Dualism." In *Gender/Body/Knowledge: Feminist Reconstructions of Being and Knowing,* edited by Alison M. Jaggar and Susan Bordo, 115–41. New Brunswick: Rutgers University Press.

Lahar, Stephanie. 1993. "Roots: Rejoining Natural and Social History." In *Ecofeminism: Women, Animals, Nature,* edited by Greta Gaard, 91–117. Philadelphia: Temple University Press.

Lorde, Audre. 1984. "Uses of the Erotic: The Erotic as Power." In *Sister Outsider: Essays and Speeches,* 53–59. Freedom, Calif.: Crossing Press.

Plumwood, Val. 1993. *Feminism and the Mastery of Nature.* New York: Routledge.

Prokhovnik, Raia. 1999. *Rational Woman: A Feminist Critique of Dichotomy.* New York: Routledge.

Siporin, Ona. 1996. "Terry Tempest Williams and Ona Siporin." *Western American Literature* 31 (2):99–113.

Snyder, Gary. 2000. "Language Goes Two Ways." In *The Alphabet of the Trees: A Guide to Nature Writing,* edited by Christian McEwen and Mark Statman, 1–5. New York: Teachers and Writers Collaborative.

Williams, Terry Tempest. 1995. *Desert Quartet: An Erotic Landscape.* New York: Pantheon Books.

———. 2001. *Red: Passion and Patience in the Desert.* New York: Pantheon Books.

craft and rhetoric

MASAMI RAKER YUKI

༅

Sound Ground to Stand On

SOUNDSCAPES IN WILLIAMS'S WORK

We call out—and the land calls back. It is our interaction with the
ecosystem; the Echo System.
—Terry Tempest Williams, "Yellowstone: The Erotics of Place"

Our modern, owned world is going deaf from listening to its own answers.
—John Hay, "Listening to the Wind"

LISTENING, SOUNDSCAPE, AND ENVIRONMENTAL SENSITIVITY

An inability to "listen" is one of the most crucial problems in unsound human attitudes toward the environment in this present age.[1] As the writer John Hay observes, human relationships with the natural world in modern dominant societies have increasingly become uprooted and abstract, making people "deaf" or unable to pay attention to the subtle, intricate interactions of different lives in a larger environmental community (1995, 47). In a similar vein, the spring 2002 issue of *Orion* offers "listening" as one of the twelve answers to "what the world needs now." Listening, Paul Hawken notes in *Orion*, "allows us to see a world we don't know, to understand experiences we haven't had, to reframe or drop a belief long held. It creates distinctions and it is from these distinctions that we create new possibilities" (26). What Hay and Hawken suggest is that the lack of listening reinforces a language of dominance that fails to grasp what Henry Thoreau calls in the "Sound" chapter of *Walden* "a broad margin," the possibility for a renewed, heightened sense of life (1992, 75). A similar perspective is presented in the work of Terry Tempest Williams, who has been exploring listening and environmental sensitivity not only as a subject to be examined but also as the matter of literary art.

The idea of listening has always been an important theme in Williams's work. *Pieces of White Shell: A Journey to Navajoland,* Williams's earliest work for adults that is grounded in her stay as an environmental educator among the Navajo of the Four Corners region, focuses on the significance of listening in Navajo society. Illustrating how their storytelling tradition helps fashion, nurture, and preserve an intimate relationship with the land, the book presents the Navajo way of listening as a possible model for revitalizing environmental sensitivity in what Williams calls "a nation suspicious of nature" (1984, 3). This paradigm of listening creates the undertone of *Refuge: An Unnatural History of Family and Place* (1991) as well. *Refuge* interweaves the process of the narrator learning to listen to her dying mother and the birds at Great Salt Lake, both exemplifying wildness of life that will not be controlled by human intervention. This process indicates that listening involves acceptance. Because a listening-acceptance interaction contradicts the dominant hierarchical social system, which controls rather than listens, Williams weaves this listening-acceptance process into an ecofeminist perspective in *Refuge*. Specifically, her ecofeminist stance evaluates the Feminine, a deep appreciation of the intimate connection between different lives. From this ecofeminist perspective evolves an "erotics of place," an idea first presented in "Yellowstone: The Erotics of Place" and further elaborated in *Desert Quartet: An Erotic Landscape*. In an erotics of place, human "flesh responding to [the] flesh" of the earth serves as an interface with the natural world (1995, 3), transforming an ecosystem into an "Echo System" in which "[humans] call out—and the land calls back" (1994, 82). This aural dimension of an erotic relationship with one's surroundings discloses an interesting transition when Williams proposes the "language of red" in her 2001 essay "Red." A linguistic embodiment of kinship with Utah's redrock desert where the writer currently lives, this recent notion of the language of red marks a shift from what a paradigm of listening is to how it is articulated. However, the writer's linguistic art in describing the paradigm of listening is already recognizable in her earlier works, as I wish to demonstrate in this essay.

In the trajectory of the development of Williams's motif of listening from the Navajo wisdom of listening to an erotics of place, and on to the language of red, a sense of humility or a recognition of human smallness in the environment is consistently predicated. It is probably because the process of listening operates in a way in which one's knowledge can never be fixed and is continuously restructured as it is being exposed to different ways of thinking, living, and of being with others. This sense of humility generated in the course of listening plays an important role in ecologically situating humans in what Aldo Leopold calls a "land-community" in which each person is a "plain member and citizen of it" rather than a "conqueror" (1968, 204). What makes this sort of heightened environmental sensitivity attainable, Williams implies, is "the deep quiet listening to the land, the river, [and] the rocks" (2001a, 17). Environmental sensitivity penetrates a topology of listening, and therefore the soundscape descriptions, in Williams's work.

The notion of "soundscape" surfaced alongside a growing sense of crisis regarding a perceived degradation of an ability to listen as well as that of environmental sensitivity. This sense of crisis was particularly intensified with the rise of environmental awareness during the late 1960s and the early '70s in North America. Defined as an "environment of sound (sonic environment) with emphasis on the way it is perceived and understood by the individual, or by a society," soundscape is not a mere registration of sounds but a perceived environment that reflects one's acoustic sensitivity toward the world (Truax 1978, 126). Acoustic sensitivity, in addition to varying from person to person, varies within and between societies in different periods of time because of particular cultural, intellectual, and emotional climates. For instance, the soundscape of a wood thrush, which may be perceived as only twitter by many today, has a distinctive transcendental tone for the nineteenth-century romantics like Thoreau, who heard the bird "speak[ing] to [him] out of an ether purer than that [he] breathe[d], of immortal beauty and vigor" (1962, 5 July 1852). How we perceive a sonic environment influences, and is influenced by, our attitudes toward the environment. Various interdisciplinary soundscape projects in countries including Canada and Japan represent efforts to improve aural sensitivity and the physical environment. Conversely, a degradation of acoustic awareness causes a detrimental sonic environment; as R. Murray Schafer points out in his landmark book titled *The Soundscape,* "Noise pollution results when man does not listen carefully" (1994, 4).

The idea of soundscape has increasingly attracted scholarly attention from diverse fields, including musicology, engineering, sociology, philosophy, and education. Soundscape is recognized as a critical starting point from which to reconsider individual and societal attitudes toward the natural environment in modern vision-oriented societies, thereby exploring a more sustainable way of relating oneself to others. Although soundscape has an obvious association with the sense of hearing, its study is not simply expected to achieve a retrieval of aural senses alone. Rather, soundscape serves as a frame of reference within which to investigate the cultural and historical significance of aural experiences, to critically reconsider the vision-centered hierarchy of the senses and relevant problems such as the preservation of natural environments on the basis of scenic value rather than ecological value, and to re-create a healthy balance among the different yet intricately connected sensory experiences. Soundscape studies are thus concerned not so much with the physical sense of hearing as with the possibility of an aural mode of understanding, inviting more-inclusive sensory experiences—or what Williams calls "erotic" experiences—with which to deepen and enhance one's intimacy with the other.

In this essay, I wish to investigate the literary and cultural significance of Williams's soundscape descriptions, examining how they record a sound web of life in a particular ecosystem, what kind of language is used for that purpose, and what contribution Williams's art of soundscape makes in a tradition of environmental literature. I should make clear that the "soundscape" that I am examining is in most cases that which foregrounds the aural physicality of language, or what Charles Bernstein calls "aurality" (1998, 13). By examining aurality, I wish to consider how literary soundscapes echo soundscapes in the biophysical environment. Schafer gives an example of an imprint of external soundscape on a literary description: Walt Whitman, he observes, sensed "the jazz rhythm produced by the short-section unwelded tracks of the American railroad" and "how the three-tone triadic steam whistle could be warped by echoes and doppler shifts to suggest blue notes"; therefore, in his poem "To a Locomotive in Winter," Whitman "penned a line of ee's: 'Thy trills of shrieks by rocks and hills returned'" (2001, 64). By focusing on how soundscape is represented more than on what soundscape is like, I hope to demonstrate the implications of Williams's literary art of soundscape in a larger environmental discourse.

THE ECHO SYSTEM OF WRITING

As I have mentioned, the "erotic" is a key notion in Williams's representations of soundscape. Soundscapes displayed in Williams's work are erotic because they are perceived by a sensual body performing as an interface between humans and nonhuman nature, transforming an ecosystem into an "Echo System." Williams's notion of "Echo System" implies the significance of an acoustic sensitivity with which to perceive the vital force of life in the environment. These elements of Williams's soundscape—a sensual body and an Echo System—are explicit in the following excerpt from the "Pink Flamingo" chapter of *Refuge*, in which the narrator is speculating on how to empathize with the devastated Earth:

> The heartbeats I felt in the womb—two heartbeats, at once, my mother's and my own—are heartbeats of the land. All of life drums and beats, at once, sustaining a rhythm audible only to the spirit. I can drum my heartbeat back into the Earth, beating, hearts beating, my hands on the Earth—like a ruffed grouse on a log, beating, hearts beating—like a bittern in the marsh, beating, hearts beating. My hands on the Earth beating, hearts beating. I drum back my return. (1991, 85)

The soundscape of this passage is gathered by a sensual body—"my hands on the Earth"—with which the palpitating earth is inwardly perceived and verbally articulated. The repeated phrase "beating, hearts beating" creates an undercurrent tone; the very rhythm of the phrase echoes heartbeats. The phrase cumulatively appears toward the end, amplifying the acoustic effect. Also, recurrent verbs such as "drum" and "beat," which stimulate with their strong aural associations, help intensify the auditory dimension of the passage. Moreover, a statement like "All of life . . . [sustains] a rhythm audible only to the spirit" adds a philosophical profundity to the aural quality of the description.

It should be emphasized that the aural dimension of this excerpt is created in the narrator's erotic relationship with the land. Because the sensual body serves as an interface with the earth, the boundary between the human body and that of the earth is blurred, as in the overlapping images of the narrator with "a ruffed grouse on a log" or with "a bittern in the marsh." The obscured division between different entities indicates a major feature of the erotic, and it is because of this blurred division that an external physical soundscape and the internal soundscape of a human perceiver may converge. As Williams herself occasionally claims, however, the word *erotic* is often misused as synonymous with *pornographic*. Yet the crucial difference between those contradictory words lies in whether different entities are in relation or separated. Being in relation, one can feel the land, its heartbeat. Being in relation, the voice of land touches; human language in turn resonates with that of the land, as the recurrent "beating, hearts beating" echoes the pulse of the earth. The prominence of erotic dimensions in Williams's soundscape suggests the underlying recognition, which I have discussed earlier, that soundscape is not an arena for aural senses alone; it enhances and is enhanced by integrated sensory experiences.

In addition to exercising a sensual body and utilizing the notion of an
Echo System, Williams also uses repetition to create a literary soundscape.
She uses both repetition of words or phrases such as "Inhale. Exhale. Inhale.
Exhale" (1995, 53) and "Wind and waves. Wind and waves" (1991, 240) and
repetition that is slightly elaborated by additional words such as "River. River
music" (2001a, 150) and "Heat. More heat" (1995, 43). In reality, repetition is
a constitutive element of the everyday world: the sun rises and sets; temperatures rise and fall; tides ebb and flow; wind blows and ceases; we wake and
sleep. Repetition is essential to life. Furthermore, as Williams observes, "the
difference between repetition and boredom lies in our willingness to believe
in surprise, the subtle shifts of form that loom large in a trained and patient
eye." Whether to perceive the sound of a river as monotonously boring or
vivaciously musical is up to a listener's sensitivity, his or her "willingness to
believe in surprise" (2001a, 149).

With such a heightened sensitivity, repetition denotes a principal cycle of
life, which in turn brings harmony. In the following passage from "River
Music," there are two different levels of repetition at work: repetition of
words and that which portrays natural cycles. Together, they represent cyclical movements of the natural world, providing the proper ambience for depicting a sonorous river environment: "River. River music. Day and night.
Shadow and light. The roar and roll of cobbles being churned by the currents is strong. This river has muscle when flexed against stone, carved stone,
stones that appear as waves of rock, secret knowledge known only through
engagement" (2001a, 150). This passage is like a piece of improvisation, unfolding a spontaneous continuity of rhythm. Particularly in the last part of
the passage, a peculiar rhythm is created by interaction among words with
the recurrent word *stones* creating the keynote.

Also, the repetition of *is* helps let the ever changing world manifest itself.
Some examples include: "The outside world is green is blue is red is hot"
(1995, 30); "The desert before me is red is rose is pink is scarlet is magenta is
salmon" (2001a, 136); "The river is brown is red is green is turquoise" (148). No
environment is static; even a seemingly lifeless desert is full of events, of
change. The strategy of listing and juxtaposing various aspects of geographical reality foregrounds a world that is alive and dynamic. Also, the rhythmical
flow created by this "is" series adds an aural quality to a written description.
This technique may not necessarily represent a soundscape of the physical environment, but it does demonstrate sonorous elements of a landscape of kinship in which the vital force of a natural environment is actively perceived.

Soundscape of the Great Basin

Among a number of Williams's representations of soundscape, the following passage from *Refuge* is unparalleled in its literary aurality. All the chapters of *Refuge* except for the prologue and epilogue display the water level of Great Salt Lake, the rise of which is suggested to be analogous to the advance of ovarian cancer in the narrator's mother—"a rise on the left side of her abdomen" (1991, 22). The chapter titled "Pintails, Mallards, and Teals," from which the following passage is taken, is one of the two chapters that indicate the highest water level. Because the flooding of Great Salt Lake is depicted, throughout *Refuge*, as a manifestation of its untamed nature or wildness, the lake described in the passage below should be considered to be at its wildest. It is the wildness of the natural environment that helps make the narrator "free" to reclaim her wild self by starting to question the social, cultural, and religious conventions of the society she belongs to:

> Once out at the lake, I am free. Native. Wind and waves are like African drums driving the rhythm home. I am spun, supported, and possessed by the spirit who dwells here. Great Salt Lake is a spiritual magnet that will not let me go. Dogma doesn't hold me. Wildness does. A spiral of emotion. It is ecstacy without adrenaline. My hair is tossed, curls are blown across my face and eyes, much like the whitecaps cresting over waves.
>
> Wind and waves. Wind and waves. The smell of brine is burning in my lungs. I can taste it on my lips. I want more brine, more salt. Wet hands. I lick my fingers, until I am sucking them dry. I close my eyes. The smell and taste combined reminds me of making love in the Basin; flesh slippery with sweat in the heat of the desert. Wind and waves. A sigh and a surge.
>
> I pull away from the lake, pause, and rest easily in the sanctuary of sage. (240)

Reading aloud, one may easily imagine how sonorous this passage is. This impression is endorsed when listening to Williams read the passage on CD; it is chanted rather than read (2001b). Particularly the second paragraph of the excerpt has an explicit melodic flow with tonal inflection, which will stimulate a listener's ears and transform the writing pinned down on paper into a sonic world of words.

There are various aural devices at work in the excerpt, devices with which to fashion soundscape by means of writing. First of all, repetition of words and phrases renders a rhythm of natural cycles and helps enhance the aural dimension of the written text. The phrase "wind and waves" appears three times in slightly different forms; as subject ("wind and waves are like African drums"), as simple repetition ("Wind and waves. Wind and waves"), and in combination with other phrases ("Wind and waves. A sigh and a surge"). The varied cumulative repetition helps evoke the throbbing pulse of life, which may imply the repetitive powers of Echo the Greek nymph, an embodiment of the eros of land.

Paula Gunn Allen observes that in the American Indian ceremony, repetition helps evoke "the specialized perception of a cosmic relationship" among all beings; repetition "integrates or fuses, allowing thought and word to coalesce into one rhythmic whole," thereby arousing "a hypnotic state of consciousness" in which one becomes "one with the universe" (1996, 248, 250). Chanting plays an important role in inducing this sort of cosmic sense. However, Allen argues that it cannot be summoned by chanting alone: "One should remember, when considering rhythmic aspects of American Indian poetic forms, that all ceremony is chanted, drummed, and danced" (251). Interestingly enough, Williams's desert dreamer associates the repetitive rhythm of wind and waves with that of drums: "Wind and waves are like African drums driving the rhythm home." Also, the narrator is "spun" to the rhythmic pattern, and the whole passage has a chantlike quality. I wonder if it is a mere coincidence that Williams incorporates chant, drum, and dance into her narrative to create a sense of unity or what Allen calls a "cosmic relationship." Or is it the product of Williams's artistic manipulation of language?

In "The Clan of One-Breasted Women," the epilogue to *Refuge,* a dream in which Shoshone women "danced and drummed and sang for weeks, preparing themselves . . . [for the reclamation of] the desert for the sake of their children, for the sake of the land" is illustrated (287). Taking this into consideration, the image of ceremony evoked in the quoted passage can be ascribed to the author's literary operation. By means of repetition and motifs of chant, drum, and dance, Williams depicts an integrated atmosphere of a woman being in physical, sensual, erotic relation with her larger surroundings, the world of cosmic relationships in which more-than-human communication can take place. It is an identical atmosphere to that of a tribal ceremony in which a "person sheds the isolated, individual personality and is restored to conscious harmony with the universe" (Allen 1996, 249).

Besides the phrasal repetition, what is perhaps more significant for the aurality of the written text is that the quoted passage contains a striking sound succession of sibilant *s*. In the first paragraph of the quoted passage, the sound *s* reverberates in the words *spun, supported, possessed, spirit, Salt, spiritual, spiral, ecstacy, tossed, across, face, whitecaps,* and *cresting,* a sound that resonates in the second paragraph with *smell, taste, lips, salt, fingers, sucking,* again *smell* and *taste, Basin, slippery, sweat, sigh,* and *surge,* and in the final sentence with *rest, sanctuary,* and *sage.* The sound *s* reverberates and echoes, providing the undertone of the soundscape. But, why *s*? What does this echo of *s* imply?

The constitutive sound of *s* can be considered what soundscape scholars call a "keynote." The keynote sound is "the anchor or fundamental tone"; like the correlation between figure and ground in visual psychology, a keynote is often obscure in its importance, yet "the fact that they are ubiquitously there suggests the possibility of a deep and pervasive influence on our behavior and moods" (Schafer 1994, 9). The keynote of a particular soundscape is provided by "its geography and climate: water, wind, forests, plains, birds, insects and animals" (9–10). For instance, different types of forests produce different keynotes. In the "sheltered English countryside," the leaves shimmer "in diverse tonalities," while in the evergreen forests of British Columbia, "there is a low, breathy whistle" because "the needles twist and turn in turbine motion" (22–23). Moreover, keynote sounds often "possess archetypal significance; that is, they may have imprinted themselves so deeply on the people hearing them that life without them would be sensed as a distinct impoverishment" (10). Then, what geographical features make the sound of *s* the keynote? What is the archetypal significance of *s*?

It is interesting to imagine that the dry, hissing sibilant *s* represents the keynote of the Great Basin with the sound of wind blowing over the ocean of sage, sending the pungent scent of sage into the air, and the sound of wind ruffling the surface of Great Salt Lake. Wind blows, swirls, and whistles in the Great Basin, the largest desert in the United States, which includes the states of Utah, Nevada, Oregon, and Idaho. It is this place that Williams claims she belongs to (1984, 1); the winds of the Basin mark Williams, who "spend[s] a lot of time in the wind," as a cosmetic salesclerk gathers from the texture of her face (1991, 26). Although in the quoted *s*-filled passage the narrator's interaction is unfolded primarily with water, it is the saltwater of the Great Salt Lake, "water in the desert that no one can drink," a part of the Great Basin wilderness (5). In fact, the passage has an overlapping image with the narrator's erotic relationships with the Basin: "The smell and taste combined reminds me of making love in the Basin; flesh slippery with sweat in the heat of the desert." In this way, the excerpt refers not so much to the narrator's relationship with Great Salt Lake alone as to that of the larger environment of the Great Basin. Consequently, the sound of *s* represents the keynote of the Great Basin desert more so than that of just the lake.

The sounds of consonants do actually have certain meanings, according to the phonosemantic scholar Margaret Magnus who observes that the "meanings [of phonemes] form a coherent whole that influences the 'meaning' of every word that contains that sound. The influence of this inherent 'sound meaning' does not merely ornament the word, but lies at the very heart of who it is and very much determine how it may be used" (1999, 38). Magnus's examination of the consonant *s* shows that about 25 percent of *s* words have some association with serpents, which serve as the phoneme archetype of *s*. Words describing serpents include *scale, skeleton, skin, slender, slight, straight, strip, satin, sleek, smooth, soft, scoot, scrape, slip, squiggle, sway, circle, sudden, swift,* and *sinew,* to cite only a few from Magnus's extensive list (72–73). Because serpents such as the rattlesnake and the gopher snake commonly inhabit the Great Basin, the archetypal meaning of *s* can be extended to include a desert. Furthermore, according to Magnus, a number of *s* words are found in the story of the Garden of Eden, such as *salt, sand, sky, spring, sultry, sun, certain, safe, seed, sod, soil, innocence, simple, sincere, sojourn, straggle, seek, secret, sinister, savvy, sacred, self, soul, spirit, speak, story, song,* and *sex,* again to list only a few (73–75). It is tempting to imagine that Williams's *s*-filled desert soundscape unveils an Edenic ambience that may be perceived only by one who deeply listens to the desert. Magnus's illustration of the sound symbolism of *s* helps reveal the layers of meanings that may always accompany the sound yet not be consciously recognized.

The sound of *s* is also dominant in the very last sentence of *Refuge:* "we were home, soul-centered and strong, women who recognized the sweet smell of sage as fuel for our spirits" (290). With a series of *s* words such as *soul-centered, strong, sweet, smell, sage,* and *spirits,* this brief sentence demonstrates the linguistic appeal of the sibilant *s*. Among the number of *s*-accompanying words employed in the above-quoted sentence and the passage I quoted at the beginning of this section, I find *sage* to be most crucial, because it represents, I wish to claim, Williams's sense of place—her physical and emotional rootedness—in the Great Basin.

In Williams's work, *sage* epitomizes both the Great Basin and the dwellers' sense of place. In "A Sprig of Sage," the prologue to *Pieces of White Shell,* sage is illustrated as an embodiment of a desert dweller's sense of home: "A few years ago, my cousin Lynne Ann moved to Boston. She could hardly wait to leave Utah and plunge into city life. I told her, 'One day you will miss these foothills.' We laughed. That Christmas I received a card from her. It read:

'Please send me some sage—'" (8). Sage, typical flora of the Great Basin, defines home to the desert dwellers; it makes Williams remember "who [she]
is," that she "belong[s] to the Great Basin" (1). Sage as symbolic of the sense
of place is displayed in the prologue to *Refuge* as well, in which the narrator
looks back at what happened to her "refuge": "I open [my journals] and
feathers fall from their pages, sand cracks their spines, and sprigs of sage
pressed between passages of pain heighten my sense of smell—and I remember the country I come from and how it informs my life" (3). Along
with feathers and sand, sage is a reminder of the Great Basin, the writer's
physical and spiritual home. In this passage, too, there is a current of *s* running with such words as *sand, cracks, sprig, sage, sense,* and *smell.*

It is common, however, to disregard sage-covered desert as monotonous,
useless, and annoying with ticks and snakes (1984, 1–2). It is such an attitude,
Williams implies, that transforms a desert into "an empty space," a "wasteland," and a perfect place for nuclear tests and harmful waste (1991, 241). For
those who do not touch the spirit of the desert, sage may simply symbolize
the arid and the barren. On the other hand, for those who listen to the ocean
of sage, being "spun, supported, and possessed by the spirit" of the Great
Basin, sage represents the spirit of the place. The deep, intimate connection
to the Great Basin—the erotics of place in the desert country—is woven in
the Echo System of *s.* Moreover, both a desert dweller's sense of place and the
keynote of the physical environment are entangled in the soundscape of *s.*
Such a multilayered soundscape is polyphonic because it represents the verbal articulation of a sense of place and the archetypal sound of the biophysical environment.

Toward Eco-logical Writing

In the polyphonic nature of soundscape lies Williams's contribution to a
new discourse of a healthier relationship between humans and nonhuman
nature. This discourse should be not only ecological but also "eco-logical,"
using the term proposed by the Italian philosopher Gemma Corradi
Fiumara. Fiumara observes that modern Western logic is one-sided because
it "knows very well how to speak practically everything and hardly knows
how to listen"; consequently, she claims, modern language has lost its "ecological" dimension, failing to listen to trees, animals, birds, mountains,
insects, rivers, oceans, and land before their cries become too palpable to
ignore (1990, 9).

Williams's soundscape descriptions offer a fine example of "eco-logical" writing in which the voice of the land is listened to, grasped, and articulated. Williams does this in such a subtle way that her polyphonic soundscape representations avoid arousing a controversy of her "speaking for nature," which would involve a political stance of advocacy. I am not suggesting that Williams's writing attempts to be nonpolitical; she is, in fact, well known as an environmental activist, being deeply engaged in environmental protection movements including that of America's redrock wilderness. However, Williams's discourse distinguishes her literary approach from political advocacy. "The environmental movement right now is not listening," she stated in an interview in 1995, criticizing a binary collision between "us" and "them," a common tactic of environmental advocacy (Jensen 1995, 316). Williams uses "listening" as synonymous with paying attention, an important attitude with which to understand intricate interactions that maintain ecological health: "If we really listen, the land will tell us what it wants, and tell us how we can live more responsively" (315). For Williams, listening represents sensitivity toward the environment. This deeper personal feeling can be evoked by means of language that "bypasses rhetoric and pierces the heart" (2001a, 3). Williams's activist stance seeks common understanding rather than advocacy. In order to attain this goal, she pursues a language with which one can listen to and be listened to by others, the language that echoes interactions between different lives and between living beings and their surroundings. In this way, Williams works toward an eco-logical language.

Williams's art of soundscape accentuates the dynamic interactions among various beings and natural forces that characterize and sustain the ecosystem of a particular environment. Because of this, her eco-logical writing may help disturb the self-contained logic of what John Hay calls "deaf" societies that have forgotten how to listen. At the same time, Williams's soundscape descriptions may touch readers and possibly expand and deepen their sensitivity and imagination toward the environment. In this way, the artistic, literary, and cultural implications of Williams's soundscape moves in an ecological–eco-logical direction toward a sound environment.

Note

1. A part of this essay previously appeared in a different form in "Narrating the Invisible Landscape: Terry Tempest Williams's Erotic Correspondence to Nature," *Studies in American Literature* 34 (1998):79-97.

Works Cited

Allen, Paula Gunn. 1996 (1986). "The Sacred Hoop: A Contemporary Perspective." In *The Ecocriticism Reader: Landmarks in Literary Ecology,* edited by Cheryll Glotfelty and Harold Fromm, 241–63. Athens: University of Georgia Press.

Bernstein, Charles. 1998. Introduction to *Close Listening: Poetry and the Performed Word,* edited by Charles Bernstein, 3–26. New York: Oxford University Press.

Fiumara, Gemma Corradi. 1990. *The Other Side of Language: A Philosophy of Listening.* Translated by Charles Lambert. London: Routledge.

Hawken, Paul. 2002. "Listening." In *What the World Needs Now.* Special issue of *Orion* 21 (2):26–27.

Hay, John. 1995. "Listening to the Wind." In *A Beginner's Faith in Things Unseen,* 38–47. Boston: Beacon.

Jensen, Derrick. 1995. *Listening to the Land: Conversations about Nature, Culture, and Eros.* San Francisco: Sierra Club Books.

Leopold, Aldo. 1968. *A Sand County Almanac.* 1949. Reprint, Oxford: Oxford University Press.

Magnus, Margaret. 1999. *Gods of the Word: Archetypes in the Consonants.* Kirksville, Mo.: Thomas Jefferson University Press.

Schafer, R. Murray. 1994. *The Soundscape: Our Sonic Environment and the Tuning of the World.* 1977. Reprint, Rochester, Vt.: Destiny.

———. 2001. "Music and the Soundscape." In *The Book of Music and Nature: An Anthology of Sounds, Words, Thoughts,* edited by David Rothenberg and Marta Ulvaeus, 58–68. Middletown, Conn.: Wesleyan University Press.

Thoreau, Henry David. 1962. *The Journal of Henry D. Thoreau.* Edited by Bradford Torrey and Francis H. Allen. Vols. 1–7. New York: Dover.

———. 1992. *Walden and Resistance to Civil Government.* Edited by William Rossi. 2d ed. New York: Norton.

Truax, Barry, ed. 1978. *The World Soundscape Project's Handbook for Acoustic Ecology.* Vancouver, B.C.: A.R.C.

Williams, Terry Tempest. 1984. *Pieces of White Shell: A Journey to Navajoland.* Albuquerque: University of New Mexico Press.

———. 1991. *Refuge: An Unnatural History of Family and Place.* New York: Pantheon Books.

———. 1994. *An Unspoken Hunger: Stories from the Field.* New York: Pantheon Books.

———. 1995. *Desert Quartet: An Erotic Landscape.* New York: Pantheon Books.

———. 2001a. *Red: Passion and Patience in the Desert.* New York: Pantheon Books.

———. 2001b. *Refuge.* CD. Boulder: Wind Over the Earth.

ROBERT MILTNER

❧

In Cahoots with Poetry

WILLIAMS AS PROSE POET IN
AN UNSPOKEN HUNGER AND *DESERT QUARTET*

What is a reader to make of the small "stories from the field" that Terry Tempest Williams has published in *An Unspoken Hunger?* Or of the four "quartet" pieces in *Desert Quartet?* Although they are strongly located in specific settings and convey themes, they are not "stories" in the traditional literary sense of fictional development, character, and plot.

Certainly, just what to call Williams's work has perplexed reviewers and readers alike. The book jacket of *Desert Quartet: An Erotic Landscape,* for example, notes how, as a writer, Williams's "experience is related with the emotional depth and in the brilliantly lyrical language we have come to expect from her" (1995). In this instance, the reference to "emotional depth" is characteristic of the expressive dimension associated with poetry, as is the use of "lyrical language." The book jacket for *An Unspoken Hunger: Stories from the Field* notes that the book offers "a series of detailed and beautifully rendered portraits," suggesting an aesthetic dimension to the character studies (1994). Stephen Lyons, writing for *Bloomsbury Review,* describes Williams's language in *An Unspoken Hunger* as "lean and intimate" (1994, 12). Alice Joyce, reviewing the same book in *Booklist,* notes Williams's affinity with something closer to poetry than to prose, identifying Williams's use of brevity ("She wastes no words"), of attention to wording ("brings a spare and poetic language"), and of lyrical focus ("brings a passionate reasoning") (1994, n.p.).

Williams herself rarely comments definitively on her writing style; in fact, she seems to be more comfortable talking about the content of her writing, though it may be possible that some of this is due in part to the interest of interviewers in her views on conservation. Even when she writes about writing, she speaks more about subject matter. In her essay "A Letter to Deb Clow," she identifies some of her reasons: "I write because I believe in words. I write because I do not believe words. I write because it is a dance with paradox. . . . I write for the love of ideas. I write for the surprise of a sentence" (2001a, 113–14). The "surprise of a sentence" is not the discovery writers feel in discoursing on the known but rather the discovery, through writing, of what was previously unknown.

In an interview with Tom Lynch, Williams does comment upon a stylistic choice in *Desert Quartet,* saying that she "wanted to create a circular text, not a linear one" (Williams 2001b, n.p.), suggesting that a text that leaps from idea to idea is organic and creates its own interior logic. This sounds more poetic than prosaic, the former being more "circular" and the latter being more "linear." Further, Williams's use of the phrase "a dance of paradox" is interesting because it can be used to consider the idea of the prose poem, a literary form that is in itself a paradox of sorts.

Arguably, Williams's stories are creative nonfictions, a reportage of actual events embellished through creative "slants" or "takes." They might equally be viewed as lyrical essays because the personal (lyric) viewpoint is foregrounded in these forays that extend the author's ideas. Certainly, any one of Williams's essays could be considered lyrical in the poetic sense, in that each is a brief, nonnarrative piece that presents "a speaker who expresses a state of mind or a process of thought and feeling" (Abrams 1988, 97). Yet the lyric is quite diverse in its literary manifestations, for in some kinds "the speaker manifests and justifies a particular disposition and set of values . . . or expresses a sustained process of observation and meditation . . . or analyzes and tries to resolve an emotional problem . . . or is exhibited as making and justifying the choice of a way of life." By definition, the lyric pertains mostly to attitude, tone, and content. Yet it occurs in different forms, for the "process of observation, thought, memory, and feeling in a lyric *may be organized in a variety of ways*" (98; italics mine). In this way, Williams's nontraditional, contemporary prose-poetic form is also packaging lyric content.

In this essay, I wish to argue that more than a nature writer of memorable prose, Terry Tempest Williams is a writer of prose poetry. By incorporating poetic techniques such as imagery, metaphor, alliteration, symbolism, and attention to language in her prose, she emerges as a writer of character, meditative, and landscape prose poems. While doing so, she delves into fugitive content—erotics and poetics of place—that take her well beyond the limitations of prose, and as a result, she is able to find a poetic voice that helps her explore her relationship to the natural world. What is evident then is that many of Terry Tempest Williams's "stories from the field" are, in fact, brilliantly crafted prose poems.

The prose poem was pioneered in the late nineteenth century by French poets Charles Baudelaire and Arthur Rimbaud who made conscious attempts to bring together into one field the best of poetry—metric or free verse—and prose, that is, any writing using paragraphs and including "all discourse, spoken or written, which is not patterned into the lines and rhythms either of metric verse or free verse" (Abrams 1988, 150). Prose poems stand as a kind of specialized prose, identified by being "densely compact, pronouncedly rhythmic, and highly sonorous compositions which are written as a continuous sequence of sentences without line breaks" (151), though stylistically, prose poems can employ sentence fragments, clauses, or individual words for effect. As poet David Young observes, prose poems are "life histories reduced to paragraphs, essays the size of postcards" or "theologies scribbled on napkins" (Drury 1991, 71). John Drury defines them further as "concentrated paragraphs, poems because of their vivid imagery, compelling prose rhythms, or stunning ideas. They may seem like stories, or essays, or descriptions, but some quality of radiance or charged language qualifies them as poems" (71–72). Thus, though written in paragraphs, a prose poem requires the attention in reading that a verse poem is given.

While the prose poem develops ideas or themes, it is prose because it uses paragraphs in two ways, both as prose paragraphs to signal shifts in ideas and as poetic stanzas to emphasize "shifts" in the content, scene, mood, tone, or point of view, or for sheer visual augmentation on the page. And because the prose poem utilizes the paragraph as its evident form, that is, the *prose* part of the equation, the only clear distinction of what constitutes the *poetry* aspect must be in its style. Thus, a prose poem employs a number of poetic elements, including concision, nonlinear development, close attention to language, and use of alliterative sound, imagery, and lyrical development.

However briefly, Williams has addressed the issue of poetics in her work. In the interview "The Politics of Place," Williams comments on the paradoxical nature of her work as writer and naturalist. Remarking on Rilke's belief that writing is about questions, not answers, she considers how her writing is about sustained inquiry: "With *An Unspoken Hunger*, it was really, How do we engage in community? Am I an artist or am I an activist? So it was, How does a poetics of place translate into a politics of place?" (Williams 2002). Irish poet William Butler Yeats too considers this issue of poetics, politics, and place, opining, "We make out of the quarrel with others, rhetoric, but out of the quarrel with ourselves, poetry" (1996). Perhaps, then, when one's quarrel with others concerns place, it constitutes politics; when one quarrels with one's self, it constitutes poetry, or the poetics of place.

Williams's *Desert Quartet: An Erotic Landscape,* with, at times, a poetic look to its pages, can be read as prose poetry, and, with narratives giving way to meditations, it can also be argued that the "stories from the field" in Williams's *Unspoken Hunger* read like prose poems. "In Cahoots with Coyote," "The Architecture of a Soul," "An Unspoken Hunger," "Redemption," "Winter Solstice at the Moab Slough," and "Yellowstone: The Erotics of Place," among others, offer a meditation on landscape through a lyrical lens via techniques associated with poetry.

This sensual and lyrical engagement with the land is, as well, the very structure of *Desert Quartet.* A collaboration with visual artist Mary Frank, *Desert Quartet* explores Williams's erotic relationship with the elemental dimensions of the landscape: earth, water, fire, air. Each section averages around ten pages of text, some with drawings as part of the page, with the longest section, "Water," fourteen pages, and "Air," the shortest, just five. In each section, Williams constructs a metaphor for the arts. The first of these, "Earth," offers an image of architecture: "The afternoon has delivered me to Druid Arch. Nothing has prepared me for this insistence of being, the pure artistry of shape and form standing quietly, magnificently in the canyons of Utah. Red rock. Blue sky. This arch is structured metamorphosis. Once a fin-like tower, it has been perforated by a massive cave-in, responsible now for the keyholes where wind enters and turns" (1995, 14–15). The tower, the keyhole, and the arch—each is a term drawn from the vocabulary of architecture. Further, the sentence rhythms are interesting; the sudden break to "Red rock. Blue sky" offers two quick stops in the midst of longer sentences, as if those brief phrases were keyholes, windows. All this seduces the eye, yet what the eye takes in goes to the body, for parts of "Earth" read like a physical seduction as well: "I relax. I surrender. I close my eyes. The arousal of my breath rises in me like music, like love. . . . [T]here is no partition between my body and the body of the Earth" (10). Williams's use of extended metaphor—the earth as a kind of architecture serving as a mimetic for the land—as well as her close attention to language through repetition demonstrate her use of poetic techniques to enhance her prose.

The music metaphor from "Earth" recurs in "Water" as Williams describes moving downstream: "Water. Water music. Blue notes, white notes, my body mixes with the body of water like jazz, the currents like jazz. I too am free to improvise" (24). Stream of consciousness, stream of jazz, this interaction brings together music of place, poetics of place, erotics of place. In addition to architecture and music, Williams appropriates yet other art forms as metaphors for engagement with the natural landscape. In "Fire," she uses dance.

In the desert darkness, where moths and bats circle like "dark angels" (43), Williams builds a fire that, as it catches, is described in a language with which one might describe a dancer. The fire "surges, sputters, and purrs. The fire holds me captive, charismatic flames wave me closer. I add two more sticks like bodies to love. They are consumed instantly. The fire shifts, then settles with new intensity; it shifts again, adjusts. The wood pops like vertebrae. The silver bark of juniper burns black, turns white. A spark breathes" (38). Shifting, adjusting, surging, holding, and breathing—each verb suggests the body in motion, the body in dance. The popping of the vertebrae imbues the flames with near-corporeal existence. One noticeable parallel with the architectural metaphor is Williams's use of the repetition of the two short phrases, "burns black, turns white," which echo the earlier use of "Red rock. Blue sky." Then, as if constructing a synthesis of the dance elements from "Fire" with the seductive quality from "Water," Williams offers this shift: "The fire explodes. Flames become blue tongues curling around each other. My eyes close. I step forward. My legs open to the heat, the tingling return of heat, inside, outside, shadows dance on the sandstone, my ghostly lover. I allow myself to be ravished" (41). Like the blue tongues of the flames curling around each other, Williams and the flames, the ghostly lover, dance, their shadows dancing on the sandstone. The dance is silent. Yet silence is overcome in "Air" as Williams discovers a fourth art: poetry.

Poetry, unlike the more physical art forms of architecture, music, or dance, is abstract. Born of ideas, then given voice, poetry must emerge out of something in order to exist in the world. "In the beginning, there were no words," Williams writes near the opening of "Air," a comment upon both the earliest people and her own craft as a writer, yet she will "try to shape a voice" (52). To do so, she will "focus on breath. Inhale. Exhale. Inhale. Exhale. The attention of breath in love, two breaths creating a third, mingling and shaping each other like clouds, cumulus clouds over the desert. On my back, I reclaim the sweet and simple ecstasy of breathing. The wind becomes a wail, a proper lament for all that is hidden. Inhale. Exhale. This is the dreamtime of the desert, the beginning of poetry" (53–54). Here Williams finds her voice, with the desert helping her to find the way to poetry, the "dreamtime" that is the eternal moment of the poetic now. This giving voice is what the animals of the desert and the Anasazi, the ancient people of the desert Southwest, knew. Fully connected to the land, the Anasazi used the animal spirits, and the voices of the animals, as a means to praise the natural world;

their own words became part of the spiritual incantations used to bridge the dream world and the waking world, thus connecting voice with an impetus that is at the core of poetry.

Gary Snyder states in "Poetry and the Primitive" that "poetry is the vehicle of the mystery of the voice" and that "[m]odern poets in America, Europe, and Japan are discovering the breath, the voice, the trance. It is also for some a discovery to realize that the universe is not a dead thing but a continual creation" (1999, 53, 58), which Williams seems here to discover. Two breaths in love create a third, the revelation of "all that is hidden." Moreover, Williams's use of "inhale, exhale" echoes comments made by Snyder in 1977 establishing the relation of breath to poetry: "Breath is the outer world coming into one's body. With pulse—the two always harmonizing—the source of our inward sense of rhythm. Breath is spirit, 'inspiration.' Expiration, 'voiced,' makes the signals by which the species connects. Certain emotions and states occasionally seize the body; one becomes a whole tube of air vibrating—all voice" (57). So it is that through the encounter of the erotics of place, Williams can expand her previous ideas of the poetics of place, constructing a nearly interchangeable relationship between the erotic and the poetic. With this expansion she encompasses the arts, blending them into the natural landscape, so that architecture, music, dance, and poetry can coexist with earth, water, fire, and air, respectively. Significantly, it is through this exploration of erotics, and through the framework of prose, that Williams is able to discover in herself the poetic breath.

Through the use of poetic breath, the speaker discovers voice and develops personality, lyricism, and character. This latter, the character prose poem, comes from literary history as a paragraph of portraiture (as in Dickens or Trollope). In the prose poem, such characters abound without any narrative element, or very little. A person may be "fleetingly glanced at in passing, or a relationship existing over a long period of time but in no definite set of specific actions" (Truesdale 1996, xxi–xxii). These can be portraits of eccentrics, of unusually original characters, crisp and precise sketches of stock characters, or the taking of a very ordinary character and writing to discover the extraordinary through close attention to detail.

An Unspoken Hunger offers many character sketches: Mardy Murie in "Mardy Murie, an Intimate Profile," Edward Abbey in "A Eulogy for Edward Abbey," Georgia O'Keeffe in "In Cahoots with Coyote," Williams's uncle Alan Dixon in "The Village Watchman," the local Kuramada family in the brief (two-page) "Erosion," even the symbolic Stone Creek Woman in the essay of the same name, "Stone Creek Woman." Yet nowhere is there a better example of the character prose poem than in the prose poem "The Architecture of a Soul," a piece about Williams's grandmother Mimi.

"The Architecture of a Soul" opens with a catalog (in the literary sense) of the names of the seashells cataloged (in a literal sense) in 1963 when Williams was eight years old: "Pink murex. *Melongena corona.* Cowry. Conch. Mussel. Left-sided whelk. Lightning Whelk. True-hearted cockle. Olivella. Pribilof lora. Angel wings" (1994, 13). Of the eleven names, only one is Latin; the others are common, as in "Cowry. Conch. Mussel." Others are more abstract, more imaginative, as in "True-hearted cockle" or "Angel wings." There is an alliterative quality to the recurring use of the *c*s and *l*s and *w*s. Williams's grandmother Mimi spent time at the ocean, something that fascinated the desert child, Terry, and although Williams says her grandmother's contemplation of shells has become her own, it is evident in the course of *An Unspoken Hunger* that it is the sense of contemplation, of meditation, that she has learned from her grandmother. Listening to the sound of the shell at her ear, she can hear "not only the ocean's voice, but the whisperings of my beloved teacher," who in this sense is her family elder, the result of an intergenerational exchange within a community of women where "beauty, awe, and curiosity were values" (13, 15). "Each shell," states Williams, "is a whorl of creative expression, an architecture of a soul" (15). We build our generalizations from our experiences with particulars, she seems to say, so that each experience we have—in this case, with the natural world—is like a brick in the construction of our environmentalist viewpoint. Moreover, the particular sounds of each shell construct a larger poetic, for the lists are not random but are constructed toward sound quality as well: alliteration, pacing, imagery, vernacular mixed with the scientific, all accrue to the fullness of language that we associate more with the poetic than with the prosaic.

Further, Williams's pieces are also meditative prose poems, offering meditations "on place, character, incidents" (Truesdale 1996, xxii). In the meditative prose poem, one ponders, considers, thinks, feels, speculates, wonders, imagines in relationship to some object, place, person, incident, so that there is something like a stream-of-consciousness movement in which the poet lets one thought move via association with another. Often, meditative prose poems are written about a short series of related objects, as in the early work of Gertrude Stein in *Tender Buttons* and a number of pieces by Polish American Nobel laureate Czeslaw Milosz, especially in his book *Roadside Dog.* In a sense, there is a kind of familiarity of tone, a kind of nonaudience awareness. Examples of these types of prose poems by Williams are the title piece, "An Unspoken Hunger," and the concluding piece, "Redemption."

The crisp visual meditation in Williams's brief (nine-line, seventy-seven-word) "An Unspoken Hunger" is imbued with poetry: "It is an unspoken hunger we deflect with knives—one avocado between us, cut neatly in half, twisted then separated from the large wooden pit. With the green fleshy boats in hand, we slice vertical strips from one end to the other. Vegetable planks. We smother the avocado with salsa, hot chiles at noon in the desert. We look at each other and smile, eating avocados with sharp silver blades, risking the blood of our tongues repeatedly" (79). Much color is evident in such a short frame: the dark black skin, the brown of the "large wooden pit," the green flesh of the avocado, the silver blades of the knife, the red of the chile salsa, the hinted red of the blood from the tongues, and the suggestion of the endless blue sky of the desert at noon. This poetic evocation offers imagery, the avocados as "green fleshy boats in hand," echoed by the "Vegetable planks" that are cut from the avocado.

Additionally, there is the tight sound quality that gels the piece, such as the alliteration of *ss*, *is*, *os*, and *bls* in "eating avocados with sharp silver blades, risking the blood of our tongues." She offers a straight narrative about a quick meal eaten in the desert, but a meditation as well on the lushness of the food eaten, augmented by the irony of an avocado "boat" eaten in a dry desert. This use of metaphor and meditation exemplifies Williams's poetic voice.

A further example occurs in the short (two-page) "Redemption," dedicated to essayist and poet Wendell Berry. A narrative about crossing the Great Basin of southeastern Oregon, "Redemption" can also be read as a prose poem, for the discovery of a coyote whose hide is "hung on a barbed-wire fence" with "the furred skin . . . torn with ragged edges" (143) jars Williams into a meditation on what endures. She considers the irony of how, named after the animal, Coyote Butte is a landscape in which one can "watch a steady stream of western tanagers fly through during spring migration: yellow bodies, black wings, red heads." The final triad in the sentence adds both musical cadence and colorful images, enriching the prose. Moreover, it hints at the American tendency to discount minorities, Asian Americans, African Americans, and Native Americans, respectively, as something to be ill-used, as is the coyote, treated as a threat to the American Eurocentric tradition. But the effective anthropomorphic presentation of the wilderness as a coyote, also personified as "Jesus Coyote," the Trickster, the Outsider, is ultimately a symbol: "My eyes return to Jesus Coyote, stiff on his cross, savior of our American rangelands. We can try and kill all that is native, string it up by its hind legs for all to see, but spirit howls and wildness endures" (144). The use of the symbolic coyote, coupled with the poetic breath through which "spirit howls"—an abstract ("spirit") expanded upon by a concrete ("howls")—allows both "Redemption" and *An Unspoken Hunger* as a whole to end on a literary and, more specifically, poetic note.

The most prominent kind of prose poem in Williams's work is the landscape prose poem, which tends toward literal description and crisp detailing and is vested with a sense of sound and lyricism, though it can be torqued by the addition of the bizarre or surreal. The place prose poem is either painstakingly real or wildly embellished; that is, a place becomes a kind of character, an emblem, or metaphor for a state of mind. They can even be imagined. Often, these are reflections, almost journal-like, of places or landscapes that the writer has visited.

According to C. W. Truesdale in the introduction to his anthology of prose poems, *The Party Train,* the landscape or place prose poem is one of the more common forms, "whether familiar landscapes are being described . . . or unique and even exotic ones" (1996, xxii). Williams's *Unspoken Hunger* includes a number of prose pieces embracing familiar and exotic landscapes in poetic ways.

"Winter Solstice at the Moab Slough" is both a landscape and a place, a juxtaposition of present and past, of heron and hawk, of Native American and "nature" American, of noun and verb, of dark and light. Williams recalls her first visit to the Moab Slough during its dedication when she returned to renew herself during the solstice; this seems to confirm what critic Helen Vendler has observed about lyric poetry: "Poems that are primarily lyric meditations on a single subject are often phrased in the present tense" (2002, 108). Writing to "celebrate remnants of wildness," Williams notes, concerning the eight hundred acres of wetlands, "It is nothing. It is everything," paralleling these two clauses with the remnants of "One red-tailed hawk. Two great blue herons." The nothing-everything dichotomy grows into a one-two expansion, parallel prose rhythms, with the herons growing into symbols. Williams calls them "feathered Buddhas casting blue shadows on the snow," offering a Snyder-like Zen moment, followed by these juxtapositions: "Páhos. Prayer feathers. Darkness, now light. The Winter Solstice turns in us, turns in me" (65). The páhos, Hopi prayer sticks decorated with feathers, are balanced by the prayer feathers of the herons, the hawk, and the "small striated feather" from the hawk that Williams found "lying on the ground" and that she took home as "a reminder of who we live among" (63).

This sense of interconnectedness, which is rooted in a sense of place and is expressed in the natural and human reflection, shows that by knowing "who we live among," the who being the creatures of the earth, the solstice is able to turn in "us" (in all creatures and people) and is cause for Williams's feeling of how it "turns in me." Her poetic epiphany is revealed as the prose poem closes: "The land is love. Love is what we fear. To disengage from the earth is our own oppression. I stand on the edge of these wetlands, a place of renewal, an oasis in the desert, as an act of faith, believing the sun has completed the southern end of its journey and is now contemplating its return toward light" (65). Love of the land leads to renewal of the individual. The winter solstice is not only one season's closure; it is also the harbinger of spring, season of renewal, as indicated by the sun's return to light. Thus, Williams follows a circular path to discover the faith that results from connecting with nature.

"Another traditional feature of poetry, which often forms a striking aspect of the prose poem," Robert Alexander notes, "involves how poems end." For support, he quotes Barbara Smith from her book *Poetic Closure:* "The devices of closure often achieve their characteristic effect by imparting to a poem's conclusion a certain quality that is experienced by the reader as striking validity, a quality that leaves him with the feeling that what has just been said has the 'conclusiveness,' the settled finality, of apparently self-evident truth" (1996, xxvi). Readers discover Williams's tight closures operating in her work. For example, the *Melongena corona* shell, part of the shell inventory that opens "The Architecture of a Soul," is held to her ear at the close of the piece so that she hears "not only the ocean's voice, but the whisperings" of her grandmother (15). Additionally, the "knives" and "sharp silver blades" that open and close "An Unspoken Hunger" (79) and the "Steam rising" that both opens and closes "Yellowstone: The Erotics of Place" (81, 87) offer further examples of Williams's effective use of poetic closure.

"Yellowstone: An Erotics of Place" opens with a paragraph rich in images and sounds that is repeated at the end: "Steam rising. Water boiling. Geysers surging. Mud pots gurgling. Herds breathing. Hooves stampeding. Wings flocking. Sky darkening. Clouds gathering. Rain falling. Rivers raging. Lakes rising. Lightning striking. Trees burning. Thunder clapping. Smoke clearing. Eyes staring" (81). When the paragraph is repeated at the end, there is an incremental change, that is, the adding of one additional line, "Wolves howling into the Yellowstone," both as the final line in the repeated paragraph and as the final paragraph of the prose poem (87). The paragraph functions similar to the way in which refrains or choruses work in songs or ballads. Moreover, the refrains are like echoes themselves, repeating units that not only accentuate the poetic but also extend and unify the work's structure.

A further example occurs when Williams considers how the Yellowstone ecosystem is an "Echo System," evoked through the constant echoing of the phrasing "Pansexual. Of Pan. A landscape . . .":

> Pansexual. Of Pan. A landscape that loves white pine, limber pine, lodgepole, Douglas fir, blue spruce, aspen, cottonwood, willow, sage, serviceberry, huckleberry, chokecherry, lupine, larkspur, monkshood, steershead, glacier lilies, spring beauties, bisort, and paintbrush.
>
> Pansexual. Of Pan. A landscape where the Bitterroot Valley, the Sawtooths, Tetons, Wind Rivers, and Absarokas loom large in our imaginations—where Henry's Fork, the Clark Fork, the Snake, and the Missouri nourish us, and revive our souls. (84)

The use of the opening and closing "refrains," both of "Steam rising" and "Pansexual," gives this piece the appearance of the echo-poem, a poem in which words or phrases refrain as echoes, one of the lyric subgenres Vendler identifies in her book *Poems, Poets, Poetry* (2002, 638). How true this seems of most of Williams's prose poems in *An Unspoken Hunger:* her convincing arguments, circularly constructed out of juxtapositions and symbols or contrasts and parallels, offer "snap shut" conclusions that leave the reader nodding his or her head in agreement.

For Williams, the renewal of the seasons, resulting from a lyrical engagement with the land, gives rise to a sensual new language, and, consequently, to a new voice. Williams also employs mythopoetics in "Yellowstone: The Erotics of Place," evoking the classical figures of Gaia, Pan, and Echo relocated into a western setting. To do so, she opens with a scientific discourse on the nature of an echo: "An echo is a sound wave that bounces back, or is reflected from, a large hard surface like the face of a cliff, or the flanks of mountains, or the interior of a cave. To hear an echo, one must be at least seventeen meters or fifty-six feet away from the reflecting surface" (82). The language used is at times anthropomorphic, employing personification in the description of the natural landscape: "face," "flanks," and "feet" all insinuate the human ways in which we describe nature. Then, Williams echoes the way in which, in Greek mythology, the gods are everywhere:

> Echos are real—not imaginary.
>
> We call out—and the land calls back. It is our interaction with the ecosystem; the Echo System.
>
> We understand it intellectually.
>
> We respond to it emotionally—joyously.
>
> When was the last time we played with Echo? (82)

This structure of a string of sentences also makes the prose passage look much like verse. Williams layers the poetic effect by using poetic devices such as anaphora, "We call out," "We understand," and "We respond," and metaphor where the ecosystem is presented as an Echo System, this latter poetic device also employing pun or wordplay. A pun works effectively in a poem, according to Vendler, when it "disrupts the expected rhythm and therefore introduces force into the line" and when it "inserts semantic surprise, on the one hand, or semantic confirmation, on the other hand, into the semantic configuration of the poem" (2002, 3).

Further, Williams uses the repetition of nonhierarchical cataloging as a means of introducing music to the paragraphs, creating a noticeable and effective prose rhythm that seems both incantational and particularly effective in a prose poem that celebrates Pan, Echo, and the gods in the landscape, which is seen as teeming with life: "A Landscape that loves bison, bear, elk, deer, moose, coyote, wolf, rabbit, badger, marmot, squirrel, swan, crane, eagle, raven, pelican, red-tail, bufflehead, goldeneye, teal, and merganser" (84). Quite a comprehensive list, this section of "Yellowstone: An Erotics of Place" includes a range of the food chain; an array of water, land, and sky creatures; and a sense of the diverse bounty of life. Yet the sounds evoked are like a song, an incantation: the *b*s in *bison* and *bear;* the echo of *deer* after *bear;* the *o*s that run from *moose* through *coyote* to *wolf;* the *r*s that begin in *rabbit,* then reverberate through *badger, marmot, squirrel;* the *s*s in *squirrel* and *swan;* the *n*s in *swan, crane,* then *raven* and *pelican;* the building from monosyllable words *(bear, elk, deer, moose)* to trisyllabics at the end *(pelican . . . bufflehead, goldeneye . . . merganser)* create an alliterative crescendo that is pure poetry. Thus, the intimate, sensual connection to the land explored in "Yellowstone: The Erotics of Place" demonstrates most fully how Williams takes on intimate content, particularly as it relates to the landscape, through her use of poetic techniques: personification, refrains, incremental repetitions, anaphora, metaphor, cataloging, alliteration, and consonance.

In "Yellowstone: The Erotics of Place" Williams exhorts readers, "It is time for us to take off our masks, to step out from behind our personas—whatever they might be: educators, activists, biologists, geologists, writers, farmers, ranchers, bureaucrats—and admit we are lovers, engaged in an erotics of place. Loving the land" (41). The standing forth unmasked, authentic and without persona, allows for a new sensual language to emerge. Robert Alexander couples this masking-unmasking tendency with the prose poem: "This ability of the prose poem to take on various registers of language, its ability to masquerade as different sorts of literary or non-literary prose, is one of its distinguishing features" (1996, xxvii). The use of this new sensual register of language is what Brooke Horvath further identifies as a distinct feature of the prose poem, its exploring of what he calls "fugitive content." "[T]he prose poem may well offer a means of saying the no-longer sayable as well as the as-yet unsaid, thus providing a home for various sorts of fugitive (unpoetic) content, an agenda enhanced by the form's fragmentary nature and marginal status, which encourage *communicative and self-exploratory intimacy:* the prose poem as the means of seeing and so saying (and so being) something new" (1992, 12–13; italics mine). If one takes fugitive content to mean erotics of place, to mean self-explorative intimacy, then both "Yellowstone: The Erotics of Place" from *An Unspoken Hunger* and the entire book *Desert Quartet: An Erotic Landscape* employ an important feature that is characteristic of the prose poem. Poets Kim Addonizio and Dorianne Laux point out, "The erotic has often been considered taboo, and even with the current abundance of sexual writing, it's under frequent attack" (1997, 46); thus, the erotic certainly qualifies as fugitive content from some realms of the poetic, for, as Addonizio and Laux further observe, it appears that more prose writers than poets are exploring the erotic in writing, and that those who do are "creating texts that are deliberately transgressive and that expand the boundaries of *what's permissible*" (52; italics mine). Williams is one of the "prose" writers who, using highly poetic prose, or prose poetry, is exploring the fugitive content of eroticism in her work, bringing together her concept of the politics of place with the erotics of place (1994, 84).

Throughout the prose poems in *Desert Quartet* and *An Unspoken Hunger,* Williams meditates on character and landscape, discovering in them vehicles for engagement and growth. These works show a synthesis of her early prose with her developing sense of the poetic, a synthesis—and symbiosis—suggested by her "In Cahoots with Coyote" anecdote of Georgia O'Keeffe and Coyote:

> Georgia stepped forward. Coyote stopped dancing. They struck a deal. She would agree not to expose him as the scoundrel he was, keeping his desert secrets safe, if he promised to save bones for her—bleached bones. Stones—smooth black stones would also do. And so, for the price of secrecy, anonymity, and just plain fun—O'Keeffe and Coyote became friends. Good friends. Through the years, he brought her bones and stones and Georgia O'Keeffe kept her word. She never painted Coyote. Instead, she embodied him. (1994, 18)

Coyote, the trickster, with his desert secrets, is the poetic; O'Keeffe, the human painter, with her bones and stones, is the prosaic; "cahoots," a friendly deal, the merger of the two: a prose poem. Most important, in *Desert Quartet: An Erotic Landscape* and *An Unspoken Hunger: Stories from the Field,* Williams "embodies" the poetic within her prose, and, in doing so, she finds a new voice.

Works Cited

Abrams, M. H. 1988. *A Glossary of Literary Terms.* 5th ed. New York: Holt, Rinehart, and Winston.

Addonizio, Kim, and Dorianne Laux. 1997. *The Poet's Companion.* New York: Norton.

Alexander, Robert. 1996. "Poetry/Prose." In *The Party Train: A Collection of North American Prose Poetry,* edited by Robert Alexander, Mark Vinz, and C. W. Truesdale, xxiv–xxxi. Minneapolis: New Rivers Press.

Drury, John. 1991. *Creating Poetry.* Cincinnati: Writers' Digest Books.

Horvath, Brooke. 1992. "The Prose Poem and the Secret Life of Poetry." *American Poetry Review* 21 (5):12–13.

Joyce, Alice. 1994. Review of *An Unspoken Hunger,* by Terry Tempest Williams. *Booklist* 90 (15 April): 1487. Available on-line at http://olc5.ohiolink.edu (25 June 2002).

Lyons, Stephen. 1994. Review of *An Unspoken Hunger,* by Terry Tempest Williams. *Bloomsbury Review* (November–December):12.

Snyder, Gary. 1999. "Poetry and the Primitive." In *The Gary Snyder Reader: Prose, Poetry, Translation, 1952–1998,* 52–61. Washington, D.C.: Counterpoint.

Truesdale, C. W. 1996. "Publisher's Preface." In *The Party Train: A Collection of North American Prose Poetry,* edited by Robert Alexander, Mark Vinz, and C. W. Truesdale, xix–xxii. Minneapolis: New Rivers Press.

Vendler, Helen. 2002. *Poems, Poets, Poetry.* 2d ed. Boston: Bedford, St. Martin's.

Williams, Terry Tempest. 1994. *An Unspoken Hunger: Stories from the Field.* New York: Pantheon Books.

———. 1995. *Desert Quartet: An Erotic Landscape.* New York: Pantheon Books.

———. 2001a. *Red: Passion and Patience in the Desert.* New York: Pantheon Books.

———. 2001b. "Talking with Terry Tempest Williams about Writing the Environment and Being a Mormon: Interview with Tom Lynch." New Mexico State University Border Book Festival, March. Available on-line at http://www.coyoteclan.com/interviews.html.

———. 2002. "The Politics of Place: An Interview with Terry Tempest Williams: Interview with Scott London." *Insight and Outlook.* Available on-line at http://scottlondon.com/insight/scripts/ttw/html.

Yeats, William Butler. 1996. *The Columbia World of Quotations.* Available on-line at http://bartleby.com.66/78/65878.html.

LISA EASTMOND

☙

When Burke Meets Williams

A STUDY OF LANDSCAPE, STORY, IDENTITY, AND POLITICS

Political courage means caring enough to explain what is perceived at the time as madness and staying with an idea long enough, being rooted in a place deep enough, and telling the story widely enough to those who will listen, until it is recognised as wisdom.
—Terry Tempest Williams, *Red: Passion and Patience in the Desert*

Petroglyphs, sage, the rise and fall of the Colorado River—southern Utah's redrock country is not a new medium or muse for Terry Tempest Williams. In fact, *Red: Passion and Patience in the Desert* is, in part, a compilation of Williams's previous work: *Coyote's Canyon* and *Desert Quartet*. The stories of poets, Navajo children, coyotes, frogs, and fire are coupled with two new sections: "Home Work" and "Red." While Williams is concerned with what stories we tell that "evoke a sense of place" (Thornton and Clark 1999, 305), her readers should consider how she is seeking their identification through the stories she tells or retells about the redrock country. This is especially important considering the political purpose of *Red*. In an era of American politics when conservation gives way to economic progress, Williams has compiled stories in hopes of reawakening the political consciousness and environmental concern of the American public and to specifically help America's Redrock Wilderness Act move safely through the halls of Congress. In an interview with Edward Lueders, she admits her political concerns over the fate of the West and, in doing so, reveals the purpose of her writings. She says, "I think there is that notion that space in the west means empty space, wasted space. I'm concerned about this" (1989, 53).

However, although there are political aspirations for *Red* as a text, it is written not in the language of legalese, but through story. With an understanding of Kenneth Burke's revised definition of rhetoric and the expansion of rhetorical experience under that new definition, it is clear that although Williams claims to bypass rhetoric with story, it is precisely through story and landscape as symbolic expression that she is able to create rhetorical experiences, encouraging identification with the western landscape and its inhabitants, and offering a chance for her readers to transcend and rethink their own identities, opinions, and actions.

Williams, at the beginning of *Red,* acknowledges her unconventional approach to political action, saying that "story bypasses rhetoric and pierces the heart" (2001a, 3). The rhetoric that Williams claims to have bypassed is most certainly that of political persuasion linking back to the traditional definitions of the art. In *On Rhetoric,* Aristotle defines rhetoric as "an ability in each [particular] case, to see the available means of persuasion" (1991, 36). He furthers this definition by breaking the art down into functioning categories for everyday use in the civic arena: judicial, deliberative, and epideictic. Whereas Aristotle's categories of judicial and deliberative rhetoric lend themselves to persuasion by demanding judgment on either past or future events, epideictic, or demonstrative rhetoric, is concerned with presenting a picture of reality to an audience and seeking their identification with that reality, albeit a constructed one. An example of this form would be a funeral eulogy where the audience is presented with a version of the deceased's life and character, which the audience may then choose to accept or reject.

It is through this epideictic form of rhetoric that Burke reconsiders rhetoric as persuasion and broadens its definition to identification. With this redefinition of rhetoric comes a significant expansion in what constitutes rhetorical experience. In *A Rhetoric of Motives,* Burke suggests that "you persuade a man only insofar as you can talk his language by speech, gesture, tonality, order, image, attitude, idea, *identifying* your ways with his" (1969, 55). Because the rhetor uses identification to persuade and persuasion to shape identity, Burke suggests that "there is no chance of us keeping apart our meanings of persuasion, identification . . . and communication" (1989, 46). In these ways, defining rhetoric as identification expands the realm of rhetorical experience, allowing such experiences to be discursive or nondiscursive, conscious or unconscious, verbal or nonverbal.

Essentially, under Burke's definition, rhetoric is not limited to the realm of oratory and gesture, but includes symbolic interaction as a whole. Greg Clark, in *Rhetorical Landscapes in America,* explains that "identification happens . . . in moments of communication, and communication occurs through rhetorical exchanges of collectively meaningful symbols. Symbols that take the form of language as well as symbols that take other forms have this essential communicative function" (forthcoming, 6). Some of these forms of symbolic communication could include alternate languages such as math or music, or cultural symbols such as dress or traffic signs. As Clark explains, even land can function symbolically: "Like words, places function as social symbols. Like words, they present people with images and experiences of collective life within which those individuals are invited to locate themselves—to make themselves at home. As words signify shared concepts to those who use them, places signify shared situations, aspirations, and identities to those who inhabit them" (70). As we encounter symbols, whether through written language or the language of landscape, we will either identify with them and what these symbols represent or we will identify away from them. This interaction constantly shapes our individual identities, and by doing so, our collective identities are molded, for we define our individual selves in relation to a whole.

This process of identification is particularly important because it not only leads to a change in thought and possibly action, but also shapes identity. Burke explains how identification leads to changes in identity, saying, "since identification implies division, we found rhetoric involving us in matters of socialization and faction. . . . We considered how imagery can figure as a terminology of reidentification ('transformation' or 'rebirth')" (1989, 18). Part of the identification process involves a reconsideration of one's opinion and place in a larger social context, making room for the shaping of identity and reexamination of belief and action. Williams uses identification through story and landscape in an attempt to influence political persuasion and possibly reshape identity.

"It is a simple equation," says Williams, "place + people = politics." This equation seems especially functional in the deserts of the American West where battle lines move daily with the grazing cattle and seismic, oil-seeking thumper trucks. In the face of this day-to-day struggle over politics and place, Williams asks, "How are we going to find our way toward conversation?" Although keeping a political conversation going through story seems unconventional, Williams admits that for her, "the answer has always been through story. . . . Story offers a wash of images and emotion that returns us to our highest and deepest selves, where we remember what it means to be human, living in place with our neighbors" (2001a, 3). Williams reveals within the first few pages of *Red* that if we are going to decide as individuals and communities what the fate of our land will be, we must be more than bystanders or travelers through the landscape—we must link ourselves to land and engage in conversation. For Williams, this means storytelling. "Story," she writes, "becomes the conscience of our communities. . . . We can transform the world through story. I write out of my life. And when Hélène Cixous says, 'I-woman am going to blow up the Law. . . . Let it be done, right now, *in* language . . .' I believe her. . . . [M]y pen is my weapon" (Pearlman 1993, 123, 132).

Certainly, Williams's belief in and use of narrative's power are demonstrated throughout *Red*. The text holds rich tales of those transformed by the landscape and the stories its inhabitants tell. The transformation of those who allow themselves to be taken in by the landscape is not simply physical. At the beginning of "The Coyote Clan," Williams challenges her reader to "pull out your pocketknife, open the blade, and run it across your burnished arm. If you draw blood you are human. If you draw wet sand that dries quickly, then you will know you have become part of the desert" (23). Through this vibrant image, she suggests that if readers let the land and its stories into their lifeblood, the change will not be a temporary one, but will forever alter their very souls.

Some of those characters in the book who have been carved by the scenery and stories of their surroundings include Navajo children who know the color of lion eyes and what songs must be sung to bring balance back to the earth; a poet who disguises his work as ancient writing and buries his poems in the ground for ranchers to find, hoping to turn their minds and imaginations to the sacredness of the land and way of life of the ancient Anasazi; a seamstress who is raped in the backcountry and returns to wander among the ridges and plains, dropping segments of crimson thread in memory of all God's creations who have been exploited and lost innocent blood. Williams also documents through story the identities and personalities of her own family members who have worked the land for more than a century, digging pipelines. She writes of family fights over the best way to use land, and the paradoxes of Mormon belief and culture. She writes of Mary Austin and Aldo Leopold, nature writers and activists, who have almost become part of the landscapes they fought so hard to capture in their writings, preserved through their vigilant attempts to defend America's wildlands. These stories all manifest rhetorical power and populate the landscape of *Red* as readers identify with or against them.

Likewise, Williams has been shaped by the landscape and stories she tells and retells, connecting her to the people and place she recognizes as home. This transformation is evident not only in her musings, but also in her descriptions of leaving the busy city (142–43) and taking up residence in "a village in the desert" (22) where there is "open space . . . [and] open time to breathe, to dream, to dare, to play, to pray, to move freely, so freely, in a world our minds have forgotten, but our bodies remember" (23). Her change is brought on by such things as watching stars (24), the landscape of the sky, and learning from the stories of Navajo children (35). This text documents not only the shifting of identity that occurs in others, but also how Williams, herself, has been and is constantly allowing herself to be molded by the land and the stories that reside within its valleys and peaks, villages and pueblos, acting as an example to her readers, hoping they allow the same process to occur within their lives.

In a joint interview, Williams and fellow nature writer and activist Robert Finch reveal the purpose and power behind their storytelling, their poetics of place. In fact, it is Finch who puts into words what Williams's writing strives to accomplish. He says "that only by storying the earth do we come to love it, does it become the place where we live, it gives us back a sense of who we are. Through stories, we literally identify with the land. We love what we come to call home. Nature writers teach us to recognize home" (Lueders 1989, 41). Williams furthers the discussion by recognizing that "within this notion of people and place, story is the correspondence between the two. It informs our lives, it keeps things known. It's the umbilical cord between the past, present, and future" (46). However, this cord is one woven by the storyteller, interpreted by audiences, and therefore must be composed of and transferred through symbols.

Burke explains the rhetorical power of story as a symbolic act, that "any verbal act, is to be considered as 'symbolic action,'" "the symbolic act is the *dancing of an attitude*," and that "implicit in poetic organization per se there is the assertion of an identity" (1957, 31). For this reason, the form, in this case poetics, plays an equally vital role as content in the symbolic interaction of rhetorical experience.

Not only do Williams's stories cover a wide range of styles, but each section also seems to contain a distinct purpose that corresponds to and gives rhetorical power to the process of identification. The stories in *Red* are symbolically expressed and infused with social and cultural meaning, asking readers to identify either with or against these snapshots of "reality." The first section, "Home Work," explores the political climate of both Utah and the nation as a whole. "The Coyote Clan," taken from one of Williams's previous books, *Coyote's Canyon*, is described by Lorraine Anderson in *American Nature Writers* as "a new mythology for desert goers, one that acknowledges the

power of story and ritual, yet lies within the integrity of our own cultures"
(1996, 977). "Red" explores spiritual and philosophical connections to land,
how it has shaped people's beliefs. The fourth section, "Desert Quartet," considers the idea of "making love to the land." Finally, the last section of the
book is a large appendix full of facts and figures, seemingly void of
Williams's storytelling voice. The appendix houses more than thirty-five
pages of this compact book, and consists of an abridged version of America's
Redrock Wilderness Act, a map of America's Redrock Wilderness, "America's
Redrock Wilderness: A Citizen's Proposal," and a list of supporting organizations. Although this section seems more like the political rhetoric Williams
suggests she has abandoned, it too is yet another form of "storying the
earth," asking us to identify with or against both its content and its form, and
certainly it fulfills the purpose of providing readers with a direct connection
to the land, even if it is written in the language of the political or legal realm.
Offering various forms of stories, symbolic interactions, and rhetorical approaches is clearly Williams's attempt to keep a politically charged conversation going. However, the rhetorical power of these narrative forms moves
beyond conversation to identification as her readers are forced to accept or
reject the realities presented to them.

The social and cultural implications of linking landscape, story, and identity are further revealed in a transcript from the NPR radio program *Insight
and Outlook,* featuring Scott London's interview with Williams. As London
describes Williams and her work preceding the interview, he explains, "[F]or
Williams, there is a very close connection between ourselves, our people, and
our native place" (1996, 1). As he reveals these connections in Williams's
work, London is introducing the notion that story can shape individual or
collective identities. He moves the conversation in this direction further as
he asks about "the power of place and the importance of a land we can call
our own" and questions Williams further about the implications of her statement that "perhaps the most radical act we can commit is to stay home" (3).
His and Williams's answers to these questions are also well thought out and
constructed. She speaks of Emigration Canyon and what it means to the
Mormon people, to her family, and to herself. She speaks of staying home "to
learn the names of things, to realize who we live among" and says, "if we
don't know sage, pinyon, juniper, then . . . we are living a life without specificity, and then our lives become abstractions" (4). When London asks about
the implications of this loss of connection with the land, Williams responds,
"I think our lack of intimacy with the land has initiated a lack of intimacy
with each other" (5). In other words, both London and Williams acknowl-

edge that a loss of landscape has social and cultural implications beyond the loss of story or place. This disconnection of people, place, and narrative ultimately leads to a loss of communal and often individual identity.

It is for this reason that Williams is not just populating the scenery with story but providing a landscape for her readers, naming and conveying the places where her characters, friends, family, and even she, herself, resides. As with story, landscape is symbolically expressed, if for no other reason than language itself is a system of symbols that we must interact with as readers. Symbolism is essentially what distinguishes land from landscape and what gives it the rhetorical power to seek identification and shape identity. Greg Clark acknowledges wilderness as symbolic of land when he explains that the "furthest reach of symbolicity is inevitably identity—place, as opposed to space, landscapes as opposed to land—[that] inevitably come to 'stand for' an identity that finally interweaves the individual and the collective" (forthcoming, 295). In *Red*, Williams supports the idea of landscape as a symbolic expression by saying that when we talk about wilderness, "we are talking about the body of the beloved, not real estate" (76). Clearly, when land is symbolically constructed, it ceases solely to represent itself and, instead, represents or translates the ideals of those who have given it meaning, making it a powerful rhetorical tool.

Throughout *Red*, Williams, herself, seems very aware of the rhetorical power of landscape and its creation. In "Home Work" she asks, "[H]ow can I convey the scale and power of these big wide-open lands to those who have never seen them, let alone to those who have?" (11). The task almost appears to overwhelm her, and rightly so, for she is not as concerned with book sales as she is with political progress through continued conversation. She is concerned with saving the redrock country of southern Utah. However, not all of her readers love southern Utah or call it home; therefore, Williams must describe this landscape in such a way that her readers identify with it, broadening it to a national level. Clearly, the shaping of identity through the rhetorical use of landscape and story is a political act for Williams and an attempt to unite readers under the umbrella of symbolic interaction and rhetorical experience to create communities of better-informed, more politically active citizens. She acknowledges her deliberate construction of landscape in literature in a question-and-answer session held after her "Erotics of Place" lecture, part of the 1995 Starker Lecture Series. Williams explains, "I write, and that exposes people to these sacred places, but I have to believe that an informed citizenry is of better use than an uninformed one" (1995, 24).

This uninformed citizenry that Williams speaks of and the political possibilities of showing how the stories and land of southern Utah relate to identity are addressed by John Beck, in his article "Without Form and Void: The American Desert As Trope and Terrain." While discussing people's perception of the use of land and the role of self based on their understanding of the landscape, Beck suggests that this understanding of land and identity is often based solely on maps, especially for those back East making important decisions about southwestern deserts. He goes on to quote Williams, saying, "'[A] blank spot on the map translates into empty space devoid of people, a wasteland perfect for nerve gas, weteye [sic] bombs, and toxic waste'" (2001, 79). Moreover, Williams reveals that identity is regional simply because landscape and story are, and because of this, she tries to convey within her stories a sense of the West to those who may make decisions about a land that has not influenced their very souls (2001b). As David Mazel further explains in *American Literary Environmentalism*, "Environmental discourse constitutes not only a specifically American *nature* but also a particular conception of an American *nation,* and ecocriticism can thus be aligned with the contemporary critique of the 'national narrative'" (2000, xviii). Yet, as is apparent through Williams's work in *Red,* this national narrative is simply a carefully chosen group of symbols portraying a landscape and community, created to convey another voice in the heated conversation surrounding wildlands. In this case, Williams has created a mythic, sensual, and sacred landscape, in hopes of shaping identity and influencing political persuasions.

Whereas landscape and wilderness, as a form of landscape, are representations of reality, this land that has been expressed through socially and culturally driven language exists in the physical realm. In fact, *Red* contains maps of the redrock region and houses a list naming actual places in this prospective wilderness area. In her stories, Williams speaks of naturalists looking for answers and understanding in the desert, family members that see the land as their livelihood and prosperity, artists that see the land as a muse and holder of history, and so on. Clearly, wilderness is a physical space, and though we may interact with it physically, we may also interact with land symbolically. At times, land ceases to simply be land and instead is imagined and treated as a narrower representation—pristine and pure, mythic and mystical, untouched and all-knowing, pleasurable and dangerous. The meanings we bestow upon the land, within story, through language, often dictate our reactions to it and our relationships with it.

Because wilderness is often symbolically expressed through human language and literature, it exists not only in the physical realm, but also as part of human imagination. In his groundbreaking "Wilderness Letter," Wallace Stegner, speaking of wildlands, writes, "[T]he remainder and reassurance that it is still there is good for our spiritual health even if we never once in ten years set foot in it. . . . [It is] important, that is, simply as an idea" (2002, 1). Williams also speaks of imagination and wilderness in *Red:* "[F]or those who have not experienced the sublime nature of Utah's canyon country, I invite you to imagine what it might be like to see and feel the world from the inside out" (17). Both Stegner's and Williams's statements suggest that we need not enter into the landscape to feel or recall what it symbolizes. Conducting that symbolic interaction with land through imagination can also afford us the "wilderness experience," without actually occupying the same space with these wildlands. Although those experiencing symbolic interaction with landscape may reside in the present time, they may be identifying, through their imaginations, with a time period or group of people not currently in existence.

What is most important about our physical or imaginary-based interaction with landscape is the ability to transcend our current life conditions and separate ourselves from present reality and reconfigure our individual and communal identities, as well as our relationships with nature. Williams suggests that wilderness is a landscape "that informs who we are, a place that carries our history, our dreams, holds us to a moral line of behavior that transcends thought" (2001a, 190) and that it "revives the memory of unity. Through its protection, we can find faith in our humanity" (69). As we interact with wilderness, we consider ourselves in terms of symbols, and as we construct idealistic cultural representations of land, we construct idealized versions of humanity to match the symbolic landscape. This transcendence allows us to separate ourselves from what we know as reality and rethink our own identities and beliefs.

Identifying with a community or concept not currently in existence plays into the idea of transcendence. As Clark explains, "Rhetorical experiences, whether discursive or not, present powerful symbols of shared identity that teach people whom they ought to aspire, individually as well as collectively, to be" (forthcoming, 9). People will naturally experience symbolic interaction personally, while connecting with the ideals of a larger group, imagined or existing. In this way, the rhetoric of politics and poetry is blurred as rhetoric encourages identification and transcendence occurs.

Whether by identification or transcendence, our identities are intrinsically linked to the scenery as we are confronted with it by way of various mediums—in *Red,* landscape and narrative as literature. In *Rhetorical Landscapes in America,* Clark suggests,

> These mythic public places [symbolically expressed landscapes] provide people with symbolic "images" of that collectivity, in the image of which—to paraphrase Burke—they are each prompted to make themselves over as they come to identify themselves with a nation. When these are images of the most spectacular features of an exceptional, and essentially uninhabitable landscape set apart from the land as a public place that anyone can inhabit temporarily, they symbolize the vast common ground that citizens must imagine themselves sharing but can never encounter. (145)

As Burke explains, "In such identification there is a partially dreamlike, idealistic motive, somewhat compensatory to real differences and real divisions, which the rhetoric of identification would transcend" (Clark 2001, 3). Understandably, this form of rhetoric has the power to bring about political action. It gives people transcendent experiences, allowing them to see, even for a moment, the type of people they could be, the type of community they could live in, the type of world they could inhabit. This type of rhetorical power is vital to the purpose and scope of *Red,* and it is therefore no mistake that Williams uses landscape and story as her medium for continuing conversation. Williams's "poetics of place" ultimately becomes "politics of place" as she strives to effectively use rhetoric as identification and a tool for transcendence.

Although transcendence can function as a higher way of looking at the world and ourselves in it, it is precisely for this reason that some consider the symbolic expression of wilderness so dangerous. In "The Trouble with Wilderness," William Cronon warns that "by imagining that our true home is in the wilderness, we forgive ourselves the homes we actually inhabit. In its flight from history, in its siren song of escape, in its reproduction of the dangerous dualism that sets human beings outside of nature—in all of these ways, wilderness poses a serious threat." However, he does acknowledge that "it is not the things we label as wilderness that are the problem," but it is the symbolic expression and our separation from reality that are the problem (1995, 81). Clearly, people are able to identify not only with symbols, but also against symbols as their individual and collective identities are shaped. The very process of identification, as outlined by Burke, is a system of drawing boundaries, and although Williams cannot ensure that shaping belief will shape the desired behavior from her audience, she attempts to reconcile the dualisms and bridge the gap between reality and transcendent vision through story and a firm call for dedication to specific landscapes. In the introduction to Burke's *On Symbols and Society,* Joseph R. Gusfield explains Burke's connecting language and rhetorical experience to action, reminding readers that "words are not empty folders, hanging in the air. They move audiences to responses and move speakers to define and redefine their contexts. . . . [E]ither identification . . . is a call—to action or inaction" (1989, 18). The rhetorical power of land and language comes through the use of symbolic interaction and identification; however, the idea of expressing landscape through culturally driven language can be problematic, suggesting that the land has no power beyond what we ascribe to it.

In fact, Williams feels that her job as a writer is not to construct symbolically charged landscapes, but to simply translate her interactions with land, the language of land, into a language her readers may understand. She writes,

> Our task as writers is to try and listen to what the land speaks in its own voice, not ours, hence, we are translators. . . . [I]n my mind and heart—what we do is not a construction, but rather a gesture on behalf of life, an exploration, a celebration of beauty and pain and mystery and awe, in the name of this beautiful, broken, blue planet called Earth. It's the questions and the contemplations of those questions through story that sustain us. (2002)

Again her choice to story the landscape as her means of providing rhetorical experiences for her readers is evident, but she maintains a strong commitment to the land she is linked to and whose language she is trying to convey to others. She says, "I will tell you that I am a naturalist first and a writer second, that the landscape came before words" (Lueders 1989, 41). This deep commitment to the land is a strong indication of her own identification with landscape and the stories of those who inhabit it; it reveals possibility for transcendence and dedication to the political cause of the redrock deserts.

Finally, in relation to poetics and politics, Williams reveals in an interview with Tom Lynch, professor of southwestern literature at New Mexico State University, her desire to make a political impact through her storytelling and writing. She cites Aldo Leopold's *Sand County Almanac* and Rachel Carson's *Silent Spring* as examples of how the poetics of place can ultimately have an impact on the politics of place, indicating that the reader is not the only one altered by the story, but that there are possibilities for political change and a revision of communal identity (2001).

Whereas *Red: Passion and Patience in the Desert* appears to be yet another title in the ever growing genre of creative nonfiction and nature writing, it is not just a simple collection of stories. By constructing a version of the current political, social, and cultural climates of both southern Utah and the nation as a whole, Williams asks readers to engage in the landscape and transcend their everyday lives to become more active citizens, hoping they will identify with her political stance. Although she claims to have bypassed rhetoric with story, she has only exchanged traditional, political rhetoric for the rhetorical power of landscape and narrative. Certainly, through these mediums, she not only provides intense rhetorical experiences for her readers under Burke's expanded definition of rhetoric, but also shapes individual and collective identities, provides opportunities for transcendence, and seeks to spark the political action needed to see America's Redrock Wilderness Act become a reality rather than just a proposal. Through landscape and story, whether physical or imaginary, Williams documents the past and present (whether real or mythical) but leaves the future in the hands of her readers. In the last entry of *Red*, "Wild Mercy," Williams writes, "The eyes of the future are looking at us and they are praying for us to see beyond our own time. . . . [W]e live only by grace. Wilderness lives by this same grace. Wild mercy is in our hands" (215). This call to arms, to transcendence, to identification is rhetorically powerful. Williams leaves her readers with stories and portrayals of a sacred landscape, hoping they are enough to alter the minds and hearts of individuals and include them in the community of those who are willing to fight for the last of America's great wild.

Works Cited

Anderson, Lorraine. 1996. "Terry Tempest Williams." In *American Nature Writers,* edited by John Elder, 973–88. Vol. 2. Chicago: Macmillan.

Aristotle. 1991. *On Rhetoric: A Theory of Civic Discourse.* Translated by George Kennedy. New York: Oxford University Press.

Beck, John. 2001. "Without Form and Void: The American Desert As Trope and Terrain." *Nepanila* 2 (1):63–83.

Burke, Kenneth. 1957. *The Philosophy of Literary Form.* 1941. Reprint, New York: Vintage Books.

———. 1969. *A Rhetoric of Motives.* 1950. Reprint, Berkeley and Los Angeles: University of California Press.

———. 1989. *On Symbols and Society.* Chicago: University of Chicago Press.

Clark, Gregory. 2001. "Rhetorical Lessons of the National Parks." Typescript.

———. Forthcoming. *Rhetorical Landscapes in America.*

Cronon, William. 1995. "The Trouble with Wilderness; or, Getting Back to the Wrong Nature." In *Uncommon Ground: Toward Reinventing Nature,* edited by William Cronon, 69–90. New York: Norton.

London, Scott. 1996. "The Politics of Place: An Interview with Terry Tempest Williams." *Insight and Outlook.* Available on-line at http://www.scottlondon.com/insight/scripts/ttw.html.

Lueders, Edward, ed. 1989. *Writing Natural History: Dialogues with Authors.* Salt Lake City: University of Utah Press.

Lynch, Tom. 2001. "Talking to Terry Tempest Williams about Writing, the Environment, and Being Mormon." New Mexico State University Border Book Festival. Available on-line at http://web.nmsu.edu/~tomlynch/ swlit.ttwinterview.html.

Mazel, David. 2000. *American Literary Environmentalism.* Athens: University of Georgia Press.

Pearlman, Mickey. 1993. *Listen to Their Voices: Twenty Interviews with Women Who Write.* New York: Norton.

Stegner, Wallace. 2002. "Wilderness Letter." *Wilderness Society.* Available on-line at http://www.wilderness.org/standbylands/wilderness/wildletter.htm.

Thornton, Deb, and Kip Clark. 1999. "Terry Tempest Williams." In *Dictionary of Literary Biography: Twentieth-Century American Western Writers,* edited by Richard H. Cracroft, 303–9. Vol. 254. Farmington Hills, Mich.: Gale Group.

Williams, Terry Tempest. 1995. "An Erotics of Place." *Re-Thinking Natural Resources: 1995 Starker Lectures,* compiled by Bo Shelby and Sandie Arbogast. Corvallis: Oregon State University Press.

———. 2001a. *Red: Passion and Patience in the Desert.* New York: Pantheon Books.

———. 2001b. Conversation with author, Salt Lake City, 4 December.

———. 2002. "Re: Returning to a draft." E-mail communication, 20 May.

MELISSA A. GOLDTHWAITE

❧

Rhetoric + Feminism = Williams's Poetic Means

TRANSFORMING TRIPTYCHS OF BODY, FORM, AND FAITH IN *LEAP*

Introduction: Reconciliation, Transformation, Possibility

Can a new alchemy bring into being a union or reunion of opposing elements, a conjunction that may produce a new guiding image? 1 + 1 = 3.
—Terry Tempest Williams, *Leap*

A place without the usual dichotomies. No phony divisions between mind and body, intelligence and passion, nature and technology, private and public, within and without, male and female.
—Carole Maso, *Break Every Rule*

At the end of her essay "Rupture, Verge, and Precipice / Precipice, Verge, and Hurt Not," novelist Carole Maso worries over a new essay she needs to write for the *Review of Contemporary Fiction:* "What to say? What can be said?" She worries, in part, because of the anger she feels over exclusion: "When thinking of literature, the past and the present all too often infuriate me: everyone, everything that's been kept out." She does not, ultimately, let the exclusion or the anger paralyze her. Maso thinks, instead, of possibility, of forgiveness: "Perhaps in my essay I will make an attempt, the first movement toward some sort of reconciliation. . . . If it's possible" (2000, 191).

Like Maso, Terry Tempest Williams, in *Leap,* seeks reconciliation, the reconciliation of corporeal experience and a tradition of religious belief—if it's possible. She seeks this reconciliation in her journey through memory and through the landscape of Hieronymus Bosch's *El jardín de las delicias* (The garden of delights). Of *Leap,* Williams writes, "Let these pages be my interrogation of faith" (2000, 5). This interrogation, for Williams, requires a questioning of orthodoxy and its effects; she asks:

> What are we told?
>
> What do we fear as a result of what we have been told?
>
> And what do we know within our own bodies? (39)

Through these three successive one-sentence paragraphs, Williams questions the effects of the orthodox Mormon beliefs passed down to her, offering the possibility of bodily experience as an additional source of knowledge. Both the content and the style/form of Williams's book bring into question the relationship between authority and experience. That is, she interrogates not only religious belief, but also the orthodoxy of form, the very structures of language that determine what can be communicated and how. Throughout *Leap*, Williams uses structures of threes, what I will call "unified triads"—a revised notion of trinity, triptychs of thought.

As reader, writer, and critic, I join Williams in both kinds of questioning and in doing so explore a related question in the context of her work: what is/what can be the relationship between rhetoric and feminism?[1] In a note explaining the equation contained in the epigraph to this section ($1 + 1 = 3$), Williams writes, "This is the formula my grandmother Mimi, Kathryn Blackett Tempest, would always refer to whenever she was talking about personal transformation, be it in our waking lives or in our dreams" (299). In this piece, too, I am interested in transformation—both personal and theoretical, the transformation of individuals and academic disciplines, the transformation I believe is possible in and through language and form. Carole Maso is not the first to rage against exclusion; Williams is not the first to question her religious heritage or to break traditional form; I am not the first to make connections between rhetoric and feminism. Many have come before; many desire transformation.

It requires no "leap" to see or analyze Williams's work in the context of feminist theory. Although there are many forms and varieties of feminism, both as a political movement and as an area of academic study, Williams's writing enacts elements of *écriture feminine,* the concepts and style associated mainly with French feminists Hélène Cixous, Julia Kristeva, Luce Irigaray, and Monique Wittig. Like these writers, Williams defies many narrative conventions, blending theory, criticism, literature, and wordplay. Williams, too, is quite familiar with these writers—all are cited in the selected bibliography at the end of *Leap.*

Whereas the feminist influence on Williams's work is clear, claiming her work as rhetoric is more controversial. Williams herself, in her books and in interviews, often distinguishes her work from rhetoric, claiming that her emphasis on story "bypasses rhetoric" and "pierces the heart." The association of rhetoric with disembodied logic (even heartless manipulation) is not new. Even rhetoricians and scholars of rhetoric often emphasize logic and downplay the importance of emotion. Edward P. J. Corbett, credited as the person responsible for revitalizing the study of rhetoric in contemporary scholarship and classrooms, forwards the wish that all audiences be persuaded exclusively by logic. When discussing logos (appeals to reason), Corbett and his coauthor, Robert Connors, write, "Ideally, reason should dominate all of people's thinking and actions, but actually, they are often influenced by passions and prejudices and customs. . . . [However,] [w]e must have faith not only that people are capable of ordering their lives by the dictates of reason but that most of the time they are disposed to do so" (1999, 32). Even in moving on to a discussion of ethos (appeals to character) and pathos (appeals to emotion), they still emphasize the ideal of logos, though they concede that we "have to deal with people as they are, not as they should be" (72). They recognize—with far more ambivalence than I do—the importance of character and the power of appeals to emotion; they also understand the persuasive potential of style, that humans respond to repetition, to figures of speech and thought, to language that is beautiful.

Perhaps it is some rhetoricians' distrust of appeals to emotion and character that has shaped negative associations with the term *rhetoric*. Or perhaps the popular pejorative dismissal "that's just rhetoric" has become so fully ingrained in common speech that it is difficult to reclaim the term. In "Home Work," her introduction to *Red,* Williams claims that in environmental debates, "abstractions of philosophy and rhetoric turn into ground scrimmages" (2001, 3). As an alternative, she affirms her belief in the power of story to create a climate for conversation, claiming, "Story bypasses rhetoric and pierces the heart" (3). This alternative, however, does not actually bypass rhetoric; rather, it emphasizes necessary components of rhetorical efficacy. Eighteenth-century rhetorician George Campbell recognized the importance of emotions; in *The Philosophy of Rhetoric,* he observes that there is no persuasion without moving an audience's passions (1988, bk. 1, chap. 7). More recently, scholars making connections between feminism and rhetoric have further elaborated on the importance of emotion in communicating with others.

In "Border Crossings: Intersections of Rhetoric and Feminism," Lisa Ede, Cheryl Glenn, and Andrea Lunsford seek to revise the traditional canons of rhetoric through the theoretical lens of feminism, illustrating their claims with examples from writers such as Gloria Anzaldúa, Audre Lorde, Toni Morrison, bell hooks, and Margaret Fuller. Acknowledging the multidisciplinary nature of both feminism and rhetoric, Ede, Glenn, and Lunsford point to both as places of "contest and difference," but also as places of possibility, as "border crossings that might allow both feminists and rhetoricians to reflect upon, and possibly even to reconsider, their disciplinary projects" (1995, 407, 408). Organized by the traditional rhetorical canons—invention, arrangement, style, memory, delivery—my essay takes a form similar to "Border Crossings," functioning as both an application of the theories Ede, Glenn, and Lunsford work out and as an extension, even revision, of those theories through an analysis of Williams's *Leap*.

Rhetoric is an art and a critical practice. By using a form of feminist rhetorical criticism as both my method and my focus, I position myself as both audience for Williams's art and as an interpreter of her text, creating a layered response that values what Williams does in *Leap* and claims her text as feminist rhetoric. I argue that rhetorical theory is a useful lens for understanding and explicating *Leap* and that *Leap* is a provocative text for expanding traditional understandings of rhetoric. Just as Aristotle based his art of rhetoric on inductive generalizations about the practice of those who spoke well and effectively, so I seek to extend understandings of rhetoric through reference to Williams's practice. Whereas throughout much of the history of rhetorical theory rhetoric has been applied to argumentative discourse, I wish to apply it, also, to literary discourse, considering the persuasiveness of forms—in this case, a mixed-genre memoir—that do not necessarily fit neatly into established categories of rhetoric.

Painting the Body of *Invention*

> Invention is the shaping spirit that re-forms fragments into new wholes, so that even what has been familiar can be seen fresh.
> —Jeanette Winterson, *Art Objects*

> I would like to write like a painter. I would like to write like painting.
> —Hélène Cixous, "The Last Painting or the Portrait of God"

Invention in rhetorical theory refers to the process of coming to discover the content of one's discourse. For some, invention is a conscious, systematic procedure, for others, an art of inquiry. In both cases, it is a starting place—using what is known to discover that which is not yet known, or at least not yet articulated. Many strategies of invention are heuristics that prompt memory and observation. Corbett and Connors deal with invention as the discovery of arguments, taking writers through the process of formulating a thesis, recognizing the three modes of persuasion, understanding various methods of definition, gaining awareness of special and common topics, and familiarizing themselves with external aids to invention (such as indexes, handbooks, dictionaries, and bibliographies). This focus on discovering material to aid in the creation of well-ordered, logical arguments assumes the kind of stable and autonomous speaker or writer that traditional rhetorical theory tends to value. In contrast, Ede, Glenn, and Lunsford point to feminist challenges to the traditional understanding of rhetors as "masculine, unified, stable, autonomous, and capable of acting on the world through language," acknowledging the important work of women who have "sought to include the intuitive and paralogical, the thinking of the body, as valuable sources of knowing, as sites of invention" (1995, 412–13). These additional sources of knowledge are especially important to Williams's text.

In *Leap*, the two main sources of invention for Williams are Bosch's painting and "the body" (including physical and emotional experiences, as well as imagination and intuition), which she draws together through metaphor. She writes of having slept under the left (Paradise) and right (Hell) panels of Bosch's triptych as a child, when visiting her grandmother: "these were the images that framed the 'oughts and shoulds' and 'if you don'ts' of my religious upbringing" (2000, 6). She then recounts the moment of coming to see the whole of Bosch's triptych as an adult:

> Standing before *El jardín de las delicias* in the Prado Museum in Spain, now as a woman, I see the complete triptych for the first time. I am stunned. The center panel. The Garden of Earthly Delights. So little is hidden in the center panel, why was it hidden from me?
> The body.
> The body of the triptych.
> My body. (6–7)

Recognizable in this unified triad is a movement from the abstract (the body: Whose body? An idealized body?) to the more concrete (the body of the triptych: Bosch's *Garden of Delights*) to the personal (my body). The invention process moves quickly from concept to object to self through the associational power of metaphor. It includes, too, as in many feminist texts, an awareness of exclusion—what has been hidden or kept out. The movement of Williams's inventive process values the paralogical, the logic of association and experience rather than the traditional logic of syllogism or even the logic of rhetorical theory's enthymeme, which assumes a syllogistic form but deals in the realm of the probable rather than the demonstrable. Unlike the deductive reasoning privileged by a syllogistic form, Williams's reasoning is intuitive, poetically suggestive.

Throughout *Leap*, Williams reflects on her associations with images in *The Garden of Delights*, often—in an act of identification—imagining herself as characters in Bosch's painting. The painting becomes her inspiration. The physical act of viewing the artwork translates into memory and observation. After counting cherries, for instance, in the center panel, Williams comments on how cherries are the state fruit of her home state, Utah, and then recalls a day when she was a child, picking cherries with her great-uncle and cousin. When her great-uncle asked which principle of the Gospel of Jesus Christ meant the most to Williams and her cousin, her cousin replied "obedience," while Williams answered "free agency" (8).

The cherries in Bosch's painting and the memory of a childhood experience trigger Williams's exploration of the concepts of obedience and free will, an exploration she carries throughout the text. Toward the end of her book, Williams returns to these concepts, placing them in a schematic form that moves away from dualism, seeking to reconcile seemingly opposing elements in order to produce something new or to see something in a new way. She writes,

> Obedience.
> Obedience as trust.
> Trust as obedience. (243)

Reflecting on a traditional way of seeing yet holding out the possibility for a new way of understanding, Williams explains, "In this dualistic world, I have seen obedience on one hand, free agency on the other. How do I bring these two hands opposed together in a gesture of prayer?" (243). The phrasing "on one hand and on the other" to demonstrate contrast is so familiar in colloquial language that it has lost some of its metaphorical power. In extending the metaphor, however, Williams helps readers see even abstract thinking as a physical act, in this case, an act with spiritual resonance.

Even when Williams provides definitions, a practice important to argument, associations with the body remain. Before alluding to religious experience as a move toward wholeness, Williams writes, "To unite, combine, form an alliance, to make whole: *ligar*" (243). From *ligar* (also *ligare* and *ligamen-*

tum) we get the word *ligament,* the tissue connecting bones and holding organs in place. Showing the body as central to her spirituality, Williams implicitly questions theologies that fear corporeal experience, that see it as potentially sinful.

Her focus on the center panel, "The Garden of Earthly Delights," further questions such theologies—their restrictions, what they exclude. And her physical interaction with the center panel is not restricted to the visual; she listens to the painting as well:

> There are three individuals talking inside a transparent dome just beyond the orchard to the right of the jay who is dropping the berry once again into the mouth that is open. Call it a bubble of conversation, a dome of conversation. I lean closer. Yes, there is an echo, a reverberation of ideas, an amplification of what they are discussing, considering, questioning. Yes, I hear the words alive on their tongues, "Above all, the senses." (143)

In this passage, Williams grounds her reader visually first, so that the reader can find her bearings in the painting itself, an object outside the imagination. She then draws the reader back into imagination, as she hears the words "alive" on the tongues of those engaged in conversation; they say what Williams seems to feel: "Above all, the senses." Looking closer, Williams figures the three conversants as the Holy Trinity and wonders, "Which one will lift the canopy to include those not allowed inside?" (144). Through this imaginative personification of the characters in Bosch's center panel, Williams suggests one of her concerns: the exclusivity of some forms of religious belief.

As an alternative, she values the "delicacy of a sensual life . . . in service of the Sacred within a shared community honoring the dignity of all its members." These members include not just humans but also the earth, for, she writes, "I accept the Organic Trinity of Mineral, Vegetable, and Animal with as much authority as I accept the Holy Trinity." In this move toward inclusiveness, Williams unites and combines, creating a spirituality of wholeness. The process of her associational invention takes readers from the painting to the religious concept of the Trinity to Williams's concept of the earth as sacred and an expansive sense of what is holy: "The world is holy. We are holy. All life is holy" (147). She unites these three sentences and their accompanying ideas through the associational power of repetition (in this case, epistrophe—the repetition of the same word or group of words at the ends of successive clauses).

Through her interaction with *El jardín de las delicias* and an emphasis on remaining faithful to spiritual imagination without betraying the knowledge of the body, Williams is able to question authority, revising the beliefs passed down to her. The voices of authorities remain—she writes, "I hear the voices of my Elders: *You can't have it both ways*"—but she answers back: "[M]ust it really be all or nothing? Right wing or left wing? Paradise or hell?" (147). Williams answers these rhetorical questions, in part, through the unorthodox arrangement of her text.

CELEBRATING UNORTHODOX *ARRANGEMENT*

> [A]s it is not enough for those who are erecting edifices, to collect stones and materials, and other things useful for the architect, unless the hand of the workman be also applied to the disposition and collocation of them, so . . . , however abundant be the quantity of matter, it will form but a confused mass and heap, unless similar *arrangement* bind it together.
>   —Quintilian, *Institutes of Oratory*

> Wish: that forms other than those you've invented or sanctioned through your thousands of years of privilege might arise and be celebrated.
>   —Carole Maso, *Break Every Rule*

Rhetoricians see arrangement as the dividing and ordering of various parts of a discourse in order to achieve a particular effect. No matter how many parts classical rhetoricians divided a discourse into, the chain of argument was supposed to be linear and logical. In considering the possibilities of feminist rhetorics, Ede, Glenn, and Lunsford argue that "we . . . have much to gain by crisscrossing the borders of rhetoric and feminism, particularly in terms of long-standing feminist attempts to disrupt the linear orderliness of prose, to contain contradictions and anomalies, to resist closure. These goals have been pursued vigorously by Hélène Cixous, whose attempts at 'writing the body' introduce forms that push against traditional patterns of discourse and closure" (1995, 418). Like Cixous, Williams breaks rhetorical norms; instead of a linear text, she creates a circuitous movement. She opens *Leap* with a suggestive epigraph from Federico García Lorca's *Blood Wedding:* "We must follow the vein of our blood." This epigraph, placed even before the table of contents, foreshadows the circuitous movement of the text, even foregrounds the centrality of the body (here, the circulation of blood). Pages later, directly before her first section, Williams includes another epigraph:

"The new can bear fruit only when it grows from the seeds implanted in tradition" (3). This epigraph, from Paul Tillich's *Dogma of the Trinity,* suggests Williams's intention to marry tradition and personal experience and, in that union, to create something new. Taken together, the imagery present in these two epigraphs merges body, tradition, earth.

Though she moves away from traditional patterns of arrangement, Williams's structure clearly forwards an argument: a nontraditional reading of both Bosch's triptych and of her own religious heritage, an argument made more persuasive through the nontraditional arrangement she chooses. I have noted already Williams's frequent use of what I have called unified triads on the level of associational invention and paragraphing. In my consideration of arrangement, I intend to broaden the picture, looking more closely both at the overall structure of *Leap* and at its patterns of arrangement within each section. In terms of overall structure and argument, we find paradise + hell = the garden of earthly delights. The argument is perhaps best represented by a unified triad:

> The gap between Heaven and Hell is fear.
> The dialogue between Heaven and Hell is prayer.
> The marriage between Heaven and Hell is Earth. (165)

For Williams, "Truth is in the mean," in the uniting of heaven and hell.

In an interview with Random House, publisher of *Leap,* Williams explains the traditional approach to Bosch's painting, a reading from left to right—from Paradise to the Garden of Delights to Hell—that corresponds to the eschatology Williams also calls into question. Such an approach, Williams argues, conceives of the world as "black and white, a dance between good and evil" in which humans "are caught inside a paradigm of dualities." Seeking to move beyond the dualities, to transform them, Williams then contrasts this reading with her own, explaining the structure she chose for *Leap:* "I chose to read the triptych, left, right, and center: Paradise, Hell, and Earthly Delights. The center panel becomes a landscape of exploration, a place where the reconciliation of opposites is possible. It is not 'either/or' but 'and.' . . . The dualistic world set into motion by Descartes becomes a landscape where we can begin to see the world whole, even holy" (Random House n.d., n.p.). The transformational unity Williams desires links the spiritual realm to the earth. She has made a similar move in her earlier texts, including *Refuge: An Unnatural History of Family and Place.* In *Refuge,* Williams seeks to revise the traditional notion of the Trinity by linking it to both the feminine and the body. She writes,

> In Mormon theology, the Holy Trinity is comprised of God the Father, Jesus Christ the son, and the Holy Ghost. We call this the Godhead.
>
> Where is the Motherbody? (1991, 240)

She then takes an additional step in imagining a grounded faith, suggesting that if "we could introduce the Motherbody as a spiritual counterpoint to the Godhead, perhaps our inspiration and devotion would no longer be directed to the stars, but our worship could return to the Earth" (241). Though she does not express this wish in the form of either a triad or an equation, the move toward combining opposites to create something new is the same: Godhead + Motherbody = earth-centered spirituality.

While Williams deals with a similar idea in *Refuge,* she emphasizes, even extends, the idea through her form, arrangement, and style in *Leap.* In *Leap,* the notion of a revised Trinity exists at the level of form in the arrangement of the book as a whole and in the smaller rhetorical units of paragraphs and sentences. Through her use of form, Williams offers an alternative logic of poetic means.[2]

The arrangement of the text in some ways mirrors the arrangement of Bosch's *El jardín de las delicias:* an overall picture and effect is created in each section, just as it is in each panel of the triptych. In her first section, "Paradise," Williams introduces her readers to her purpose: to interrogate her faith through "traveling in the landscape of Hieronymus Bosch"; through the whole of Bosch's triptych, which she compares to "a great medieval butterfly flapping its wings through the centuries" (5); through the panel of Paradise itself; and her interaction—through vision and memory—with it. The overall effect of this section is a sense of innocence, as Williams recounts her baptism into the Mormon faith at age eight; the sacrament of communion with a religious community (and with birds); her spiritual connection with Joseph Smith, first prophet of the Mormon faith; her own spiritual vision at age seventeen; and her marriage in the Salt Lake Temple at age nineteen. Williams enters into images in the painting, finding herself; she recognizes Eve in Paradise, and is transported back in memory: "I am Eve standing in the Temple of the Lord. Across from me is Adam, the man I am about to marry; his name is Brooke" (37). The inventive power of the painting itself—its images, colors, composition—helps Williams communicate different pictures, effects, and feelings in each section.

In her second section, "Hell," Williams abandons the innocence of Paradise, taking up the madness of Hell. The imagery—both in Bosch's panel and in Williams's chapter—is dark. The arrangement is confused and confusing, taking the reader-viewer through hell. The arrangement is disconnected, offering few transitions, moving from suggestions of physical and mental torture to sensory overload to panic attacks to environmental destruction to clips of disturbing stories from the news to an explicit description of a Damien Hirst art installation to a conversation on an airplane to fears of cancer (which took the lives of many women in her family) to the conjugation of the verb *destroy* to isolation to the death of her grandfather to fire to torture to her and Brooke burning their marriage certificate and throwing their wedding bands in the Great Salt Lake to more fire to hallucination to disconnection from her religious community. The movement within this section—like the other sections—is associational, but my use of the word *to* and the linear nature of sentences mask the chaotic feeling of Hell.

Still, in this section, Williams continues to use unified triads. For example, her unification of Damien Hirst and environmental destruction reads:

> A shark in a box.
> Wilderness as an installation.
> A human being suspended in formaldehyde. (68)

In this triad, Williams through images shows the wild tamed, enclosed; she unifies art, preservation, and wilderness, but does so in a way that foregrounds death. In "Hell," the connections between the three one-sentence paragraphs are not healing; the transformations are often grotesque, yet this form allows Williams to explore and engage the full range of human creativity and experience, even its destructive powers. She makes the point that "[w]e are all complicit in the destruction of life" (86). Instead of placing blame, she allows herself to embrace the multiplicity of experience, an act central to Williams's argument.

In the midst of chaos, the characters in Bosch's Hell lead Williams; she writes, "I follow El Bosco's soldiers in Hell over the charred bridge around the blood-soaked soil surrounding the River of Sorrows to the site of the Universal Battlefield, where the bodies of all the war dead through time are stacked" (80–81). Like Bosch, Williams leads her readers, even through the disconnections and ruptures. Note, for example, the prepositions in the previous quotation: *in, over, around, through.* She guides her readers through the chaos, winding her themes of body, faith, and earth throughout. At one point, Williams questions, "Is Hell nothing more than the tortured chambers of our own hearts?" (82). Though she doesn't make the connection explicit, this question fits well with her circuitous form, that image of following the vein of one's own blood.

The vein of Williams's blood, of her experience, of her interaction with *El jardín de las delicias* does not end in Hell; it carries her to the Garden of Earthly Delights, "offering me," she writes, "the chance to live after I was almost dead" (132). The Garden of Earthly Delights is the poetic mean between Paradise and Hell, a place of joy and sensory language, where the body occupies a central place. Williams writes of the fruit in Bosch's center panel, "To partake of these fleshy fruits is to swallow the seeds of our own inquiry born of the body, sensed of the body, the body broken open through beauty" (134). Like more traditional Christian theologies, Williams links fruit and knowledge, but her link does not lead to chastisement, expulsion, or death. Likewise, the nakedness of the people in the garden causes no shame. Rather, Williams figures both the fruit and the naked bodies as beautiful. Just as the center panel is the largest panel of Bosch's triptych, so "Earthly Delights" is the longest section of *Leap*. Indeed, the arrangement of Williams's "Earthly Delights" mirrors the arrangement of the center panel. In an interview with John Nizalowski, Williams explains the connection: "The Garden of Earthly Delights is very sensual. It breaks down the world so the viewer can enjoy it piece by piece. I wanted to slow down the reader in the same way, to allow the reader to pick up the book anywhere and begin reading in the same way that you can begin looking at a painting anywhere" (2001, n.p.).

In direct contrast to the claustrophobic feeling created in her section on hell, Williams uses an open and playful form throughout "Earthly Delights"; she emphasizes such qualities in a triad:

> To open is not a sin.
> To play is not a sin.
> To imagine is not a sin. (137)

Her imagination finds its expression in movement. In one place, she shifts from first person to third person,[3] telling of the traveler and her companion being served plates of seafood; they eat in a sensuous act of play, lifting their forks "to explore, to taste, to tease, to touch, to play, to romp, to knead, to court, to want, to do, to dare, to ride, to rock, to swim, to float, to fly, to feed, to toy, to try, to say, to hear, to see, to dare, to do, to break, to burn, to eat, to be eaten" (139–40). The repetition of the active form of each infinitive creates a galloping sensation, a quick movement, before slowing at the end of the sentence to the passive "to be eaten." "To dare" and "to do" are repeated in the list, giving daring and doing a place of prominence. Williams also emphasizes movement through a focus on change. For instance, she transforms the seven deadly sins by metaphorically figuring them as caterpillars metamorphosed into earthly delights: bodies, doctrines, and texts transformed through earth-grounded metaphors.

In "Earthy Delights," Williams works to transform her religious tradition into a faith she can live with and by. She creates this transformation through a process of picking and choosing, adopting and discarding according to her own ethical standard: "to help more than harm and contribute to the well-being of my community with love, good works, and compassion" (147). In this process of picking and choosing, Williams identifies with certain spiritual mentors over others; Joseph Smith and Saint Teresa become her guides. Significantly, the spiritual seekers Williams names as authorities are those who trust the authority of personal experience. Her experience leaves her at once connected to and cut off from her own religious community, yet the images in Bosch's painting help her define the spirituality she desires:

> A woman savors a cherry. Delight for the Body.
> A man rides a white stag high. Movement for the Mind.
> A man listens intently from the headdress of a hoopoe. Inspiration for the Soul. (188)

This sensory approach to spirituality, for Williams, is Bosch's middle path, a path she both fears and desires, for it requires considerable individual responsibility.

In her final section, "Restoration," Williams deals with the concept of personal responsibility. More straightforward and linear than the other three sections, Williams writes of returning to the Prado with her father, only to find that the painting is gone. She learns that *El jardín de las delicias* is being restored. When she sees the painting being restored, Williams is shocked by its vulnerability: "How had this damage to the Garden escaped me? How had I been so blind to the painting's perilous condition? Had I been so in love that I failed to see its deterioration?" (246). She sees this object, her spiritual guide, for what it is: painted wood in need of restoration.

Williams's own spiritual restoration requires a recognition of her own responsibility. On finding Bosch's painting gone, Williams faces the empty wall:

> The empty wall.
> Look at the shadow.
> Face the shadow. (242)

In facing the shadow, Williams is able to return to the theme of free agency that she began to explore in the first few pages of *Leap*. The empty wall and agency merge in another triad:

> The painting is gone.
> A white wall remains.
> What will I create for myself? (242)

The question, for Williams, is personal, but it also extends to the reader. At the end of *Leap*, Williams comes full circle. She's followed the vein of her blood back to her heart—her home in Utah. She returns home transformed after having traveled through a painting; she returns home believing "we are the creators of our own worlds" (266). By putting this observation in an inclusive form—by using the plural pronouns *we* and *our*—Williams includes her reader in the creative process. What will she, the reader, create for herself?

EMPOWERING *STYLE*

> The effect of speech upon the condition of the soul is comparable to the power of drugs over the nature of bodies.
> —Gorgias, "Encomium of Helen"

> I write knowing I can be killed by my own words, stabbed by syntax, crucified by both understanding and misunderstanding.
> —Terry Tempest Williams, *Red*

Style has been used purposely for rhetorical effect for thousands of years. Scholars of rhetoric might point to Gorgias of Leontini (ca. 480–380 B.C.E.) as one of the earliest practitioners of what later came to be codified as stylistic schemes and tropes. Gorgias recognized—both in his content and in his use of style—the power of language, knowing words to be as potent as magic or even drugs. Through using patterns of repetition, Gorgias was attentive to the aural dimensions of language and how audiences respond to sound and rhythm. He recognized the sensual pleasure of listening to a well-delivered speech. Though Gorgias used style for effect, as a means to persuasion, the extension of his drug metaphor demonstrates what many have recognized as the power of style for both good and ill. According to Gorgias: "[J]ust as different drugs dispel different secretions from the body, and some bring an end to disease and others to life, so also in the case of speeches, some distress, others delight, some cause fear, others make the hearers bold, and some drug and bewitch the soul with a kind of evil persuasion" (2001, 46). I quote this section from Gorgias's "Encomium of Helen" for several purposes: to introduce my comments on the contested place of style in rhetorical theory, to retain the centrality of "the body" in this analysis, and to foreground my consideration of how these points relate to feminist rhetoric in general and, in particular, to my analysis of Williams's use of style in *Leap*. As the epigraph from Williams in this section suggests, language affects not only its audience but also its users. The image of being "stabbed by syntax" personifies style, suggesting the power and risk of words.

Throughout history, rhetorical theorists have tended to focus on the ways speakers and writers use style to affect audiences, investing the power of persuasion in the speaker's intentional use of words to communicate or to manipulate through style. Ede, Glenn, and Lunsford point to style as "a site of tension and contest within rhetoric" and comment on Aristotle's "anxiety about the extent to which language can be used to obscure and mislead, to play upon the emotions of the audience" (1995, 420). They, like other scholars of feminism and rhetoric, also consider the ways derogatory considerations of style (and dismissals of rhetoric on the basis that it is inherently manipulative) are gendered.[4] For example, they comment on style being seen as merely "the dress of thought" (421), Plato's understanding of rhetoric as "'pandering' akin to 'cookery' and 'beauty-culture,'" and how a rejection of the significance of style "has generally necessitated the exclusion of women from the rhetorical scene" (422). When seen as seductive without substance, dishonest, or trivial, the true power of style—not only in relation to audiences but also in relation to speakers and writers—is obscured.

Ede, Glenn, and Lunsford more productively define style as "the material embodiment of the relationships among self, text, and world" (423). It is this definition of style that I wish to apply in my analysis of Williams's writing, for it recognizes what Corbett and Connors refer to as the "integral and reciprocal relationship between matter and form" (1999, 338). Throughout *Leap*, Williams explores moments from history, her past, her experience, and the present just as she explores images in the painting: imaginatively, episodically, poetically, allowing her argument to emerge from a colorful composition of both stylistic delights and even, at times, torture.

I make this point about "torture" because acceptance of the full range of experience is significant to Williams's argument, and she uses a range of stylistic options—perhaps style uses her as well—to textually embody and communicate that experience, allowing readers to experience both delight and pain in their encounter with her text. For example, through both syntax and sensory language, Williams brings the reader into the crowded Prado to face Bosch's panel of "Hell"; she brings the reader, too, into her noisy mind and tense body. Using the shape of a screw to form her sentence, Williams tells the reader she finds herself "screwed in place":

> t i g h t e r
>
> a n d
>
> t i g h t e r
>
> a n d
>
> tight
>
> er (50)

Through her use of a concrete form and tightening repetition, Williams elicits a physical response from the reader, engaging here the reader's sense of
sight. She then draws on additional sensory experiences: "The column of
voices rises, raises, razors, I am sick to my stomach, shadows bleed on the
pages, darken my words, all I can see are shoes, legs, voices, more voices"
(50). Through the alliteration, assonance, and consonance in "rises, raises,
razors," readers can feel the cutting and grating sounds of voices. Just as
"shadows bleed on the pages," Williams's sentences bleed into each other; she
forsakes the separation, the strong pause, of semicolons or periods, providing only weak commas to separate independent clauses and sensory experiences. In terms of sentence structure, "voices, more voices" seems to be included in the list of what she *sees*. Although this description may not make
perfect logical or grammatical sense, it does effectively render the jumble of
sensation in a syntactical form that communicates the sickness and tension.

At the end of "Hell," pushed past the pause and safety of commas and
even white space, Williams's words bleed together in sickeningly powerful
repetition: "Whataboutheconvenantswehavemadenottobebrokenwearebro-
kenwearebrokenthisrecordofoursisbrokenisbrokenisbrokenwearebrokenthis-
recordofours" (126). Using no end punctuation to bring the repetition to a
close, readers get the sense of continued brokenness and repetition: the sentence is broken, just as we are broken. Matter and form are one.

John Nizalowski comments on Williams's unification of style and content
in *Leap*. He writes, "Along with her challenge to the conventional worldview,
Williams detonates classic non-fiction patterns in *Leap*. For her, a revolution
in concept is a revolution in style." He then quotes Williams's own reflection
on style and form, her desire "to have an experience on the page instead of
rhetoric" and her claim that breaking orthodox form can be frightening for
both writer and reader. She alludes to the direct, physical effects of her style:
"'You feel it in your body first. Then it's an understanding'" (2001, n.p.).
Though Williams contrasts having "an experience on the page" and
"rhetoric," her stance—her use of style—is clearly rhetorical, especially when
viewed in the context of feminist rhetoric.[5]

Like Cixous and Kristeva, her theoretical predecessors, Williams resists "traditional western stylistic conventions of unity, coherence, linearity, and closure," and her text like theirs challenges "traditional distinctions between poetry and prose" (Ede, Glenn, Lunsford 1995, 426). Williams's writing mirrors her description toward the end of "Earthly Delights" of Antoni Gaudí's "unfinished cathedral in Barcelona known as El Templo de la Sagrada Familia" (227). She uses a bodily metaphor to describe the experience of entering this Church-in-Progress: "Bone by bone, ligament by ligament, an idea, now a collective belief" (228). Her text seems to have been created in the same way, exhibiting the qualities of the "biological style" she attributes to Gaudí's architecture and to the earth itself: "freedom of form, voluptuous color, texture, and organic unity" (229).[6]

In the section on entering Gaudí's church, for example, Williams's syntax mirrors the physical acts of climbing and descending the stairs. In the form of a labyrinthine sentence, she writes of ascending the spiral staircase:

> My heart is pumping, my head is throbbing, my mind is reeling, steeling against the fear, the claustrophobic fear, mirror of doubt, nothing else to do, one foot in front of the next, around and around, curling, whorling, swirling thought, spinning thoughts, this is freedom, freedom of form, freedom from mind, freedom in beauty, man-made on Earth, our daily bread, thread, do not panic, there is an invisible thread, pulling me up, up, do not panic, do not waver, one foot in front of the other, up and up and up and up. (229)

In this sentence, Williams makes connections between body and mind, detailing her physical and mental responses to the act of climbing. Though this sentence is not punctuated in a standard fashion, readers can still follow the careful rhetorical construction, Williams's use of traditional schemes and tropes. We are led through the first three clauses by the parallel structure: "My heart is pumping, my head is throbbing, my mind is reeling." And then Williams connects the third and fourth clauses through the rhyme of "reeling" and "steeling." The fifth clause functions as an appositive, modifying the fourth, and these two clauses are further connected to each other syllabically (each has six syllables) as well as through epistrophe, the repetition of "fear" at the end of each clause. The remainder of the sentence demonstrates other schemes of repetition: the simple repetition of "around and around"; the rhyme of "curling, whorling, swirling"; anaphora in "freedom of form, freedom from mind, freedom in beauty"; the rhyme of "bread" and "thread"; the repeated phrase "do not panic"; and the deliberate repetition of "and," the polysyndeton, in "up and up and up and up." When Williams repeats the phrase "do not panic," she speaks to herself and potentially also to readers, for there is "an invisible thread" guiding our reading.

Williams's next sentence, more than five hundred words long, is held together by the same stylistic features of sound, movement, repetition, and association. Readers are then led back down the stairs through Williams's spiral, DNA-shaped poem;[7] we are led down and around, through the writer's imagination and our own imagined sense of Gaudí's staircase until the chapter ends with the stabilizing: "feet on the ground" (234).

Sometimes with her feet on the ground, other times flying like one of Bosch's winged creatures, Williams moves through Bosch's painting. She uses the metaphor of a "traveler" to explain: "Over the course of seven years, I have been traveling in the landscape of Hieronymus Bosch" (5). That she spent seven years traveling in this landscape shows that she is not a weekend tourist, not one to be herded along with a group, told how to see and experience. She experiences the painting for herself—first observing, then allowing the observation to take over her other senses. In a triad, she unifies mind and body, artist and painting:

> It is quiet in the Prado.
> Hieronymus Bosch is a hallucination.
> *El jardín de las delicias* is a fever. (190)

The painting infects her. She gives herself over to it, both in moments of pain (in "Hell") and in moments of joy, as demonstrated in "Earthly Delights": "I am a traveler hovering in place, watching, watching pleasure, pleasure pursued through the body, my body rising and falling, rising and falling, until I am carried away. Let us be carried away" (136). In this sentence, readers will recognize the schemes of repetition and balance Williams uses elsewhere: anaphora, anadiplosis, epanalepsis, alliteration, and antithesis. These rhythmic structures create an emotional effect; like Williams, readers can be carried away.

There are, of course, readers who will resist. Brian Doyle, in a review of *Leap,* points to it as a difficult text, commenting that readers "unused to a taleteller who leaps from image to idea to dream in the space of a couple of lines will be rattled" (n.d., n.p.). If *Leap* were categorized as prose poetry, the movement among image, idea, and dream would not necessarily be cause for warning readers. Many readers expect to be challenged by poetry yet find themselves disconcerted, rattled, or frustrated by mixed-genre prose. Just as Bosch's feverish painting asks something of its viewers, so Williams's style asks something of readers: "Let us be carried away."

It is difficult here to remain abstract, to talk about readers in a general sense. I can tell you this: though I read *Refuge* and some of Williams's other books in one sitting, my first reading of *Leap* took several months; the structures of "Hell" were stomach turning; I resisted the hallucinations.[8] But after fits and starts—after picking the book up and putting it down many times—instead of resisting its effects, I began to pay attention to what the text was doing to me as reader. I paid attention to how a seemingly endless sentence about climbing a spiral staircase could make my heart pound, as if I too were climbing. I paid attention to my own sense of feeling tense, screwed in place. Williams writes of counting the cherries in Bosch's center panel (8); I counted the words in Williams's sentences and lists: the thirty-five kinds of birds she recognizes in Bosch's painting (17–18), the seventy-nine different colors in the panel of paradise (34), and the thirty-five Latin names of trees (34–35). Williams responds to Bosch's painting as both naturalist (paying incredibly close attention, even viewing the birds in his painting through her binoculars) and lover, allowing herself to rise and fall, to be carried away. In a similar way, I saw my positions as reader and critic merge, both experiencing the text emotionally and physically and charting that response through close rhetorical analysis of Williams's text—body and mind, one.

The Fruit, Fire, and Gesture of *Memory*

> The Memorie . . . must be cherished, the whiche is a fast holdyng, both
> of matter and woordes couched together, to confirme any cause.
> —Thomas Wilson, *The Arte of Rhetorique*

> The whole world—luminous, luminous. We are lucky to be here. Even
> in pain and uncertainty and rage and fear—some fear. And exhaustion.
> —Carole Maso, *Break Every Rule*

Though few rhetorical theorists have provided sustained treatises on the canon of memory, many recognize its importance, for without the faculty to hold knowledge, nothing can be learned or communicated. In his 1553 *Arte of Rhetorique,* Thomas Wilson defines rhetoric as the application of apt words and sentences to the matter that will confirm one's cause, yet he observes that when "all these are had together, it availeth little, if manne have no Memorie to contein theim" (2001, 708). The notion of "containing" memory is also seen in other rhetoricians' metaphors, such as Aristotle's idea of memory as the storehouse of knowledge and Quintilian's related conception of memory as the treasure-house of ideas. In order to help speakers gain access to these houses of memory, classical rhetoricians suggested various mnemonic strategies, including superimposing ideas or words on mental pictures of familiar places (a house or a street) or remembering parts of a speech through devices such as rhyme, association, or homonyms. Ede, Glenn, and Lunsford link "invention, the heart and soul of inquiry, with memory, the very substance of knowledge" (1995, 410), recognizing the overlap of these two canons, an overlap significant, too, in approaching *Leap*.

Earlier, I discussed Bosch's *El jardín de las delicias* and Williams's bodily experiences as two primary sources of invention in *Leap*. In a sense, images in Bosch's painting function as mnemonics for Williams, prompting her—through association and imagination—to draw on memories of specific experiences. In terms of arrangement, memory is the storehouse for specific sites of knowledge in *Leap:* "Paradise" stores Williams's memories and experiences of innocence, "Hell" houses descriptions of pain and chaos, and both sites come together in "Earthly Delights" in Williams's embrace of both innocence and pain—as well as joy and love, an acceptance of the full range of experience. Williams recognizes, like Maso, that despite fear, rage, and pain, the world is luminous.

In her section "Paradise," the fire-red image of cherries serves as a mnemonic for childhood memories.[9] In Bosch's garden, "Cherries are flying in the air, dangling from poles, being passed from one person to the next, dropped into the mouths of lovers by birds, worn on women's heads as hats, and balanced on the feet as balls" (8). For Williams, cherries are the fruit of her home—a love crop, the state fruit of Utah, and the fruit of her childhood. In "Paradise," she recounts many childhood memories, from picking cherries with her cousin to her baptism into the Mormon faith to her marriage at the age of nineteen. Williams shares the fruit of her memory, the sweet and the tart, yet the end of "Paradise" foreshadows the pain to come. On seeing the figure of Christ in the center of "Paradise," Williams writes, "I fear His pink robes might suddenly ignite" (42). Readers turn the page, and they are, with Williams, in the fires of hell.

In "Hell," readers get a sense of the pain of memory, its effects, through Williams's associational connections among memory, fire, and fear: "The flare-ups of thought, the glowing coals of fear, the aftermath" (109). She tells readers that "there are no cherries in Hell" (47), and in both a question and a description of her condition writes, "Do I dare to extend my hands to that which will burn, I am burning . . . ?" (47). The imagery of fire, of burning, repeats throughout the chapter—especially in the image of the burning eyes that witness destruction. In "Hell," Williams lists the names of beautiful places that have been destroyed and in the same long sentence writes, "Coyote watches with burning eyes, burning eyes Bosch's owl with burning eyes in Paradise" (53). She repeats "burning eyes" three times in these two clauses, emphasizing the significance of the connection between fire and eyes.

The fire of memory, Williams suggests, will—through the capacity to witness—have an effect on the future. Indeed, she makes the connection among memory, fire, and vision explicit through a unified triad, one that brings memory and future together through the image of fire:

> Staring into fire.
> Staring into memory.
> Staring into the future. (109)

To witness destruction, to name it, to remember the names of all that is lost, requires daring, but this daring is also the impetus for change. In another triad, she asks,

> Why look?
> Do we dare to look?
> If we look can we change what we see? (105)

The implicit answer to the final question of the triad is "yes," for although Williams links fire and fear, she also figures fire as means to change: "Fire as torch; fire as illumination; fire as that which initiates change" (108); through anaphora and association, Williams is able to demonstrate the transformative power of fire and, by extension, the transformative power of memory.

Transformation, however, can come about only if she is willing to confront the destructive potential of both fire and fear. Williams writes:

> I strike a match and stare into the small flame.
> What am I afraid of?" (91)

She then follows this rhetorical question with a list of fears, ones that might, for Williams, be linked to specific memories, though as readers we don't know all the details:

> A shattered glass broken in rage.
> The dismantling of family.
> A loss of hearing. (91)

Williams writes of the "dismantling of family, the crumbling of community, the careening of our senses, a blade between our ears" (104). She writes in more detail of sitting on the shore of Great Salt Lake with her husband, together burning their marriage certificate, watching the flames consume their names and the names of their elders. She writes of her own swell of emotion, the fear. Yet she follows this fear with a symbol of hope: a phoenix, "the firebird rising from the ashes" (118). And we see this hope for restoration fulfilled in Williams's final section when she and Brooke "deliver new vows in whispers by the authority of [their] own remembered hearts" (261). In this scene and others, memory is communal.

Hope is transformed into joy in "Earthly Delights" when Williams returns to the image of fruit: "I taste the joy, explode with joy, smear the joy all over my face. Feed me cherries, and I will feed you grapes" (132). This act of feeding—a shared communion[10]—is linked later in the chapter to memory when Williams writes, "Feed me. Nourish me. Remind me what I have forgotten" (136). What has been forgotten can be restored only through a physical act, and consuming the fruits in Bosch's garden becomes for Williams a means to knowledge—a source of invention, "a responsible inquiry into the fruits of our own experience, the knowledge transmitted through a blackberry placed on our tongue" (146). Memory, for Williams, is restored through a physical act, the gesture of sharing fruit.

In the final section, "Restoration," when Williams returns to the Prado and discovers that *El jardín de las delicias* is missing, she must use the powers of her memory to restore it. She writes, "I can restore the painting in this moment, this very moment, through my mind's eye. One by one, I transfer each tableau, each face, each gesture, each piece of architecture El Bosco has created from my memory to the white wall before me." She faces the white, blank wall, but she does not stand still, lost in memory. Rather, she reconstructs "the triptych with both hands," creating a "shadow dance on the wall" (241). Williams embodies her memories of the painting; her shadow creates images: "I lift my arms. I become a cross. I raise and lower my arms slowly and become a bird" (242).

This image of the shadow bird is important because I see birds as another mnemonic in "Earthly Delights." Williams suggests the metaphorical significance: "Memory, a bird, flies to the place where I was born" (216). She also relates birds and fruit in the text, writing, "Communion in *El jardín de las delicias* is administered through the birds one berry at a time" (136). Williams, as shadow bird, administers the fruit of memory to her readers, a gesture of communion, one berry at a time.

ETHOS AND *DELIVERY*

> *Delivery* is by most writers called *action;* but it appears to derive the one name from the voice, and the other from the gesture; for Cicero calls action sometimes the *language* . . . and sometimes *the eloquence of the body.*
> —Quintilian, *Institutes of Oratory*

> The artist is a translator; one who has learned how to pass into her own language the languages gathered from stones, from birds, from dreams, from the body, from sex, from death, from love.
> —Jeanette Winterson, *Art Objects*

Delivery is the art of performing a speech, usually before an audience. As the quotation from Quintilian suggests, it involves both language and the performance of the body—voice and gesture. It is also an act of translation—translating the many languages that occupy us into a form (whether textual or bodily) that communicates. In this section, I consider two forms of delivery: the body of the text and physical performance, as well as the importance of ethos in considering both kinds of delivery.

Although ethos is often discussed in relation to invention, the task—as Aristotle puts it—of discovering all available means of persuasion, it seems fitting in this context to discuss ethos as it relates to performance, both textual and in person. Throughout history, rhetorical theorists have disagreed about the nature of ethos, about whether it comes from the speaker or writer (a kind of prerequisite, intrinsic virtue) or whether character is constructed in texts, providing the appearance of credibility and goodwill, but having little relation to the speaker or writer herself. Whereas Plato, like Quintilian, believed an orator's persuasiveness depended on intrinsic virtue, Aristotle held that ethos was dependent not on the speaker's reputation but rather on the speech itself. Cicero's view was similar to Aristotle's, but instead of seeing ethos as a matter of invention, he saw its relation to style and delivery.

The canon of delivery encourages attention to successful practice in form and performance. On the debate concerning where ethos comes from, I take a middle ground, seeing ethos as both embodied and crafted—and also affected by the perception of audience members. In my discussion of the body of Williams's text, I consider the ways that ethos is created in Williams's inclusion of multiple voices. Then, in my consideration of one physical performance of *Leap,* a reading by Williams, I analyze the ways extratextual choices also embody ethos and affect the persuasive possibilities of particular rhetorical moments.

In analyzing Williams's textual delivery, it is important to consider what she includes in the body of the text and also to note the additional resources she includes. At the end of my section on arrangement, I ask the question, "What will she, the reader, create for herself?" I end the section on arrangement discussing Williams's final chapter, "Restoration," but it is important to note that the book does not end with "Restoration." Rather, it ends with forty-nine pages of endnotes, a twenty-two-page bibliography, seven pages of acknowledgments, and a color fold-out copy of *El jardín de las delicias*. In the body of the text, Williams presents her sources, interpretations, and experiences, but with the argument that "we are creators of our own worlds," the responsibility for interpretation shifts to the reader. What will she create from this collection of sources? [Where] will she find herself in Bosch's painting?[11] Through writing *Leap,* Williams becomes artist and translator— as well as a source for other writers and thinkers—inviting her readers to create their own interpretations.

Through acknowledgments, extensive notes, a bibliography, and inclusion of the painting, Williams brings in the world. In addition to being a personal memoir and one woman's idiosyncratic connections with a painting, *Leap* is scholarship, art criticism, history, theology, science, rhetoric, environmental writing, feminism, and more. In bringing in such diverse sources of knowledge and working with them in respectful ways—in allowing all these texts and ideas to circulate through her—Williams demonstrates the qualities associated with appeals to ethos: knowledge and goodwill. The notes explain certain aspects of the text—often allusions to other texts or additional information about the environment or her Latter-day Saint references; they demonstrate the depth and breadth of Williams's study and knowledge. For example, Williams writes that she accepts "the Organic Trinity" (147). In her note on this phrase, she draws from the work of T. A. Strand to explain "a trinity of design at work in the universe," noting "a trinity of color: red, yellow, blue"; how "the atmosphere is made up of three gasses: nitrogen, oxygen, and hydrogen"; and numerous other natural groups of three (296). And her extensive bibliography further demonstrates the depth of her study.

While the notes and bibliography demonstrate Williams's knowledge, the acknowledgments demonstrate her gratefulness to others: her sources, her friends, her family, the multitudes who have contributed not only to her book but also to her life. In the acknowledgments, she lovingly points to writers, editors, friends, family, even places—the many who contributed to her life and her text—reciting their names, their gifts, and contributions. These kind acknowledgments demonstrate her goodwill.

Just as ethos can be created in and by a text, so it can be reinforced—or destroyed—by embodied performance. In Williams's case, her ethos is strengthened by her delivery in person. She seems attentive, yes, to voice and gesture: her reading is lyrical, her voice clear and calm, though simultaneously passionate. She makes eye contact with her audience and appears to practice many of the very details that teachers of rhetoric and oratory have included in their manuals throughout the ages, even though those manuals were addressed almost exclusively to men: pronunciation, grace, management of breath, decorum, appropriate countenance, and so on. There are additional aspects of delivery that I wish to consider in this analysis as well: what Ede, Glenn, and Lunsford—in their discussion of "delivery informed by feminine/feminist ethics"—refer to as "embodied examples of inclusion, cooperation, and identification" (1995, 436, 437).

With these qualities in mind, I now move to the discussion of one rhetorical performance: Terry Tempest Williams's reading from *Leap* at the Wexner Center on the campus of The Ohio State University on May 7, 2001. Although, for illustrative purposes, I concentrate on one particular reading, those who have been present at Williams's other readings will recognize many of the characteristics of her performance that I describe, for she embodies similar inclusive and generous practices in nearly all of her public performances, always inviting identification.

When Williams walked into the film and video room of the Wexner Center on a rainy May evening before most of the people had arrived for her reading, she surveyed the scene: the stage, the spotlight, the large lectern off to one side, and the microphone. She then asked if the lectern could be moved closer to the audience. Unable to move the fixed lectern, she opted instead for an unstable music stand and positioned it closer to the audience. And instead of the spotlight, she asked to leave the house lights on.

When people began to arrive, Williams met each person at the entrance, shook hands, and said, "Hello, I'm Terry, and this is Bosch," as she handed each person a copy of the painting. Her sense of connection with the audience can be illustrated further by the fact that during the introductions before her reading, she sat in the audience, rather than onstage.

When Williams did stand to read, she opened with sustained acknowledgments, devoting more than ten minutes to thanking others—from those who helped prepare for her visit to those who walked with her at a local park, Blendon Woods, the preceding evening. She recognized each person by name and a short anecdote and also spoke about the wonders and delights of place—in this case Columbus—and about seeing that very day a scarlet tanager for the first time. Each of these acts, these gestures toward audience and place, helped establish her goodwill.

During her reading of *Leap,* Williams moved gracefully between journal entries and sections from the book (both the body of the text and the endnotes), alternating between the public, published versions and presumably more private journal entries that were a source for the published version. In doing so, she connected public and more private realms of experience and writing, showing the ways they interact with and inform each other.

Throughout both the reading and the following question-and-answer time, Williams also gestured to Bosch's painting, grounding her audience and facilitating their participation in the reading, indeed encouraging identification with the painting. She asked the audience to make their own connections and then to share their knowledge and responses during the question-and-answer time, inviting—with an open hand rather than a pointed finger—comments from those who wished to speak. At one point, she specifically asked a professor in the audience, Lisa Klein, what a medievalist might note about the painting. In every case, she listened intently to whomever was speaking, again demonstrating an invitational ethos.

As Ede, Glenn, and Lunsford observe, "Just as the history of rhetoric cannot be written from rhetoric books alone, neither can the canon of delivery be theorized beyond the point of successful practice" (1995, 437). I believe that Williams's practice is successful as a form of feminist rhetoric in both its textual and its embodied performances because of its inclusiveness and generosity. By embedding invitations to identification in her text and in her public readings, Williams strengthens her ethos, demonstrating her knowledge and goodwill in ways that draw others in.

MERGING CATEGORIES

> Write, dream, enjoy, be dreamed, enjoyed, written.
> —Hélène Cixous, "Coming to Writing"

> I have two eyes and they see the world as one.
> —Terry Tempest Williams, *Leap*

Williams counts the last line from Auden's "Leap before You Look" as inspiration; it reads, "Our dream of safety has to disappear" (1966, 201). There's a sense of safety that comes from pure categories: this is rhetoric; this is feminism; this is literature; this is criticism. The purity of categories, however, is only an illusion of safety. Writers can write, dream, and enjoy, yet through reading and response they are also dreamed, enjoyed, and written.

The world seen from various positions (as writer, reader, critic; informed by feminism and rhetoric) is whole, even in all its contradictions. Feminism plus rhetoric equals, for me, a revised understanding of where knowledge comes from, of the possibilities of form, of the power of style as argument. It means valuing experience and memory and finding new ways of being and interacting with others. Seemingly discrete categories are transformed through interaction. Interaction assumes two-way (or multidirectional) communication: comment and response, speaking and listening, giving and receiving. And, as Williams expresses in a powerful triad, no one—nothing is immune to change:

> Art is not immune.
> The body is not immune.
> The greatest sin is the sin of indifference. (56)

One goal of both feminism and rhetoric is change—a move away from in-difference.

At this conclusion, questions remain: How will you respond? What will you create for yourself?

Notes

1. In seeking to define my terms in the context of this piece, one connection be-tween rhetoric and feminism became clear to me: many people have negative associ-ations with both terms. Although most academic audiences have at least a cursory understanding of feminism as an area of academic study, many still use "rhetoric" pejoratively. "Rhetoric" in this essay refers to the field of study concerned with the art and practice of human communication.

2. In using the term *poetic means,* I wish to suggest many senses of the word *means:* intention or purpose (That's what I mean), the middle ground between ex-tremes, and a method of accomplishing (a means to an end).

3. In May 2001, speaking to a group at The Ohio State University, Williams ex-plained that she wrote an earlier draft of *Leap* entirely in the third person. The main character was the traveler. An experience with the Playwright Lab at the Sundance Institute in the summer of 1999, however, encouraged her to rewrite in the first per-son. She retains a part of that earlier version, though, on pages 137–40.

4. See Jarratt 1991, Sutton 1992, and Foss and Griffin 1992.

5. Though generally known as feminist theorists or philosophers, the works of Cixous and Kristeva have also been anthologized as rhetorical theory. See, for

instance (in addition to Ede, Glenn, and Lunsford 1995), Bizzell and Herzberg 2001 and Ronald and Ritchie 2001.

6. Writing of biology, feminist theories of writing, and the earth in the same paragraph, I know will—for some—raise flags of essentialism. Such critiques against Williams's writing have been well rehearsed and responded to by others. Despite the critiques, I find the body metaphor illuminating, helpful in considering the rhetorical features of Williams's text.

7. For a reproduction of the poem and further discussion of this section of Williams's work, see Bart Welling's essay, pages 153–174, of this book.

8. Williams told me a similar story in May 2001. She said she gave the book to her father and when she didn't hear from him for a couple weeks she called to ask how he liked the book. His response: "I'm stuck in 'Hell,' and I don't want to talk about it."

9. Though the cherries are actually represented in Bosch's center panel, Williams includes them, too, in her section on "Paradise."

10. The link between memory and eating in communion is, of course, also spiritual. Most of Williams's readers will be familiar with Jesus' words to his disciples in Luke 22:19: "This is my body given for you; do this in remembrance of me."

11. In a workshop for faculty and graduate students at The Ohio State University in May 2001, Williams offered participants an opportunity to find themselves in Bosch's painting through an invention exercise. She handed out color copies of *El jardín de las delicias* and asked each person to find him or herself in the painting and to write from that place. After several minutes of writing, each participant read his or her piece, a litany of voices re-creating personalized versions of Bosch's images. Williams listened and wrote, selected and ordered. She then read her translation aloud.

Works Cited

Auden, W. H. 1966. *The Collected Shorter Poems, 1927–1957.* Reprint, New York: Random House.

Bizzell, Patricia, and Bruce Herzberg, eds. 2001. *The Rhetorical Tradition: Readings from Classical Times to the Present.* 2d ed. Boston and New York: Bedford, St. Martin's.

Campbell, George. 1988. *The Philosophy of Rhetoric.* Edited with a revised and expanded introduction by Lloyd F. Bitzer. Landmarks in Rhetoric and Public Address. 1776. Reprint, Carbondale: Southern Illinois University Press.

Cixous, Hélène. 1991. *"Coming to Writing" and Other Essays.* Edited by Deborah Jenson. Translated by Sarah Cornell, Deborah Jenson, Ann Liddle, and Susan Sellers. Cambridge: Harvard University Press.

Corbett, Edward P. J., and Robert Connors. 1999. *Classical Rhetoric for the Modern Student.* 4th ed. New York: Oxford University Press.

Doyle, Brian. N.d. "The Power of Restoration." *Nimble Spirit.* Available on-line at http://www.nimblespirit.com/html/leap_review.htm.

Ede, Lisa, Cheryl Glenn, and Andrea Lunsford. 1995. "Border Crossings: Intersections of Rhetoric and Feminism." *Rhetorica* 13 (4):401–41.

Foss, Sonja K., and Cindy L. Griffin. 1992. "A Feminist Perspective on Rhetorical Theory: Toward a Clarification of Boundaries." *Western Journal of Communication* 56 (4):330–49.

Gorgias. 2001. "Encomium of Helen." In *The Rhetorical Tradition: Readings from Classical Times to the Present*, edited by Patricia Bizzell and Bruce Herzberg, 44–46. 2d ed. Boston and New York: Bedford, St. Martin's.

Jarratt, Susan C. 1991. *Re-reading the Sophists: Classical Rhetoric Refigured.* Carbondale: Southern Illinois University Press.

Maso, Carole. 2000. *Break Every Rule.* Washington, D.C.: Counterpoint.

Nizalowski, John. 2001. "Terry Tempest Williams: The Emerson of the West." *Inside Outside Southwest.* Available on-line at http://www.insideoutsidemag.com/archives.asp.

Quintilian. 1891. *Institutes of Oratory.* Translated by Rev. John Selby Watson. London: George Bell and Sons.

Random House. N.d. "A Conversation with Terry Tempest Williams, Author of *Leap.*" Available on-line at http://www.randomhouse.com/catalog/display.pperl?isbn=0679752579&view=qa.

Ronald, Kate, and Joy Ritchie. 2001. *Available Means.* Pittsburgh: University of Pittsburgh Press.

Sutton, Jane. 1992. "The Taming of the *Polos/Polis*: Rhetoric As an Achievement without Woman." *Southern Communication Journal* 57:97–119.

Williams, Terry Tempest. 1991. *Refuge: An Unnatural History of Family and Place.* New York: Pantheon Books.

———. 2000. *Leap.* New York: Pantheon Books.

———. 2001. *Red: Passion and Patience in the Desert.* New York: Pantheon Books.

Wilson, Thomas. 2001. "From *The Arte of Rhetorique.*" In *The Rhetorical Tradition: Readings from Classical Times to the Present*, edited by Patricia Bizzell and Bruce Herzberg, 702–35. 2d ed. Boston and New York: Bedford, St. Martin's.

Winterson, Jeanette. 1996. *Art Objects: Essays on Ecstasy and Effrontery.* New York: Alfred A. Knopf.

BART H. WELLING

❧

One Wild Word

LEAP AND THE ART OF RESTORATION

> There is no such thing as immaterial matter. All spirit is matter, but
> it is more fine or pure, and can only be discerned by purer eyes.
> —*Doctrine and Covenants of the Church of Jesus Christ*
> *of Latter-day Saints*

> Now at last that process of miraculous verisimilitude, that great
> copying which evolution has followed, repeating move for move
> every move that it made in the past—is approaching the end.
> Suddenly it is at an end. THE WORLD IS NEW.
> —William Carlos Williams, *Spring and All*

As even its more sympathetic readers have acknowledged,[1] Terry
Tempest Williams's *Leap* poses serious interpretive challenges to its diverse
audience—challenges as daunting, in their way, as those facing viewers of the
Hieronymus Bosch triptych, *The Garden of Delights,* upon which the book
literally and metaphorically hinges. What are Bosch critics to make of the
book's blending of scholarship and mystical response, precise natural history
and visionary aesthetics? How are mainstream members of the Church of
Jesus Christ of Latter-day Saints to respond to Williams's call to "Ignite the
hymns" and bow to their own authority? (2000, 125). How should they react,
for instance, to the news that Williams and her husband have burned the certificate from their temple sealing, remarrying themselves under the aegis of
Native American pictographs she calls the "Elders of Time"? (117–18, 261).
Where do ecocritics place a text so torn, it seems, between the categories art
and wilderness? What is *any* reader to make of this apparent jumble of criticism and memoir, republished and original material, graphic and literary
art, scripture and graffiti?

We might begin, following Williams's lead—binoculars in hand—by making a catalog of literary genres similar to her checklists of the birds, colors, and trees of Paradise (17–18). This catalog would have to include

Confession
Prose Poem
Exhibition Catalogue
Field Journal
Travelogue
Conversion Narrative
Manifesto . . .

and many other forms. In one sense, as Williams's experience shows, this would put us on the wrong track: by the end, her work has proved itself no more a simple *Kunstkammer,* no more a cabinet of curiosities and still-lifes, than Bosch's (see 196). In fact, the tempering of this encyclopedic rage to catalog natural, human, or other "objects" with spiritual vision is one of the book's main projects. But in linking our interpretive strategies to Williams's in this way, in learning to "watch" and "travel in" the landscape of *Leap* as she interacts with Bosch's *Garden,* we would be making other crucial discoveries.

In the first place, we would notice that *Leap* is a highly self-conscious (logo)graphic performance in its own right. From its careful choice of typeface to its incorporation of newspaper headlines and wildly different poetic forms—even a mushroom spore print (see fig. 1)—to its overall typographical commitment to "deep acts of play" (Caldwell 2000–2001, 51)[2] and improvisation, culminating in the four-page DNA-staircase-shaped riff at the end of "Earthly Delights" (see fig. 2), *Leap* tirelessly declares its linguistic text's embodiment in the material environment of the book, its own "elegance of form in the context of function" (36). By doing so, it simultaneously not only acknowledges but also actively celebrates its imbrication in a network of art and knowledge production, its intellectual *and* material engagement with the human and unbuilt landscapes around it. These, in turn, are figured as existing not beyond the reach of the text, not somehow magically (or scientifically) separated from the "taint" of the words used to describe them, but locked in mutually constructive dialogue with language.

In *Leap,* Williams thus succeeds in the Hélène Cixous–inspired enterprise of "writing out of the body," including the book's body. She teaches us to read out of the body as well. Not only is the book a "marriage of text and image" (as Williams has described *Desert Quartet* [1995] [Bartkevicius and

Hussmann 1997, 4])[3] between Williams and Bosch, linguistic and graphic textuality, but it invites us to join in the dance of creative interpretation. In *Leap,* the erotics of place and the erotics of the page become inseparable. By this, I mean that Williams achieves something running directly counter to most popular definitions of the "erotic," which tend to equate passion with the solitary (male) possession and imaginary sexual consumption of desirable (female) "objects," whether women or endangered panthers. A beautiful book, but no mere objet d'art, *Leap* offers an alternative to the pornographic economies at the heart of much writing about the body and the environment by calling for and enacting a different kind of eros between text and reader, reader and land: a dialogue of shared desire.

In these ways *Leap,* though hard to place within the Williams canon and manifestly impossible to catalog with any degree of precision according to the Library of Congress system, does in fact align itself with at least two larger (if appropriately incongruous) "New World" traditions: modernism and Mormonism. Virginia Woolf and Ernest Hemingway, with their intimate connections to Spain, the natural world, and (at least in Hemingway's case) Bosch, are the modernist writers Williams draws on most heavily in *Leap*—the title of which was inspired by Auden's poem "Leap before You Look"—but she might just as well have found inspiration in a book written by another Williams, William Carlos Williams, during a period of emotional turmoil similar to the post-*Refuge* crisis[4] that precipitated *Leap:* "In the imagination, we are from henceforth (so long as you read) locked in a fraternal embrace, the classic caress of author and reader. We are one. Whenever I say, 'I' I mean also, 'you.' And so, together, as one, we shall begin" (1970, 89).[5] The "new world" triumphed by the two Williamses is not just the American landscape, site of previously unthinkable convergences and couplings, but this landscape as informed by and informing the perpetually self–re-creating collaborative landscape of the modernist imagination, bodied forth on the printed page. It is a situated exchange rich with performative—and *transformative*—potential: "Suddenly it is at an end. THE WORLD IS NEW." Like William Carlos, Terry Tempest Williams applies Pound's famous dictum "Make it new" to land as well as language. Or rather, by struggling to fashion an unalienated vocabulary of word-acts, reawakening language to its material "whereness," she cleanses her readers' doors of perception in environmentally vital ways. "How can we learn to speak in a language that is authentic, faithful to our hearts?" she asks, and *Leap* performs as well as provides the answer to its own question: "The ceiling is raised by our imagination. Authentic acts reform" (118).

Leap

death angels. One must key out a mushroom in order for proper identification. I kneel in the woods and separate one cap from its stem and place it on the forest floor. Finding another I know to be edible, I partake of its earthy flesh. I fall asleep, dream. I am riding inside a milkweed pod balanced on the hump of a camel. There is no escape. Hieronymus Bosch meets me at every turn, his eyes etched on the trunks of trees, watching, hidden in tall grasses, watching. If I am the woman who stares at Bosch, he is the man who is stalking me, haunting me. When I awaken, I lift the mushroom's cap to find a spore print dropped from its gills.

Inside my apartment in Madrid, I sauté some morels in garlic and olive oil.

No one ever told me olive oil was a blessing on the tongue. It belonged to men in the priesthood and to whom they chose to touch. These men who unscrewed the black lid from the tiny glass bottle had been anointed by other men in positions of power within the Melchizedek Priesthood of the Mormon Church. These men who had access to this consecrated oil looked like any other men. But these men were of God.

Within our household, the sacred oil was a secret inside the refrigerator and used by our father for special occasions, most often in times of sickness when one of us needed to be healed.

Figure 1.

Earthly Delights

The person being anointed would sit on a straight-backed chair with family members gathered round. As we bowed our heads, the one receiving the blessing would look to our father as he drew a small circle on their forehead with the oil. They would close their eyes and he would deliver the blessing by the authority vested in him. After the prayer, they would rise in belief and patiently await the cure. The oil was quietly returned, hidden from eyes of gentiles.

Standing over the stove, my senses are bathed in olive oil. I think of my father's fingers. When I was twelve years old, riding too fast on my bicycle down the steep hill of Commonwealth Avenue, the front wheel of my Sting Ray fell off. I hit head first on the asphalt and flew into a coma. At the hospital, my father gave me a blessing, that I might regain consciousness with all my faculties restored. When I awoke the next day, I smelled olive oil. I knew I had been saved.

I spoon the morels over a bed of pasta and say grace.

WOMEN: OLIVE OIL MAY BE AN
ALLY VS. BREAST CANCER

CHICAGO—A new study adds to growing evidence that eating monounsaturated fats—the kind found in olive oil—may significantly reduce the risk of breast cancer. . . . The findings by researchers who studied more than 60,000 women in Sweden appear in today's issue of *Archives of Internal Medicine,* published by the American Medical Association.

"Our results indicate that various types of fat may have specific opposite effects on the risk of breast cancer," wrote the authors, led by researcher Alicja Wolk at Karolinska Institute in Stockholm. Epidemiologists at Harvard's School of Public Health also participated.

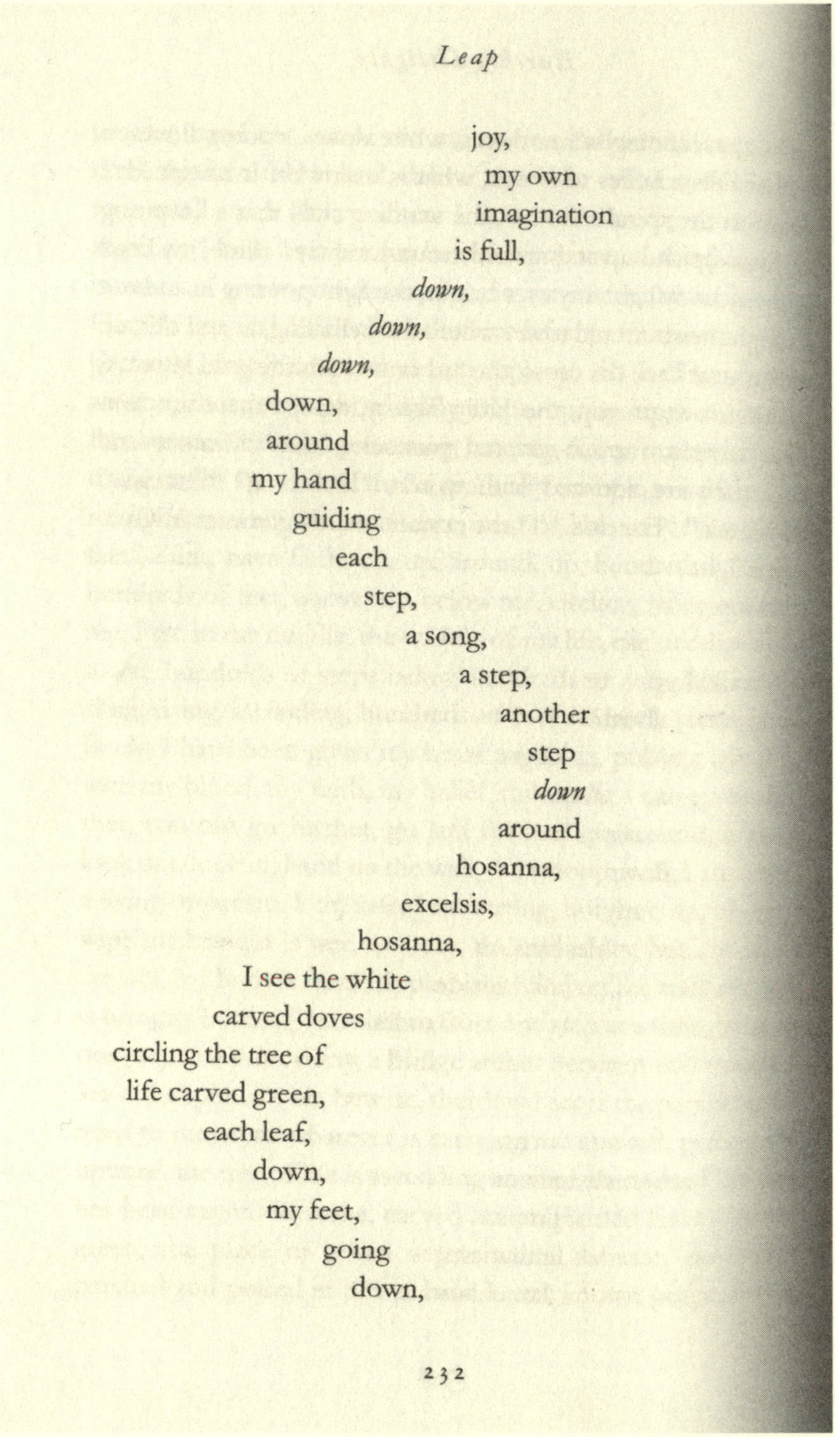

Leap

joy,
my own
imagination
is full,
down,
down,
down,
down,
around
my hand
guiding
each
step,
a song,
a step,
another
step
down
around
hosanna,
excelsis,
hosanna,
I see the white
carved doves
circling the tree of
life carved green,
each leaf,
down,
my feet,
going
down,

232

Figure 2.

Earthly Delights

                    my head,
            spiraling
    down,
                    around,
            around,
                    down,
                        down,
                            down,
                        down,
                    down,
            down,
                down,
                        down,
                        down,
                            around,
                            how
                            many
                        more
            steps
            around
        in beauty
        descending
            in a shell
                of my own
                        making by
                            making a shell
                            Gaudì wraps
                                his
                                imagination
                                around
                                every

    233

In becoming the creator of this bibliocosmic new world, Williams is, perhaps ironically, as adept a student of her religious roots as her literary ones. As a polyvalent act of spiritual restoration and revolution that frequently sites itself within the Joseph Smith tradition, *Leap* takes certain aspects of Mormon theology very seriously: its relentless literalism and materialism ("There is no such thing as immaterial matter"); its vision of this earth as a potential Celestial Kingdom; its emphasis on personal revelation, or what Harold Bloom calls, paradoxically, the "doctrine of experience" (1992, 63); its faith in the healing power of language; even its investment in what some see as heretical and deformative readings—Bloom would say "creative misprisions" (84)—of sacred texts. In *Leap*, of course, the tables have been turned, and it is a corporatized, globalized Mormonism itself being challenged by the vision out of the garden. "Besides being a way of thinking," Williams has said, in words that apply equally well to theology and writing, "orthodoxy is a form[.] The old forms are not working anymore, and I wanted to break form in *Leap*, to play with it, to have an experience on the page instead of rhetoric" (Nizalowski 2001, n.p.).[6] In her sacramental vision of the marriage of Paradise and Hell, body and soul in the here-and-now of the earthbound page, Williams gladly drinks the wine reserved by temple-going Mormons for the Second Coming.[7] But it would be foolish to read this experimental intervention in the "living theology" (2000, 88) of the Latter-day Saints as a mere attack. *Leap*'s faith "born out of questions," which takes the shape, like the Book of Mormon, of an "alchemical text" pulled from the earth (23, 145), demands to be considered as its own kind of restoration document: modern revelation.

In what follows I approach *Leap*'s wild art of restoration from several interrelated standpoints, all based on the multiple hermeneutic possibilities inherent in the book's title: as a gathering of reformative language acts (a self-advertising leap forward for the literary arts); as an embodied leap of faith into the abyss of doubt; as an unfinished prayer—a study in disjunction, incoherence, and improbability ("*That's* a leap") almost as much as in middleness, fulfillment, and reconciliation; and as an invitation to its readers ("Leap!") to participate in the construction of wholeness, holiness, from both the material fragments of the book and the damaged gray and green landscapes around us.[8] This task is both enriched and complicated by my own position as, like Williams, a student of modernism and the natural world, but especially as a fifth-generation Mormon. I can't presume to judge whether in the cosmic scheme of things Williams ultimately will manage to *have it both ways*"—a feat the stern voice of her "Elders," as of mine, often tells us is impossible (147). Rather, my concern here, as I hold *Leap* in my hands, is with her art of the printed page: a place where in very literal terms THE WORLD IS NEW. But maybe, just for now, that will be enough.

ꝏ

Williams's desire to "literally be in relationship on the page" with readers and landscape, to create a "physical experience, not just an intellectual experience," announces itself from the start of *Leap* on every bibliographic and semantic level.[9] On opening to the title page we are greeted with the title (verb? noun? nominalization?) set in Garamond in bold capital letters. No subtitle takes away from the monumental force and spare elegance of the four letters in their white space, accompanied only by Williams's name and the mark of Pantheon Books in diminishing order. In fact, the absence of a subtitle, rare in Williams's oeuvre, is a conscious decision: as it turns out, the working title was "Leap: A Traveler in the Garden of Delights" (Lynch 2000). Flipping through the book, we notice that all of the text except for the mock-gilt lettering on the ornate dust jacket is set in Garamond, generously spaced and on fine paper. It is a thoroughly integrated performance. *Leap*'s colophon (341), which includes the names of the book's composers, printers and binders, and designer, helps explain the significance of the choice of type, focusing on the use of Garamond in the Antwerp printing of the famous Polyglot Bible commissioned by Philip II of Spain, to whom Williams devotes considerable attention in "Earthly Delights."

—"Wait a minute!" the voices of some of my scholarly "Elders" break in. "What business do you have indulging in that kind of pedantry here? This is a critical essay! Does anyone really care anymore who *makes* our books? Get on with the text!"[10]

—With all respect, that's what I was doing. As the colophon makes clear, the choice of Garamond involves more than "elegant" ornamentation, although that's part of it, too. It joins with the passages set in Philip II's El Escorial in "Earthly Delights" in collapsing distinctions between our day and Philip's Counter-Reformation, aligning *Leap* with a sacred text, the Polyglot Bible, that was nonetheless considered heretical by many of Philip's ecclesiastical subjects. The presence of the colophon itself gestures toward the revival, under figures like William Morris and (in the American book trade) Pantheon's corporate cousin Alfred A. Knopf, of Renaissance typographical procedures and standards, including the idea that a book's author, rather than being the sole arbiter of its appearance and meaning, is just one part of an involved communal process. The Paul Tillich epigraph to "Paradise" sums it up in bibliographic as well as in religious and artistic terms: "The new can bear fruit only when it grows from the seeds implanted in tradition" (3). Williams's elaborate endnotes, bibliography, and particularly her acknowledgments, written in a style similar to that of the main body of text, likewise embrace an ethos of collaborative work, distinguished craftsmanship, and spirited dialogue in the service of revolutionary thoughts. An explicitly "made" rather than transparently "written" book, *Leap* challenges our postmodern disembodiments and ahistoricisms and other orthodoxies, in part, by so beautifully incarnating the textual Word in this bibliographical and intertextual Flesh. But can we honestly attribute all of these decisions, motives, and achievements to Williams? Of course not. Her book revels in the fact that these are tasks she could not have accomplished alone.

And not without the reader's participation, either. From the beginning of its text proper (or not-so-proper), *Leap* foregrounds the reading experience and both demystifies and erotically charges the author-reader relationship in a number of illuminating, often disquieting ways. Some lines from the book's opening bear extensive quotation:

> Over the course of seven years, I have been traveling in the landscape of Hieronymus Bosch. A secret I did not tell for fear of seeming mad. Let these pages be my interrogation of faith. My roots have been pleached with the wings of a medieval triptych, my soul intertwined with an artist's vision.
>
> This painting lives in Spain. It resides in the Prado Museum. The Prado Museum is found in the heart of Old Madrid. I will tell you the name of the painting I love. Its name is *El jardín de las delicias.*
>
> The doors to the triptych are closed. Now it opens like a great medieval butterfly flapping its wings through the centuries. Open and close. Open and close. Open. (5–6)

How many kinds of embodiment can an author, or for that matter language, practice at once? Here we have the embedding of a linguistic text within a system of graphic representation (Garamond) chosen for its simultaneously traditional and revolutionary qualities, but we also get a narrator within a painting within a museum within a city within a book: a book that speaks in the first person, describing its own anatomy ("My roots have been pleached with the wings of a medieval triptych") and inviting exploration in erotic terms; and a narrator whose intimate game of secrecy and disclosure plays itself out not only in her entrances to and exits from the painting, museum, city, and expository level of the text, but also in the reader's tactile experience of flipping between the text and the gatefold reproduction of Bosch's *Garden* at the back of the book. It is an erotic experience both instigated and recapitulated by words ("Open and close") to which Williams returns at key junctures. "Erotic," that is, not "pornographic." Although the passage does promise the revelation of more secret knowledge, appearing to license the reader's roving hands and eyes to explore the book in ways discouraged by more conventional texts, this same emphasis on mutual engagement rather than passive, voyeuristic consumption disrupts the one-way geometries that govern pornography. *Leap* talks back, it looks back at us (so to speak), it dwells on its relationship with us, and in fact it invites secret-sharing of our own. Not surprisingly, Williams has defined *eroticism*, in the short piece "The Erotic Landscape," as "being in relation" to wild places and to the wildness in each other (1999, 28), a process that makes the viewing of pornographic images seem tame by comparison.

In that same essay Williams writes, "We need a context for eros, not a pedestal, not a video screen" (28). Her use of the Spanish title for Bosch's painting in the opening passage (as elsewhere) is thus appropriate, because it prefigures further acts of location as she struggles to understand its place within its unusual Spanish cultural and historical contexts. Spanish itself, particularly through its verbs, becomes the imagination's medium of transformative conversation with place and art as Williams travels back and forth between Spain and Utah in search of the kind of "nakedness [that] allows the body to be in open dialogue with the world, not hidden" (2000, 134), Utah being (at first) the site of hidden knowledge, hidden bodies, "records hidden in stone" (5). The culminating point of Spanish usage in the book happens in "Earthly Delights," when "the traveler" shares her dinner of paella with a mysterious guest (Bosch? a secret lover? us?) in a sacramental transport of verbs: "They lift their forks and begin to explore, to taste, to tease, to touch . . . to eat and be eaten. With saffron-stained fingers they break open the last mussels, blue-orange, and feed each other what is inside moving to the outside . . . *Explorar. Probar. Agitar. Palpar.* . . . *Comer y ser comida.* . . . To desire. *Desear*" (139–40). At such moments, which occur with startling frequency in "Earthly Delights" and elsewhere, the act of reading is refigured not as the passive reception of the Word from above but as a charged zone of *mutual* consumption and transformation.

Why is this sort of refiguration, possibly discomforting for some readers, necessary? Why this incredible stress on mutual nakedness, bibliographic immediacy? The same questions, along with performative answers in the same vein as Williams's, swirl in and around the modernist canon. "All this paper between us. What a weariness," writes D. H. Lawrence. "I am I. Here am I. Where are you? Ah, there you are! Now, damn the consequences, we have met" (1977, 51). It is largely a problem of vision, on both sides of the paper. Writers like D. H. Lawrence, Virginia Woolf, and William Carlos Williams struggle to pierce the haze of "demoded words and shapes" (W. C. Williams 1970, 100) blocking the imagination from metamorphic contact with the Other, whether the sky, an animal, or the human beings they write about and for. At the same time they often militate, as in Woolf's "Lady in the Looking-Glass: A Reflection," against the realist and other conventions that seem "like some acid to bite off the unessential and superficial and to leave only the truth" about characters and their surroundings, particularly women and "female" (that is, domestic or natural) settings, leaving them pinned down and dead in the harsh light of mimesis, the traditional mirror of nature (1989, 225). A contemporary creative nonfictionist like Terry Tempest Williams obviously has her own challenges to confront, including the expectation that as a "nature writer" she will deliver on the genre's stock-in-trade (at least as Joyce Carol Oates has seen it) of "REVERENCE, AWE, PIETY, MYSTICAL ONENESS" (Lyon 1989, xiv). But Williams—the kind of visionary naturalist played by Woolf's narrator and by Bosch in *Leap*—shows that the modernist struggle for collaborative intimacy and thus against the disembodied, murderous gaze of Western history in all its avatars is very much alive. By offering this brief comparison I do not mean to argue for *Leap* as a modernist text per se, but rather to sketch a place for it in a context toward which it makes frequent gestures of solidarity. And in *Leap*, as in many of the modernist texts it revisits, context is everything.

At the same time, it is important to note that Williams's struggle, like the modernists', isn't always against an external foe. One of *Leap*'s primary metadramas centers on her failed attempts to make sense of Bosch using her skills as a naturalist. It is a failure realized in prose lists that threaten to make a "death walk" of both Bosch and her narrative, one comparable to the "trail of trophies" she visits in the natural history museum in Madrid: *"Pinus pinea, Quercus robur, Acer pseudoplatanus, Pseudotsuga menziesii"* (32, 34). Her experiences with the Japanese painter Mariko Umeoka Taki likewise make it clear that finding prose equivalencies for Bosch, essentially cataloging or copying his art on the printed page, will not suffice. *Leap* clearly aspires to the condition of Mariko's *Homenaje a El Bosco* rather than her *Copia* (see 164). From Mariko, and other guides living and dead, Williams learns to imaginatively inhabit rather than merely view and interpret the *Garden*. And the relocation of subjectivity encapsulated in some of the book's opening lines—"I once lived in the City of Latter-day Saints. I have moved. I have moved because of a painting" (5)—comes to be mirrored by a move both rhetorical and factual away from the Utah Museum of Natural History and toward the aptly named Paradox Basin (191, 266). Williams thus fulfills at least two goals of modernism at once. She surrenders the privileged, eminently safe gaze of the scientist or the voyeur for that of a questioning fellow traveler in Bosch's triptych, and by so doing creates an intimacy with readers that in turn thwarts the all too common urge to read the erotic as the pornographic, which for Williams (as we have seen) means to read out of context, out of place. "The Erotic Landscape" deserves to be quoted at greater length here: "To be in relation to everything around us," Williams writes after visiting a Copenhagen museum of pornography,

> . . . is to see the world whole, even holy. But the world we frequently surrender to defies our participation and seduces us into believing that our only place in nature is as spectator, onlooker. A society of individuals who only observe a landscape from behind the lens of a camera or the window of an automobile without entering in is perhaps no different from the person who obtains sexual gratification from looking at the sexual actions or organs of others. (28)

All of this is not to obscure the fact that Williams sometimes toys with invisibility in *Leap*, wondering whether she has become "simply a traveler, a voyeur who casts no shadow," an escapist or "'spiritual tourist'" (19, 121). Neither is it to ignore that she mixes lived experience with fabrication, as in her creation of the historian Jennings, the human storehouse of dates and statistics she "meets" at El Escorial, by synthesizing passages from different books. In fact, it is precisely this interplay of self-exposure and self-concealment ("Open and close") that prevents us from occupying a purely spectatorial role in relation to Williams's narrative persona and the painting in which she lives. "I am a presence in the physical world and I am a traveler in the world I am creating"; this paradox neatly captures, if it can never resolve, the book's fully materialized conditions of narratorial presence *and* absence (226). When Williams isn't "there," the world she is creating (the book) still *is*, and our role as cocreators of meaning becomes that much more vital. We learn to see through other eyes but also touch with other hands: artist's hands. This is a crucial step, Williams demonstrates, in beginning to imagine any kind of restoration.

To look at it another way, the "restoration of nature, even our own," may require a Rimbaudian derangement of the senses turned to redemptive purpose: "To see with our heart. . . . To touch with our mind. . . . To smell with our hands. . . . To taste with our eyes. . . . To hear with the soles of our feet" (261).

How does *Leap* attempt to bring this about? For that matter, how much of a sensory revolution can a book, *one* book in a crowded field, really promise? Every reader will, of course, offer different answers, but it seems clear to me that *Leap*'s stretching of literary-bibliographical boundaries successfully engages and reenvisions multiple senses at once where it really matters: in the embodied imagination. This is the kind of imagination that Williams attributes to Damien Hirst, the "bad boy of British art," as well as to Bosch, the kind that can blur the lines between that other great Western antinomy, Art and Nature (see 61–68). It is also the kind that her experiments call into being in us. Consider her pages on mushrooms and olive oil in "Earthly Delights," passages that bring Williams closer than any other part of the book to catching the spirit of the Damien Hirst installations she explores in "Hell" (see fig. 1 for the rest of the passage): "Where it is wet, look for mushrooms. Where a fire has roared, look again, more mushrooms. Feel the top of the mushroom with your hand, moist and smooth, note the curvature of its head, soft and fleshy, wet with dew. . . . Now wrap your hand around its stem and decide whether or not this is the one you wish to eat" (221).

Do we label the spore print she makes from a dreamed mushroom "art" or "wilderness"? For that matter, how do you read a mushroom? How do you write one? Variations on these questions have vexed and animated natural theologians, poets, and other students of the "Book of Nature" for centuries, particularly in the disturbingly "chaotic" wilderness ecosystems opened up to intellectual as well as commercial exploitation by Western imperialism. But instead of treating the mushroom as a living hieroglyph either of God's power or of the ultimate illegibility of the universe, as Cotton Mather (on the one hand) or Herman Melville (on the other) might do, Williams lets the mushroom do its own bibliographical work—she yields the page, as far as possible, to the mushroom's mysterious "print"-making agency—and then brings orders of knowledge traditionally rejected by mainstream science and religion to bear on the problem of what, and how, nature means.

Make no mistake, Williams implies, this is no simple academic exercise. Reading mushrooms correctly is a life-or-death matter in more ways than one. Its importance is reflected in the sheer diversity of ways of knowing she brings to the project: not only the visual but also the tactile, the kinetic, the chemoreceptive, the digestive, the oneiric, the painterly, the poetic, the magical, the Mormon, and, most of all, the erotic. It isn't so much that Williams's mushrooms are phallic symbols; her methods have the powerful effect not only of deanthropomorphizing and detranscendentalizing the natural "sign," but also of ascribing to it its own being, of restoring to it both an autoreferential and a sacramental dignity. Mushrooms are not incomplete without the human body part or divine attribute we take them to "represent": like all organisms, they mean themselves; they are ontologically and semiotically whole, autonomously holy. But as potential food or poison for humans, as reproductive organs in their own right, and even as "food" for metaphoric invention, they can—if we have the minds to touch them, eyes to taste them—evoke powerful kindred feelings from the human body for its terrestrial home and for the other bodies, human and otherwise, around it.

Sharing mushrooms (the fruit of death) with each other, cooking them in olive oil, "finger[ing]" unbroken olives and letting a loved one "suck each one off slowly, joyously" (224) in Williams's vision become ways of giving and receiving the blessings of life: not only feeding and curing each other, but also participating consciously in the myriad small acts of networked creation and re-creation that constitute life. The book's physicality won't let us forget that Williams's words and images—a shared dream, a performative utterance, a feast of the senses—are literally a blessing, too. They provide us, as much as is bibliographically possible, with the found material (whether dreams, spore prints, or newspaper clippings) of her collagist's art, reeducating us in the natural foundations of *all* art (larkspur, rabbit glue, animal grease, human dialogue) and equipping us with the materials and senses to create new worlds.

But the voices of some of my scholarly, and now Mormon, "Elders" are simply getting too strident to hold off any longer. . . . —"Whatever happened to your critical distance? How can Williams say there's no difference between book, body, and landscape? And why would you believe her?" "Those sound like 'carnal, sensual, and devilish' mushrooms to me. Don't forget what happens to the 'natural man.'"[11] "Death of the author!" "What's this you say about women giving blessings?" "If faith is what heals us, why does she need to cite the breast cancer study?" (see fig. 1). (In paradoxical unison:) "You can't have it both ways!"

I'm not saying we always can, or that Williams always does, even in "Earthly Delights" and "Restoration." As she admits, some of her revelations can sound at first like "cheap antiperspirant jingle[s]" (150) or other nostrums of the Mind-Body-Spirit variety (although this self-consciousness itself saves the book from becoming yet another New Age bible). I'm fully aware, too, that thinking or saying that the world outside the text is new doesn't necessarily make it so. But try to grasp what Williams is after—not the erasure of *difference* between mind and body, humanity and environment, but rather a condition of "no separation": a linguistically and

otherwise physically articulated state of connectedness and mutual correspondence in which she, like Bosch, tries to model reintegration and the living of paradox by using the "same muscles" to write as to pray (79). As she
frequently claims about Bosch, over the disapproving commentary of
tourists and their guides in the Prado, this is anything but pornography. Neither is the "middle path" she travels in *Leap* comfortable, for us or for her,
even if it is the "path of movement" (188). What if we don't believe in the efficacy of language, let alone prayer, or disagree with the version of God she's
praying to or how she does it? At those points it's important to see how
vividly *Leap*, true to its word, interrogates its *own* as well as its author's beliefs, even at the risk of incoherence or madness for both of them.

So far my description of *Leap*'s pilgrimage has followed a reasonably
straightforward trajectory, a kind of modern *Life of St. Terry:* Midway
through life's journey, the Traveler leaves her husband and the City of Saints
for the company of her "ghostly lover" Hieronymus (126) and passes through
the illusions of Paradise, the sufferings of Hell, and the delights of the garden,
learning to cast aside her naturalist's tools for the "blood instruments of pens
and pencils" (19) on the way to rejoining her husband and finding her true
home with a more environmentally aware community of Saints in the Paradox Basin. In this critic's allegory, as in Mormon theology, Hell functions not
as an "endless" condition in the temporal sense of the word but as a potentially limited period of alienation from the Endless—that is, God or the sacred (see *Doctrine and Covenants* 1981, 14:9–12). But is this structure true to
Leap's complexities? Can the questions and methods conjured up in Hell be
laid to rest with the words "God forbid. God forgive"? (126). (We might just
as well ask what kind of closure *The Waste Land,* which Williams's vision of
Hell parallels in key respects, achieves with the words "Shantih shantih shantih"). "W e a r e s l o w l y c o m m i t t i n g s u i c i d e . . . we all start un-
raveling u n r a v e l i n g . . .": in sentences like these Williams's narrative taps
the resources of visible language to record its own *dis*integration and the rupture of the author-reader bonds it elsewhere sanctifies—or perhaps the cor-
ruption of these bonds in mutual insanity (53, 104).[12] In "Hell," you can read
and feel the book's cry of pain, even as Williams lays bare exactly what she is
doing to the pages she has written so far: "I am decomposing" (93). But
"Hell"'s fragmentary makeup is not unique in the book. Does Williams's art
of *de*composition overwhelm her art of restoration?

One answer to these questions, paradoxically (of course), is fire. Fire, for
good or bad, is the agent of change in "Hell." It can be wielded either by the
slash-and-burn farmers destroying monarch butterfly habitat in Mexico or

by the neighborhood satirists of Valencia, "not voyeurs to change, but participants" committed to "striking the match" against the "ills of society" in the form of the large *fallas* they ignite on St. Joseph's Day (123, 121). "Hell" very neatly proceeds to consume itself as scenes from the Night of Fire in Valencia alternate more and more rapidly with fragments from Bosch's triptych, Utah, and elsewhere; the "ills of society" Williams has spent much of the section gathering up, especially through newspaper clippings ("EYE SCANNING TAKES ATMS HIGH-TECH"), are partially exorcised in the flames created by a pile of gathered beds. "Hell" *almost* ends in the communal abandon of the *fallas*. But Williams is left alone—her solitary voice, in multiple ways, a broken record—praying to her gods, "male and female, human and animal, recalling privately the vows I once made and burned" (124, 126): "Whatabout thecovenantswehavemadenottobebrokenwearebrokenwearebrokenthisrecord ofoursisbroken . . ." *Leap*, "thisrecordofours" we have been creating with Williams, is left broken at this point, not least of all because the reference to private covenants between Terry Tempest and Brooke Williams effectively shuts readers out. It relocates the "we" from the universal plane of the rest of the book to the innermost granite chambers of the Salt Lake temple, and to the most intimate spaces of a marriage in crisis.

Of course, Williams has told us elsewhere about her sealing to her husband, as well as their burning of the record of this, the highest LDS temple ordinance, signed by the General Authority of the Church who performed it, on the shores of Great Salt Lake. But that scene is at the heart of the book's problems for practicing Latter-day Saints, like me. Is there room in the LDS church today for someone who feels a "soul-stirring disconnect as [he or she is] preached sermons spoken from the dead" (118), who prays to a plurality of gods, who engages in and teaches subversive marriage practices, plays with seer-stones, communes with dead saints, regularly invents new rituals, and rewrites hymns and scripture? Is there a place for those who come bearing "the Spirit of God like a fire," heralding a new Restoration?

Trick questions, of course. Harold Bloom puts it very mildly indeed when he observes that Joseph Smith and his successor, Brigham Young, "*might* not flourish in contemporary Utah" (1992, 116). But these are questions *Leap* insists on asking, connections with Mormon history and theology it keeps on drawing, even at the risk of excommunication—a more-than-spiritual exile: a placelessness—for its author. And I have a secret suspicion of my own. A book I have been traveling in for some time now gives me courage to voice it. I suspect that many of us who will never break and refashion our temple covenants, or choose to leave our lifelong home with the main body of the

Saints (in Utah or out), but who have nonetheless shared in the Terry Tempest Williams and Joseph Smith kind of "soul-stirring disconnect" on reading the official histories, on floundering (with great guilt and inner turmoil) in a sea of kindred faces proclaiming with cheerful certainty, "I know the Church is true," or on feeling ourselves "unhing[e]" (like Williams and her book) on hearing the crowds chant "baptize, baptize, baptize" (180)—I suspect that we (we are more than you might think) will make a place for books like *Leap* by living the paradoxes and engaging in new *Leap*s of our own, in commitment to a "Church-in-Progress" (228). We can "Protect the flame" (125). We, too, can create new worlds.

And why not the rest of us? That reference to the "Church-in-Progress," nominally made to Gaudì's Sagrada Familia in Barcelona, brings us to *Leap*'s crowning act of restorational disobedience, alongside Williams's unauthorized participation in conservation work on the Bosch triptych: the "'endless'" (read: "sacred") sentence and vertiginous shaped poem that climb "up, up, up" and

> down,
>   down,
>   down

the DNA strand–bell tower at the end of "Earthly Delights" (see fig. 2). Here the walls of separation are once again knocked down between Williams and the mind of another artist (Gaudì), between that artist and his precursor (Bosch), between author and reader, text and book, the natural and the constructed, Creation and Creator, artifact and performance ("in beauty . . . descending . . . in a shell . . . of my own . . . making by . . . making a shell"), inscape (DNA) and outscape (la Sagrada Familia). But we also see the schizophrenic up-and-down motion of "Hell" channeled to productive artistic and spiritual use as the lines between Mormonism and modernism, as well as the LDS Church and "non-Mormon" faiths (and doubts), are erased in a structure capable of marrying, if never fully reconciling, all the dualities in the world. "Open and close." Here exiled or excommunicable language finds a home in the dialogic "paperspace" of the text, as in *Ulysses* and so many other modernist works. Williams may have left behind her key to the LDS temple, but working with her we can create a "skeleton key made to fit many locks" (91) in the shape of Gaudì's "Expiatory Temple" (228). In the collective reconstruction of beauty, we achieve the forgiveness so fervently desired, at the end of "Hell," for our individual failures of vision.

To return to the questions I asked at the beginning of this essay, questions that have indeed been asked many times about *The Waste Land* and Pound's *Cantos,* as well as the Book of Mormon—where does *Leap* fit, then? How does it cohere, if at all? Where do we "place" it in literary, artistic, spiritual, and scholarly terms? What do we *make* of it? I've attempted to enact as well as enumerate a few answers here, making a leap (however awkward) of my own, in the hope that readers similarly inclined but perhaps a bit puzzled by the book may feel motivated to look again, creating responses to its challenges appropriate to their individual circumstances. I don't mean to diminish its challenges, the substantial effort it demands on our part both on the page and in place. That, I think, is actually one of its greatest contributions to contemporary literature *and* religion. Call it a Book-in-Progress. I like to think of it as Williams's self-thematizing example of what she means when she calls for the transformation of *descansos,* traditional Spanish markers that "locate the place of death," into shrines that instead mark "beloved lands, lands where a spirit is located, moments in place where someone felt whole or where a mountain lion was seen. Places of inspiration." She continues:

> Must death be the only thing we honor? There are other forms of passage. That a shrine could be constructed in the name of a salmon's return in fall, or the nesting grounds of curlews, the baptism of a child by wings, an altar could be raised stone by stone to make prayers to creation, full of fruit, El Bosco's cherries, a piece of turquoise, poems, shells, feathers, the white handkerchief of a mother, in the name of all we surrender when we choose to love, these gestures could be a way to revest ourselves in place, a personal honoring of where we live, how we live and whom we live among, our hearts rejoined in wonder. (225–27)

Refuge is unquestionably a book (or *descanso,* literally a "place of rest") that memorializes particular deaths and confers honor upon death in general, providing, like *Leap,* recursive emblems of the kinds of functions it hopes to perform for its author and readers, beginning with its title. *Leap,* however, turns out to be a different kind of "shrine" than the earlier book. The montage of real and imaginary fragments of things in the passage above speaks to its greater formal complexities, aimed at honoring a wider range of "forms of passage" by bringing what we sometimes assume to be binary opposites into dialogue (some might say violent collision) with each other: art and nature, belief and doubt, the spiritual and the erotic. Without our collaboration, Williams's eclectic "shrine" might bear a greater resemblance to one of the natural history mausoleums whose dead and brittle objects she condemns as "remnants of the real" (205). But with this participation—

which is what Mormons generally mean by "faith"—the book starts looking like more of a whole than at first sight. Placing the book in our respective bioregional contexts, we are tempted to imagine a more whole, more holy world. We begin to see with what Joseph Smith called "purer eyes." And in our day, that kind of clear-sighted hopefulness may be the wildest thing of all.

Notes

1. See, for instance, Anderson 2001.

2. Interestingly, Caldwell traces her idea of organizing this issue of *Whole Terrain* under the rubric "Serious Play" to the experience of hearing Williams read from *Leap*.

3. In the interview, which was conducted while *Leap* was in its formative stages, Williams's descriptions of her collaboration with the painter Mary Frank on *Desert Quartet: An Erotic Landscape* often read like passages in *Leap* on her relationship with Bosch—for example, "That's why I love collaboration because in a way one plus one equals three, the creative third. It's not a consensus, but a communal response" (14; compare with the equation "1 + 1 = 3" presented in *Leap* [167], along with the surrounding text and accompanying note). As in *Leap,* Williams also discusses her debt to Cixous in this interview.

4. Terry Tempest Williams has described the crisis in political, artistic, and religious terms, noting in one interview that after her mother's death, "I was absolutely seized by the question of what I believe" (Nizalowski 2001, n.p.), and elsewhere that, during the battles over the Utah Public Lands Management Act of 1995 and related legislation, "I developed a shrill voice. I lost my art[ist's] and poet's soul" (Wolterbeek 2001, n.p.).

5. In *I Wanted to Write a Poem,* Williams notes that *Spring and All* "was written when all the world was going crazy about typographical form and is really a travesty on the idea," and goes on to say, "It made sense to me, at least to my disturbed mind—because it *was* disturbed at that time—but I doubt if it made any sense to anyone else" (1978, 36–37).

6. Also from Nizalowski, on the composition of *Leap:* "I used endless sentences, a spiral poem in the shape of DNA, a spore print from a mushroom, newspaper articles, stories within stories. *I brought in the world.* This is scary to the reader and to the writer. Each word carries you to the next. It's like love. You feel it in your body first. Then it's an understanding. It was a frightening book to write, to take the jump into it" (n.p.; italics mine).

7. One of Joseph Smith's early revelations from the Lord on alcohol (1830) reads, in part, "Wherefore, a commandment I give unto you, that you shall not purchase wine neither strong drink of your enemies; Wherefore, you shall partake of none except it is made new among you; yea, in this my Father's kingdom which shall be built upon the earth. Behold, this is wisdom in me; wherefore, marvel not, for the hour cometh that I will drink of the fruit of the vine with you on the earth" (*Doctrine and Covenants* 1981, 27:3–5).

8. Of course, other readers will discover valid uses for the title on their own; I don't pretend to have exhausted the many possibilities. Nizalowski writes, for instance, that the title "refers to three transitional experiences: the metamorphosis of Williams' prose into unconventional forms, Williams['s] passage through her crisis of personal faith, and the looming transformation of planetary culture into an environmentally sound civilization" (2001, n.p.). Williams has explained her intentions for the title in similar terms.

9. The first quote refers to *Desert Quartet*, the second to *Leap*. See Bartkevicius and Hussmann 1997, 3; and Wolterbeek 2001, n.p.

10. With due thanks to Jerome McGann, upon whose revolutionary theories of textuality and interest in reviving ludic modes of scholarship this essay draws heavily. See especially McGann 1991 and 1993.

11. The "natural man," observes King Benjamin in Mosiah 3:19 in the Book of Mormon, "is an enemy to God, and has been from the fall of Adam, and will be, forever and ever, unless he yields to the enticings of the Holy Spirit, and putteth off the natural man and becometh a saint through the atonement of Christ the Lord."

12. For references to "visible language" in its different forms, see McGann 1993, 8 and throughout.

Works Cited

Anderson, Lorraine. 2001. Review of *Leap*, by Terry Tempest Williams. *ISLE: Interdisciplinary Studies in Literature and Environment* 8:221–22.

Bartkevicius, Jocelyn, and Mary Hussmann. 1997. "A Conversation with Terry Tempest Williams." *Iowa Review* 27:1–23.

Bloom, Harold. 1992. *The American Religion: The Emergence of the Post-Christian Nation.* New York: Simon and Schuster.

The Book of Mormon: Another Testament of Jesus Christ. 1981. Rev. ed. Salt Lake City: Church of Jesus Christ of Latter-day Saints.

Caldwell, Susie. 2000–2001. "Lighting the Match: An Interview with Terry Tempest Williams." *Whole Terrain* 9:48–51.

Doctrine and Covenants of the Church of Jesus Christ of Latter-day Saints. 1981. Rev. ed. Salt Lake City: Church of Jesus Christ of Latter-day Saints.

Lawrence, D. H. 1977. *Studies in Classic American Literature.* 1923. Reprint, London: Penguin Books.

Lynch, Tom. 2000. "Talking to Terry Tempest Williams about Writing, the Environment, and Being a Mormon." *Southwestern Literature* (January). Available on-line at http://web.nmsu.edu/~tomlynch/swlit.ttwinterview.html.

Lyon, Thomas J., ed. 1989. *This Incomperable Lande: A Book of American Nature Writing.* Boston: Houghton-Mifflin.

McGann, Jerome. 1991. *The Textual Condition.* Princeton: Princeton University Press.

———. 1993. *Black Riders: The Visible Language of Modernism.* Princeton: Princeton University Press.

Nizalowski, John. 2001. "Terry Tempest Williams: The Emerson of the West." *Inside Outside Southwest* (September). Available on-line at http://www.insideoutsidemag.com/archives/articles/2001/09/terry_tempest_williams.asp.

Williams, Terry Tempest. 1991. *Refuge: An Unnatural History of Family and Place.* New York: Pantheon Books.

———. 1995. *Desert Quartet: An Erotic Landscape.* New York: Pantheon Books.

———. 1999. "The Erotic Landscape." In *Literature and the Environment: A Reader on Nature and Culture,* edited by Lorraine Anderson, Scott Slovic, and John P. O'Grady, 27–30. New York: Longman.

———. 2000. *Leap.* New York: Pantheon Books.

Williams, William Carlos. 1970. *Spring and All.* In *Imaginations,* edited by Webster Schott. 1923. Reprint, New York: New Directions.

———. 1978. *I Wanted to Write a Poem: The Autobiography of the Works of a Poet.* Edited by Edith Heal. 1958. Reprint, New York: New Directions.

Wolterbeek, Mike. 2001. "Terry Tempest Williams Enthralls Fans." *Zephyr* (15 March). Available on-line at http://zephyr.unr.edu/arts/archives/art_wolt_williams.html.

Woolf, Virginia. 1989. "The Lady in the Looking-Glass: A Reflection." In *The Complete Shorter Fiction of Virginia Woolf,* edited by Susan Dick, 221–25. 2d ed. 1929. Reprint, San Diego: Harcourt Brace.

faith, ethics, politics

RICHARD HUNT

༁

Integrating Science and Faith

WILLIAMS AND THE EROTICS OF PLACE

Writing in the summer 2002 issue of *Nature Conservancy*, Steven J. McCormick notes that we once thought "'utility' was the best way to make conservation . . . more relevant to people" (2002, 4). Such a position may be "laudable," he continues, but it misses a "more profoundly elemental and compelling rationale for preserving natural diversity," which is the ability of wild nature "to nourish our souls" (4, 5).

McCormick, of course, is not the first writer to connect our physical needs with the nourishment of our souls in seeking to preserve wild nature. What he does not address, though, is that these two sets of needs often appear contradictory. In one infamous case, for instance, physical needs ("jobs") are placed into "competition" with the desire to preserve the habitat of the spotted owl in the Pacific Northwest. The issue is generally presented as an "all or nothing" conflict, with the aesthetic or spiritual desire to maintain the spotted owl's habitat directly opposed to the physical needs of loggers to maintain their jobs, and only one "side" may be the "winner." Thus framed, there can be no resolution: the conflict continues. While heavily polarized conflicts of this sort are hardly the sole source of tension between what we might describe as the two realms of science and faith, the failure to account for that tension, much less to resolve it, will not lead us to successful preservation efforts.

The need for such preservation forms the basis for much of the work of Terry Tempest Williams, who echoes Henry David Thoreau's "wish to speak a word for nature."[1] Williams is not the only writer with that desire. Nor is she the only writer to employ elements of both science and faith in her calls for environmental reform. What sets her apart from many of her

contemporaries, however, is the unique way she brings science and faith together as she seeks to preserve the wildlands of southern Utah. In the following pages, I intend to examine how her notion of an "erotics of place"
functions as a locus of integration between those two seemingly conflicted
realms of understanding.

The tension between the realms of science and faith often stems from a
fundamental divergence of worldview. As such, it often appears insurmount-
able, except by way of one worldview conquering the other in what amounts
almost to a kind of final solution.

So virulent a hostility between science and faith need not, and indeed
cannot, exist. So, at least, is the view of the late Harvard paleontologist
Stephen Jay Gould, who offers a fresh way to understand the relationship between those disparate realms. In *Rocks of Ages: Science and Religion in the
Fullness of Life* (1999), Gould argues that science and religion ought not to be
seen in conflict and, indeed, *cannot be* in conflict. They are, he insists, separate "magisteria" entirely, and when properly understood can never interfere
with one another.

Gould defines a magisterium, which he admits is "a four-bit word," as a
"domain where one form of teaching holds appropriate tools for meaningful
discourse and resolution" (5). Science, in this system, "covers the empirical
realm, what the universe is made of (fact) and why does it work this way
(theory)," whereas religion covers "questions of ultimate meaning and ultimate value." It is through the imposition of one magisterium upon the other,
Gould writes, that misunderstandings and conflicts occur. What he calls "the
false conflict between science and religion" (6) stems, in this view, from mis-
guided or unprincipled attempts to make these distinct magisteria somehow
fuse. Gould's principle offers, instead, "a respectful, even loving, concordat
between the magisteria of science and religion" (9). "The magisteria will not
fuse," Gould argues; "so each of us must integrate these distinct components
into a coherent view of life. If we succeed, we gain . . . one of the most beautiful words in any language: wisdom" (58).

At this point, I need to say a word about terminology. Where Gould
speaks of *religion,* I prefer to use the more or less analogous term *faith.*[2] Faith
contains more than just religion; it is a domain of understanding not necessarily bound by dogma. Gould, in fact, equates dogma with "superstition, ir-
rationalism, philistinism, ignorance, . . . and a host of other insults to human
intellect" (209). I will not go quite that far, but the fact that questions of
dogma can generate extreme responses makes it seem only appropriate for
me to avoid the problem with a simple vocabulary adjustment. This distinc-

tion—between *faith* and *religion*—seems especially useful in describing Williams's work.

Between her academic training in the sciences and her strong religious heritage, Williams might seem particularly susceptible to the problems caused by any tensions between science and faith. And, indeed, she frequently refers to such tensions in *Refuge: An Unnatural History of Family and Place* (1991). But she distinguishes between *faith* itself and the dogma of her *religious* heritage as she seeks to establish for herself a way to integrate the two magisteria.

Her personal faith derives more from her participation with and observations of the natural world than from any formal religious structures of her cultural heritage. She takes the lessons nature provides her and applies them to the larger community, what Aldo Leopold simply calls "the land," in the form of environmental activism. For instance, in "The Clan of One-Breasted Women," Williams argues against the continuance of nuclear testing in the Nevada desert, and though she offers pragmatic or *scientific* reasons for this position, her primary rationale stems from her *spiritual* connection to the land itself (1991).

Before we can consider how Williams establishes that connection, however, we need to step back a moment and consider the matter of individual identity. The magisterium of science is indifferent to the individual; what falls within that realm is the same for each individual: gravity always operates in the same fashion, regardless of what one knows or believes about it, for instance. On the other hand, what falls within the magisterium of faith can be quite different for each individual: we each have—or can have—a unique ethical or moral structure that need not resemble that of any other individual.[3] Thus, we each must *choose* our own ethical bases.

Williams has chosen an ethical basis that includes the needs of the natural world alongside our personal needs. But as the Australian philosopher Warwick Fox has pointed out, without addressing the very human tendency toward self-interest, no true environmental reform can be possible. Fox argues that the most effective method "*invites* the readers' interest rather than . . . *demands* the reader's compliance" (1995, 243). "Rather than dealing with moral *injunctions*," he suggests, "transpersonal ecologists are therefore inclined far more to what might be referred to as experiential *invitations:* readers or listeners are invited to experience themselves as intimately bound up with the world around them, to such an extent that it becomes more or less impossible to *refrain* from wider identification" (244–45). By identification, Fox does not mean to suggest that he *becomes* a tree in the woods, but rather

that he shares with it "a single unfolding reality" (232). By learning to identify the tree with the "me," in other words, we become less able, or at least less
willing, to accept damage to that tree.

Williams offers a practical method for such an extension of her individual sense of self in her formulation of an erotics of place by developing an
identity intentionally devoid of specific cultural reference, but rather lodged
within the magisterium of science (which for Williams especially includes
the realm of physical experience), and in which the boundaries between
human and nonhuman become highly permeable. When Karla Armbruster
writes that Williams defines herself "primarily [by] her positioning in our
culture" (1995, 218), she constructs her reading in terms of social and gender
politics, a nod toward contemporary academic cultural positioning. Although this reading is useful in a general sense, I cannot entirely accept the
limitations it imposes upon Williams in the particular.

Williams subsumes her individual identity in a sensual connection with
nature, immersing herself in the physical realm as she might immerse herself
in a desert stream. The erotics of place Williams elaborates in those immer-
sions might be seen as her response to the convergence of Gould's magisteria. The passion Williams feels for wilderness is clearly a physical process and
thus occurs within the magisterium of science; in contrast, as we will see
shortly, what she does with that physical experience, the argument for
wilderness preservation, occurs within the magisterium of faith.

Unlike Annie Dillard, whose practice of faith often seems to interfere with
her ability to engage with the natural world, Williams uses her own practice
of faith to enhance her relationship with the magisterium of science.[4]
Thomas Moore describes this process as "natural spirituality," which "transcend[s] the limitation of your personal life . . . by sensing the whole of the
body and with the blood-swirling testimony of your emotions the fact of nature's eminence" (1998, 32). Williams makes full use of "the whole of her
body" in articulating her own relationship with the natural world.

Inspired rather than revolted by natural processes, Williams brings to
mind the work of the more scientific nature writers such as John Hay rather
than Dillard, despite the important role religion plays in the lives of both
women. Like the early Puritans, Williams is loath to stray too far from the
structures of her faith, but unlike the Puritans she continually challenges
those religious—and cultural—orthodoxies. Psychologist Abraham Maslow,
writing in *Religions, Values, and Peak-Experiences,* marks a distinction between religious orthodoxy and a personal, largely private faith such as that
suggested by Moore, arguing that "[i]f the sacred becomes the exclusive

jurisdiction of a priesthood, and if its supposed validity rests only upon supernatural foundations, then in effect, it is taken out of the world of nature and of human nature" (1970, 14). Approaching the matter from a different direction, Gould argues that "traditional ways of thought often block understanding" (1993, 15). More to the point, perhaps, science writer K. C. Cole notes that "any view of nature or human nature that views one 'side' as dogma and the other as heresy is probably wrong, or at least dangerous. . . . [T]he domination of one idea has inevitably led to abuses—whether it was the dominance of religious dogma during the Middle Ages or the excessive influence of technology today" (1999, 84). Cole's note might be seen, then, as a corollary to Gould's argument that even "the doctrine of unstinting self-promotion, whatever the cost to other people" is an "ethic" within the magisterium of faith (1999, 58). To label the results of such an ethic "abuses" is to argue implicitly in favor of a harmonious relationship between the magisteria. Williams addresses this relationship with her discussion of one particular abuse: the nuclear tests that Williams suspects led to the prevalence of cancer in her family and to the endangerment of wild places both around the Great Salt Lake and in the southern Utah deserts.

In *Refuge,* Williams describes her often troubled opposition to both religious and cultural dogma. Within the cultural bounds of her church she feels more constrained than she does in the presence of wildness. "Once out at the lake," she writes, she experiences a sense of release: "I am free. Native. Wind and waves are like African drums driving the rhythm home. I am spun, supported, and possessed by the spirit who dwells here. Great Salt Lake is a spiritual magnet that will not let me go. Dogma doesn't hold me. Wildness does" (1991, 240). Here Williams blends her identity with the lake in their shared refusal ever to be tamed. Like herself, the lake is "wilderness, raw and self-defined" (92), a reference to the difficulty she has with the Mormon church over her growing reluctance to accede to authority. "We are taught not to trust our own experiences," she says. "Great Salt Lake teaches me experience is all we have" (92). Unlike wildness, dogma is restrictive; as Maslow points out, dogma frequently results from an effort to codify mystical experience.[5] Because the magisterium of faith includes both religious and cultural concerns, we can understand both religious and cultural dogma as codifications of faith. It is through such a codification of, or imposition of rules upon, the natural world that the magisterium of faith can usurp—and thus control—the magisterium of science. Gould, for instance, writes that at one time the magisterium of science was entirely subsumed within that of faith; not until the Enlightenment did science emerge in its own right. That emergence has often been resented by organized religion: consider the continuing efforts to install "creation science" as an "alternative theory" to Darwinian evolution in high school biology classrooms. As a Mormon, Williams is culturally immersed in that struggle. Thus, when she writes that wildness means more to her than dogma, she uses that distinction to reestablish a balance between the two magisteria.

Only through an understanding of wildness, as Williams implicitly argues, can we accommodate our cultural desires (within the magisterium of faith)[6] with what the natural world (within the magisterium of science) shows to be possible. The possible, as Emerson reminds us, must always be limited by what accords with the natural world. Likewise, as Alison Deming writes, "to be civilized at this point in history must mean to set limits, to understand when our comfort and freedom exact too extreme a cost on the overall well-being of others and on the planet that sustains us all" (1998, 46). Aldo Leopold's famous Land Ethic suggests the need for similar limits on how we interact with the land.[7] But those limits need not necessarily be constrictive: we might liken a progressive ethical framework to the traditional twelve-bar blues, in which a strict formal structure allows and in fact encourages a virtually infinite range of artistic expression. In *Testimony: Writers of the West Speak on Behalf of Utah Wilderness* (1996), a more overtly political work than her more personal books, Williams strongly reflects on the honesty and love she develops in her earlier work.[8] In its multiple calls for preservation of Utah's wild places, *Testimony* demands that the nation, as represented by our legislators, live up to Leopold's legacy. This plea clearly emerges from Williams's own practice of faith, which requires her to transcend a received dogma too often out of alignment with the natural world. Her erotics of place results from the integration of observations in nature (the magisterium of science) with spiritual and ethical realizations about our relationship with nature (the magisterium of faith).

Refuge marks the clearest illustration of this integration of science and faith as Williams interweaves the simultaneous stories of the destructive flooding of the Bear River Migratory Bird Refuge, due to the rising level of the Great Salt Lake, with her mother's death from ovarian cancer. It also demonstrates her own uncertain relationship to orthodoxy; Williams most clearly demonstrates this subversion in "The Clan of One-Breasted Women." After recounting her family's history of cancer, which Williams believes derives from their status as *hibakusha,* a Japanese word meaning "explosion-affected people" (1995b, 661), she argues that for the usually obedient and patriotic Mormons of downwind Utah, "the price of obedience has been too high" (1991, 286). Here we see a writer suddenly free to explore alternative ways to experience that all-important relationship with the natural world. Williams later translates that experience into the erotics of place, the highly suggestive phrasing of which is, I suspect, intentionally contrary to the restrictive culture—both in the narrow sense of Mormon culture and in the broader sense of American culture in general—from which she charts her departure.

One representation of the restrictiveness of that culture occurs early in *Refuge*. At the bird refuge, Williams encounters two "beergut-over-belt-buckled men" who destroy a burrowing owl mound. The men are shooting up the mound, but point out to her that the birds have been removed by "[t]hose boys from the highway department [who] came and graveled the place." Although Williams reports that these men are not personally responsible for the loss of the birds, she admits that she "knew rage" at their casual dismissal of the "messy little bastards" (1991, 12). Yet in this incident she does not so much castigate "men" as she does their *attitude* toward nature, an attitude all too prevalent but hardly something by which all men might effectively be measured. The attitude demonstrated by these men is primarily *cultural*: it is not inherent in male biology (or more men would have those characteristics). These men represent a set of prevailing cultural attitudes that, as Masami Yuki argues, Williams tends to subvert throughout her work in "an effort to restore intimacy" to our relationship with the land (1998, 87). When we recall that Gould links cultural attitudes with the ethical magisterium (another name for the magisterium of faith), we can see how Williams distinguishes between magisteria. For were the "beergut-over-belt-buckle" attitudes somehow *inherent* in men, their attitudes would fall within the magisterium of science, a claim Williams subverts throughout *Refuge*.

To further illustrate the distance between her practice of faith and that required by traditional dogma, Williams notes that the Mormon General Conference meets in the tabernacle, where "pews are stained to look like oak, even though they are pine" (1991, 239). What is significant about this illustration is not just the artifice she describes, but that she sees a need to mention it. The implication is that the church, the embodiment of the traditional magisterium of faith, is not what it seems, that its appearances are unreliable. The pine is native to Utah, the oak is not; the staining, the simulation, is indicative of a tendency to look at the land as an abstraction, malleable, something to do with as we please. This is, of course, the reaction of the city and church fathers to the flood itself: they propose draining and pumping; one person even (seriously?) suggests atomic bombing the lake to deepen it, thus making room for more water. And although what Williams values in the desert, what makes it "sacred" to her, is often its connection to human culture and habitation, that habitation must respect the land; one cannot, for example, imagine the ancient cultures she has studied staining pine to look like oak. In the heightened state of awareness brought on by her mother's illness and the threats to the bird refuge, Williams might well regard the pews as fraudulent, one more instance of "pornographic" disconnection.

The effects of that disconnection are readily discernable in the way Diane Tempest adjusts to the certainty of her own death. Williams writes that once her mother came to accept death as part of a natural process, "suddenly, the shackles which have bound her are beginning to snap, as personal revelation replaces orthodoxy" (136). That is, the magisterium of faith has returned to its proper position alongside the magisterium of science; when her own faith no longer seeks to impose itself upon science, Diane Tempest is able to move more freely in exploring the ramifications of it. Williams will often allow others to speak for her, as surrogates for her own thought: the effect is to say "not I alone have these thoughts." In this instance, her mother's sudden absorption in "Zen, Krishnamurti, and Jung" (136) parallels her own unshackling from orthodoxy. Thus, if the dialogue in *Refuge* is often stilted, we can see that its true importance is to expand—to communalize, if you will—Williams's own inner dialogue. The various letters, conversations, and reports scattered throughout *Refuge* serve both to illuminate the other figures Williams describes and to enhance her own "personal revelations" within the magisterium of faith. The restrictions imposed by Mormon orthodoxy—and by extension any dogmatically-based tradition—must be overcome to allow one the direct experience of the magisterium of science.

Throughout *Refuge,* Williams's use of surrogate speakers to present information she may not be able to offer under her own authority demonstrates another of the book's central themes—the importance of community. While riding with Sandy Lopez, for instance, the two women speak of their "rage" at the way "our bodies and the body of the earth have been mined." The conversation takes on tones of an inner monologue as the voices merge in thought: "Men define intimacy with their bodies," Williams begins; Lopez completes the thought: "Many men have forgotten what they are connected to" (10).

Though this conversation resolves into the idea that men have lost their intimacy with the land, we can also see the beginning not of a divergence between men and women but of the rejoining Williams seeks always to initiate.

Later, in both *Refuge* and *Desert Quartet* (1995), Williams defines her own intimacy with the land through her body. It is not the act of definition, then, that she and her friend lament, but that the act is too often forgotten, ignored, or dismissed. The cartoonish "beergut-over-beltbuckled men" who destroyed the burrowing owls' mound represent to Williams the sort of disconnection that leads to devastation, and with the lake rising of its own accord, that human-caused devastation is all the more troubling (12–14). For the most part, Williams presents the lake's flooding as naturally occurring. But she also hints that human development around the lake has played a part in the problems the flood causes for the birds. "In a normal cycle of a rising Great Salt Lake," she writes, "the birds would simply move up. New habitat would be found. New habitat would be created. They don't have those options today, as they find themselves flush against freeways and a rapidly expanding airport" (112). That the birds too have become, in effect, refugees lends Williams one more point of identity with them. Watching the mating practices of grebes—which involve a particular form of head-shaking—she unconsciously identifies with the birds, conforming her own movements to those she studies. A passing fisherman asks her a question, to which she shakes her head "in a rather grebelike way." She then blushes, "hoping he has not been watching the amorous birds and mistaken my behavior as flirtatious" (143). Williams uses such encounters as a means of reinforcing that ever present sense of interconnection that informs all of *Refuge*. But I suspect, too, that she uses it—not so much in the book as in her life—as a distancing move: to connect so fully with the "self-defined wilderness" represented by both birds and lake assuages the sense of loss she experiences with the cancer so prevalent in her family.

Williams describes her previously obedient uncle's initial engagement in civil disobedience at an antinuclear rally in an essay titled "A Patriot's Journal." The uncle, former Utah state senator Richard Tempest, is orthodoxy personified. Williams reports that his "voting record was erratic" as he sponsored bills for recycling and air quality, but opposed wilderness and social-reform measures (1994, 99). But at the Nevada Test Site with Williams and his daughter Lynne, he finds himself "unexpectedly gripped by emotion" as he contemplates the energies that have devastated the women of his family (106). In showing his movement away from the orthodoxy of his previous positions, Williams is using Richard Tempest, in effect, to speak for her own concerns, to add the legitimacy of a skeptical observer to her own more subjective arguments.

Richard Tempest's abandonment of orthodoxy mirrors Williams's own.

The physical realities before him at the Test Site—the land itself, the family's history with cancer—overcome the restrictions of cultural dogma to elicit a *new* practice of faith, one more consistent with the magisterium of science as represented by those physical realities.

In "Narrating the Invisible Landscape: Terry Tempest Williams's Erotic Correspondence to Nature," Masami Yuki draws on the work of Kent Ryden to distinguish between "homogenous space" (undifferentiated by human resonances) and "experiential place" (seen in terms of the human stories associated with it) in her reading of Williams's work (1998, 82).[9] Williams, Yuki argues, operates primarily within the second of these realms, articulating her sense of Great Salt Lake or the southern Utah deserts as "places" distinguished by what humans have done, or have felt, there.

I would argue for a third element in Williams's work as well, one within the magisterium of science, which I would call a *biological* "place." John Daniel, writing of old growth forests in Oregon, "feel[s] the forest keenly as *place*," referring not to *human* stories but to the history inherent in the ancient trees themselves. Like Williams, Daniel chooses not to hierarchize human-nonhuman presence on the land as he sees the forest as "distinctively placed" without the need to invoke human presence (1992, 92). For Daniel, as for Williams, such perceptions suggest that a "more-than-human" story, no less than the more traditionally positioned human story, can inscribe the land. For both writers, and for their readers, such a realization necessarily leads toward a Leopoldian ethic: if we understand the land in terms of story, and if that story no longer need be limited to *humans*, we are closer to the idea of a "community instinct in-the-making" with which Leopold concludes "The Ethical Sequence" section of *A Sand County Almanac* (1987, 203).

Williams, I believe, operates primarily from such a "community instinct." The reliance of cultural geographers on a strictly *human*-defined sense of place, along with its opposite sense of a homogenous, undifferentiated sort of "no-place" devoid of human presence, is entirely anthropocentric, leading to the culture-nature and male-female dichotomies described by Cassandra Kircher as "simplistic" (1996, 98). But in *Refuge,* these dichotomies are far from simple: as Williams uses them, they tend more to be corrective than divisive or oppositional. If "men" have a poor connection with nature, Williams wants not to slap them but to offer them a means for adjustment. And with the publication of *Desert Quartet* in 1995, the erotics of place has come to suggest a potential adjustment for women as well—they too should be able to make use of the physical as a means of establishing a fundamental connection with nature.

The book opens with the section titled "Earth," in which Williams describes hiking on the slickrock desert of southern Utah. She shuns maps, preferring to rely on rock cairns to show her the way to the distant Druid Arch. "Many resist cairns in the desert," she tells us, "believing each traveler should walk on their own authority" (1995a, 6). Williams understands that the faith she seeks must come from the land itself; she also knows that she needs to envision herself in terms of the land in order to realize that faith. Thus, when she chooses "[t]o walk in this country [as] an act of faith" (7), she declares her willingness to bypass the representation of a map in favor of the direct experience of the ground. A map is a representation of the ground, not the ground itself, of course; boundaries drawn on a map suggest a construction, an imposed story if you will, having primarily a coincidental engagement with the land the map represents.

One might argue, though, that a rock cairn is also just another form of map. Certainly, it is "constructed," a pile of rocks with a distinct and discrete purpose. But in another sense, the cairn is a *part* of the land in a way a map may never be. For one thing, the rocks come from the same trail they mark. They are of the same land, are what we might call an *inherent* marker, relying on the natural terrain to show the way to a particular destination. A map, on the other hand, relies on the constructs of latitude and longitude, of political borders (state lines, or the edges of federal explosive reserves). In much of her other work, Williams makes it clear that she has little regard for such artificial lines on a map. Trust, however, is quite another matter. Though a cairn might be "designed to fool people, to trick them off the trail so they will be lost forever," because they are real, physical markers derived from the ground she walks upon, she chooses to trust them (6). The cairns, she says, "give me the courage to proceed in a landscape mysterious, unpredictable, and vast" (7).

Once she has entered that landscape, she begins quickly to merge with it. On the trail, she feels as though she were "walking through the inside of an animal"; the very canyon becomes a living entity for her, as her "hands search for a pulse in the rocks" (8). Barry Lopez suggests that were we to offer our "heart and soul," we might attain "sanctity, companionship, wisdom, joy, [and] serenity" in our quest for a new relationship with the land (1992, 21). As she moves through the canyon, Williams presents a clear illustration of such an offering as she passes through "sacred hallways," in which "there is no partition between my body and the body of Earth" (10).

She walks on through "meadows of serenity," thinking about "how necessary it is to live without words, to be satisfied without answers" (12). To live in that manner would require a level of trust in the world, "no matter how illusory," through which she can locate herself. Only after realizing such trust does she feel able to begin to add to the cairns; if they are, as I believe, what amounts to an *organic*, an *inherent* map, she would have to feel herself an integral part of the landscape before she could allow herself to engage with that trust which both the cairns and the desert entail.

Having established for herself the aura of trust, she comes to a small body of water. As she contemplates this rarest of desert phenomena, she for the first (but not the last) time in *Desert Quartet* reflects on the erotic: "Why is it for most of us the vision of the erotic comes as a rare event, a shooting star, a flash flood, a moment of exotic proportion and not in a stable condition?" (14). This conjunction of the erotic and desert water is not a coincidence. If each is rare, each is also necessary to our survival. We might expect her to remark on this connection, but she does not. This is what she means when she suggests that art strives to "bypass rhetoric and pierce the heart" (1995c).[10] She does not (rhetorically) drive home the point of the correspondence between water and eroticism, as I do above, but rather allows the reader to discover it, to experience it in terms of what David Abram refers to as "sensory interactions with the land around us" (1996, 56).

In "Water," Williams tells of bathing in a desert stream. Having already established a linkage between water and the erotic, the imagery is now more direct than in the previous section. Still, she retains some uncertainty about her erotic impulses: "I dissolve. I am water. Only my face is exposed like an apparition over ripples. Do I dare? My legs open. The rushing water turns my body and touches me with a fast finger that does not tire. I receive without apology." The water is transmogrified into "a liquid hand that cools and calms the desert" (1995a, 23). It "cools and calms" her as well, further enhancing the correspondence between her body and the land. Immersed, she leaves behind both thought and control, and when she emerges from the water, "there is moss behind my fingernails" (24). Once again, she blurs boundaries, this time between herself and the stream. Yet she continues to view both herself and this place from within the magisterium of science. The correspondence she describes remains physical and does not seek to impose any sort of dogma upon the land with which she is conjoined.

In "Fire," Williams continues the development of her relationship with nature, always, however, remaining within the magisterium of science. While she becomes the flame, the flame becomes almost human, popping "like vertebrae" (38). "Bones of juniper and pinyon" feed the flames, and "[t]he fire is aroused" (39). She *is* the fire: "the white heat of my heart," she says, becomes "a prayer" (40). Once more, she merges with an elemental force, in which the flames are "bodies," with "tongues curling around each other" (40–41). She is "ravished" by the fire, "my ghostly lover" (41). At last, the reverie of the fire ends, and she realizes that "love is as transitory as fire" (44).

Love: the great theme in so much of Williams's work. Or perhaps I should say: passion. Her immersion in the things of the magisterium of science allows her also to "unshackle" herself from received cultural dogma. This in turn frees her to see that passion, so often attached to the magisterium of ethics and faith, is a *physical* process, and thus occurs within the magisterium of science. "It is our nature to be aroused," she says, "not once but again and again. Where do we find the strength not to be pulled apart by our passions?" (44). At this mention of passion, Williams steps briefly from the particulars of a single sojourn in the desert and into the realm of her own activism. One object of her passion—and we can see this throughout her work—is wildness. Absent protection, as Barry Lopez reminds us, the desert stands little chance against the forces of greed and venality. We need courage, we need love, if we are to stand up for the land. Protection of the desert asks that we stand away from the imperatives of the dominant culture if we are to, as Williams says, "step outside and defy custom" (46).

In "Air," Williams is more diffuse than she has been; the effect of her merging with the elements builds to this climactic segment, in which she discovers "the simple ecstasy of breathing" (54). From her mildly sensual immersion in the water, she has progressed to an identification with the elements, and both she and they are transformed. Steeped now in the eros of the landscape, Williams is able to find erotic connections in the simplest, most basic parts of life. By listening to the land, to its elements, she has discovered what I would call an "everyday erotics," which brings one both to a peace with the natural world and to an appreciation—in a far deeper sense than usually perceived—for it. The subtle connections Williams evokes here, exemplified by her erotic connection to the air itself, become "the dreamtime of the desert," and "the beginning of poetry" (54). *Desert Quartet* ends with Williams pressing her hands to the rock ("feeling its pulse") and pressing her mouth, as though in a kiss, to an opening through which the wind blows. She hears it speak and becomes "drunk with pleasure." "Listen," she says at last; listen to this land: "This is all there is" (58).

Certainly, the land itself speaks to Williams in *Desert Quartet.* New England nature writer John Hay writes that "there is reason to suspect the assumptions of the human brain when it becomes too elevated from the earth that nurtured it" (1986, 7). I would suggest now that Williams's "erotics of place" works as an antidote for that tendency toward elevation. The thought Hay refers to is not the analytical thought by which we articulate our practice of science, but those abstractions by which we articulate our practice of faith; when such thinking "becomes too elevated from the earth," it can seek to impose imperatives upon that earth that the earth cannot long sustain.

There's an old joke about a man who spends an hour one night helping a stranger search a grassy area for lost car keys. At the end of the hour, having turned each blade of grass at least twice, the man asks the stranger, "Are you sure you lost your keys here?"

"Hell no," the stranger replies, "I lost them down the street." He points to a dark area half a block away.

"Then why are you looking for them here?" the man asks. "Because the *light's* better here."

❧

I suspect that while the light may be better in an "elevated" world, that's no reason to assume the keys are there. Some readers may be put off by that chaos, expecting that things should be orderly in nature, that the conscious mind should be able to envelop the natural world in its entirety. But any solace we might hope for in the face of multiple and perpetual threats to the natural world will be found not in the world of the mind, but in what Abram calls "the sensuous world," consisting of "our direct, unmediated interactions" with nature (1996, 54). Williams connects the erotic impulse in its pure form with the land; this sort of "erotic connection," she says, "is a life-engaged, making love to the world that I think comes very naturally" (Jensen 1995, 310). Seeking always to reinforce the connection between the human heart and the land, in *Desert Quartet* Williams offers us entry into a love and passion that our culture has declared, somehow, unseemly, inappropriate.

The physicality of the sensual occurs within the magisterium of science, and suggests to Williams necessary limitations on what the magisterium of faith might require of us. That is, it suggests to her an ethical stance. Gould argues that ethics ought not to derive from nature or natural facts—that is, from the magisterium of science. By implication, then, there can be no "intrinsic value" to nature, which would seem to eliminate a major source for establishing a moral stance as to the natural world. Yet perhaps we might find an accommodation between his principle and an intrinsic value to nature in the very separation Gould demands between magisteria: though nothing in nature "obviously" indicates intrinsic value, there still remains sufficient space to derive an ethic *relating* to nature out of our observations of the natural world. This ethic would include the notion of nature being "worthy" in its own right. That is, if we *choose* to hold nature worthy of ethical or moral consideration, then the imperatives of nature—broadly stated, the freedom of species and habitats to continue to exist on their own terms—must be part of our ethical or moral systems.

By establishing the erotics of place as a locus of integration between science and faith, Williams successfully establishes a basis for formulating her own ethical and moral system. In *Red: Patience and Passion in the Desert,* Williams describes what she calls "a strike moment," referring to that instant when a match drawn along a flint suddenly bursts into flame. This event, she writes, creates both "the moment of illumination for the viewer" and "a fire in the mind believing it is possible to read . . . the world differently" (2001, 191). The first step to change, after all, is to believe that it is possible. The erotics of place offers a radical vision of what may be possible.

Though the language of her call for environmental preservation remains essentially gentle, lacking the heat that characterizes such writers as Rick Bass or Jack Turner, her rage at those who seek to spoil wilderness is immense. But the vision she locates in *Desert Quartet* and develops in *Red* elicits a new shape for rage—a gentle jeremiad if you will, though one no less vehement than those of her friend and contemporary Rick Bass. And even Bass is discovering that his own rage is more effective when it becomes firmly grounded in both science and faith as part of an integrated whole.

Much of *Refuge* is about personal healing and discovery; in *Desert Quartet,* Williams links the personal with the public, for both discovery and healing. She shifts from an explicit argument for environmental activism to an implicit argument, in which she combines her sense of an intimate identification with the land to an unspoken plea to honor and protect it as we would honor and protect a human lover.

Alison Deming writes that "[t]o be an animal is to know this sensation of wildness, electric as sexual arousal" (1994, 45). This animal nature, something often dismissed in contemporary culture, is central to Williams's eroticism in *Desert Quartet.* In "Living Like Weasels," Annie Dillard suggests that she "could very calmly go wild" (1982, 33). I suspect Dillard is only having fun with her readers; in any case, she chooses—both in that essay and in her subsequent work—to *not* go wild. Williams, however, has no hesitation; the erotic relationship she develops recalls the observation of art critic Arthur C. Danto, who suggests, "An area of animal response which bears comparison with the aesthetic sense . . . is that of sexual response" (1981, 97). But where Danto speaks of "the aesthetic sense" within the structured world of art,

Williams's aesthetics responds to a decidedly less structured world of south-ern Utah.

Williams says that "whenever we try to make sense of the mysteries it is always a human construct. . . . I think there is something older, something deeper, wiser, that has its own authority, and that is the land itself" (Robin-son and Walker 1995, 9). In *Desert Quartet,* it is clear that the land "has its own authority," one that Williams both appreciates and loves. In a new sort of way, the land has become *real,* as real as any human lover.

And like any love, we risk losing it when we allow it to become one-dimensional. This, I believe, is the heart of both Gould's magisterium for-mulation and Williams's erotics of place. When science and faith operate at cross-purposes, with little or no regard for the other's necessities, the resul-tant confusion leads only to environmental disaster. When they *integrate,* as they do in the erotics of place, they foster the authority of the land itself as something to love. We protect the things we love; be then, Williams argues, in love with the land.

Notes

1. The phrase is from the opening lines of Thoreau's 1863 essay "Walking" (1980, 93).

2. Gould supports such a move when he alternately labels the magisterium of re-ligion as that of faith and that of "ethics and values" (1999, 14).

3. This is not to argue in favor of moral relativism. I intend only to point out that all morality is a matter of individual choice. Society proceeds by way of selecting a *range* of choices to call acceptable. (I might, though, ask that we make those selec-tions more carefully than sometimes seems to be the case.)

4. Dillard's religious presuppositions interfere with her ability—or perhaps with her willingness—to appreciate the natural world. This process is most clear in the "Fecundity" chapter of *Pilgrim at Tinker Creek* (1974).

5. In *Religions, Values, and Peak-Experiences,* Maslow writes that "the mystic expe-rience" from which religions originate is often "forgotten" as it is transformed into a "set of habits, behaviors, dogmas, forms, which at extremes become entirely legalistic and bureaucratic, conventional, empty, and in the truest meaning of the word, anti-religious" (1970, viii).

6. Gould explicitly links such desires with the magisterium of faith when he ar-gues that "every one of us must reach some decisions about the rules we will follow in conducting our own lives (even if we only pledge ourselves to the doctrine of un-stinting self-interest, whatever the cost to other people)" (1999, 58).

7. The best statement of Leopold's famous "Land Ethic" comes from his posthu-mous book, *A Sand County Almanac:* "A thing is right when it tends to preserve the

integrity, stability, and beauty of the biotic community. It is wrong when it tends otherwise" (1987, 224–25).

8. Williams coedited this anthology with Stephen Trimble in support of efforts to preserve southern Utah wilderness areas. Though the book originated as a pamphlet delivered to select members of the media and to every member of Congress, in 1994 Milkweed Editions published it under the title of *Testimony: Writers of the West Speak on Behalf of Utah Wilderness*.

9. In *Mapping the Invisible Landscape: Folklore, Writing, and the Sense of Place,* Ryden describes "an unseen layer of usage, memory, and significance—an invisible landscape if you will, of imaginative landmarks—superimposed upon the geographical surface and the two-dimensional maps" (1993, 40).

10. I first heard Williams use this phrase at a symposium, "Environmental Art and Activism," held on the campus of the University of Nevada, Reno, on 27 November 1995. Since that time, the phrase has become something of a mantra for Williams.

Works Cited

Abram, David. 1996. "Turning Inside Out." *Orion* 15 (1):54–58.

Armbruster, Karla. 1995. "Rewriting a Genealogy with the Earth: Women and Nature in the Works of Terry Tempest Williams." *Southwestern American Literature* 21 (1):209–20.

Bartkevicius, Jocelyn, and Mary Hussmann. 1997. "A Conversation with Terry Tempest Williams." *Iowa Review* (spring):1–23.

Cole, K. C. 1999. *First You Build a Cloud.* San Diego: Harcourt Brace.

Daniel, John. 1992. *The Trail Home.* New York: Pantheon Books.

Danto, Arthur C. 1981. *The Transfiguration of the Commonplace: A Philosophy of Art.* Cambridge: Harvard University Press.

Deming, Alison Hawthorne. 1994. *Temporary Homelands: Essays on Nature, Spirit, and Place.* New York: Picador.

———. 1998. *The Edges of the Civilized World: A Journey in Nature and Culture.* New York: Picador.

Dillard, Annie. 1974. *Pilgrim at Tinker Creek.* New York: Harper's Magazine Press.

———. 1982. *Teaching a Stone to Talk: Expeditions and Encounters.* New York: HarperPerennial.

Fox, Warwick. 1995. *Toward a Transpersonal Ecology.* Albany: SUNY Press.

Gould, Stephen Jay. 1993. *Eight Little Piggies: Reflections in Natural History.* New York: Norton.

———. 1999. *Rocks of Ages: Science and Religion in the Fullness of Life.* New York: Ballantine.

Hay, John. 1986. "The Nature Writer's Dilemma." In *On Nature: Nature, Landscape, and Natural History,* edited by Daniel Halpern, 7–10. San Francisco: North Point Press.

Jensen, Derrick. 1995. Interview with Terry Tempest Williams. In *Listening to the*

Land: Conversations about Nature, Culture, and Eros, 310–26. San Francisco: Sierra Club Books.

Kircher, Cassandra. 1996. "Rethinking the Dichotomies in Terry Tempest Williams's *Refuge.*" *Interdisciplinary Studies in Literature and Environment* 3 (1):97–113.

Leopold, Aldo. 1987. *A Sand County Almanac.* 1949. Reprint, New York: Oxford University Press.

Lopez, Barry. 1992. *The Rediscovery of North America.* 1990. Reprint, New York: Vintage Books.

Lorde, Audrey. 1978. *Uses of the Erotic: The Erotic As Power.* Freedom, Calif.: Crossing Press.

Maslow, Abraham. 1970. *Religions, Values, and Peak-Experiences.* New York: Viking.

McCormick, Steven J. 2002. "Landscapes That Sustain Us, Body and Soul." *Nature Conservancy* 52 (2):4–5.

Moore, Thomas. 1998. "Natural Spirituality." *Resurgence* 186 (January–February): 30–32.

Robinson, Joanna, and Casey Walker. 1995. "Interview with Terry Tempest Williams." *Wild Duck Review* 2 (1):8–11.

Ryden, Kent. 1993. *Mapping the Invisible Landscape: Folklore, Writing, and the Sense of Place.* Iowa City: University of Iowa Press.

Thoreau, Henry David. 1980. *Natural History Essays.* Salt Lake City: Peregrine Smith.

Trimble, Stephen, and Terry Tempest Williams, eds. 1998. *Testimony: Writers of the West Speak on Behalf of Utah Wilderness.* Minneapolis: Milkweed Editions.

Turner, Jack. 1992. "The Abstract Wild." In *On Nature's Terms,* edited by Thomas J. Lyon and Peter Stine, 87–104. College Station: Texas A&M University Press.

Williams, Terry Tempest. 1991. *Refuge: An Unnatural History of Family and Place.* New York: Pantheon Books.

———. 1994. *An Unspoken Hunger: Stories from the Field.* New York: Pantheon Books.

———. 1995a. *Desert Quartet.* New York: Pantheon Books.

———. 1995b. "A Downwinder in Hiroshima." *Nation* 269 (19):661–64.

———. 1995c. "Environmental Art and Activism." Symposium held at the University of Nevada, Reno. 27 November.

———. 2001. *Red: Passion and Patience in the Desert.* New York: Pantheon Books.

Yuki, Masami. 1998. "Narrating the Invisible Landscape: Terry Tempest Williams's Erotic Correspondence to Nature." *Studies in American Literature* 34:79–97.

KATHERINE R. CHANDLER

❧

Potsherds and Petroglyphs

UNEARTHING LATTER-DAY SAINT SOURCES
FOR WILLIAMS'S ENVIRONMENTAL VISION

If you think you can grasp me, think again:
my story flows in more than one direction
—Adrienne Rich, "Delta"

"I think of all the years I have taken the formal sacrament in my church," Terry Tempest Williams writes, remembering "the beautiful hymns sung with solemnity prior to the blessing on the bread and water." Such details of Latter-day Saint (Mormon) practices and beliefs abound in Williams's prose, providing readers with vivid renderings of the culture and theology of the Church of Jesus Christ of Latter-day Saints. Williams accompanies descriptions with responses that manifest her reverence for her faith: "the communal silence that permeated the chapel as silver trays were passed; the silence I loved. . . . I hold these moments of reflection dear" (2000, 14). There is no question that Williams has drawn much from the Mormon beliefs with which she was raised. What resound most memorably among Williams's reactions to the Latter-day Saint religion, however, are her criticisms. Mark Allister characterizes Williams's relationship to her church in a manner that echoes what other critics observe: "Williams is an influential Mormon woman who refused to have children and who challenges Mormon religious and patriarchal beliefs but does not renounce her religion" (2001, 59). The question is why—why, given the extent of her criticisms of her church and her tussles with her faith, Williams still declares when she publicly speaks or reads, "I am a Mormon woman"?

The question is not irrelevant nor is the query irreverent because Williams wrestles with it in public. In a recent interview, Williams illuminates the source of some of the questioning and misunderstanding: "One of the curious situations I have found myself in as a writer is that outside of Utah, I am seen as Mormon, whereas inside Utah I am seen as an 'edge walker,' an unorthodox Mormon" (2002, 19). Thus, critics, who are predominantly not Mormon and not residents of Utah, are obliged to ask, echoing what Williams asks of the petroglyphs she encounters in the Cabeza Prieta National Wildlife Refuge in Arizona, "Who is this artist, this scribe?" (1994, 124). There are, of course, multiple reasons Williams resists wholly severing her affiliation with the Church of Jesus Christ of Latter-day Saints, and over the years she has provided various answers, reviewing myriad ways in which the Latter-day Saint church entwines with her family, heritage, and culture. "Mormonism is one of the lenses I see the world through," Williams says. "We cannot escape our conditioning. Why would we want to? I grew up in a Mormon household where that was the focus of our lives. It was the fabric that held everything else together. I think it's still so much a part of me. I cannot separate out the various strands again: it's my connective tissue" (2002, 19).

One of the most compelling connections Williams feels with her religion is through place. Her writings clearly signal that the Salt Lake valley to which Brigham Young, the Mormon prophet who succeeded church founder Joseph Smith, led the exodus of his people from Illinois to the Utah Territory and which he declared was "the place," their new home, is, resoundingly, Williams's place as well. "Each of us harbors a homeland," she writes, and the "stories that are rooted there push themselves up like native grasses and crack the sidewalks" (1984, 8). Regardless of experiences that may tend to pave over and obscure Williams's past, her sense of homeland, her origins, and the ecological ethic arising from them, are inextricably bound to her Latter-day Saint faith and tradition.

In *Leap* (2000), Williams cross-examines faith-derived reasons that it is impossible for her to divorce herself from the church, but I would like to investigate a motive that has been overlooked: Latter-day Saint sources for her ecological vision. Core concepts that Williams advocates as part of her environmental philosophy—that all nature, animate and inanimate, is spiritual; that duality of body and spirit is a false divide; that the earth is home for all living things; that humans need to work toward a relational community—have tended to be portrayed as emerging predominantly from Native American traditions or ecofeminist thought that Williams has embraced as an adult, yet all of these concepts also have referents in Latter-day Saint doctrines. Williams provides a great deal of information about the church in her works, but she does not specify all of the Latter-day Saint sources that contributed to the shaping of her environmental vision. Those doctrines will be the focus of my examination.

The Church of Jesus Christ of Latter-day Saints (commonly called the Mormon Church) is a relatively new religious tradition, founded in New York in 1830 by Joseph Smith, who, in the midst of a time of great religious foment in America, claimed to have been divinely inspired to bring forth a restored gospel. Although the existence of the Mormon Church is widely known, its history, doctrine, and practices are not. Understandably, readers unfamiliar with these may fail to associate aspects of Williams's ecological vision with her upbringing and so may find her criticisms of Mormon culture and practices particularly, sometimes inordinately, conspicuous. Indeed, literary criticism that references Williams's Mormonism most commonly points out what she writes against. Cheryll Glotfelty, when elucidating ways in which Williams has been on the leading edge of ecofeminist methodologies, notes how men, including church leaders, are satirized in *Refuge* (1996, 165). Lynn Ross-Bryant suggests that Williams's self-designated "unnatural history" is "a history of resistance" (1997, 100). And Mark Allister observes how Williams joins other women "consciously ridding themselves of the orthodoxy, making for themselves a modified religion" (2001, 66).

Direct statements from Williams justify critics' focus: "I resist," Williams writes in *Red* (94), and in *Leap* she states, "Never trust the artist, the writer, the philosopher. They will betray the truth that raised them. Through their curiosity and the fire of their imagination, they will evoke change. They are religion-breakers" (144). However, with a fuller appreciation of the context for these claims, namely, the religious background informing them, critics and readers will be able to have a concomitantly fuller comprehension of the development of her ecological vision and of areas in her writings now clouded or unexplored.

I would like to direct attention to Williams's early Mormon beliefs, with an eye toward investigating Latter-day Saint nuances in Williams's environmental vision and the ways in which Williams alters the direction of one of Thoreau's most familiar dictums: "in wildness is the preservation of the world." Some one hundred fifty years after Thoreau, Williams maintains that a new dictum is in order: "preservation of wilderness is not so much a political process as a spiritual one" (2001, 187).

SPIRITUAL NATURE OF NATURE

Understanding Williams's particular ecological philosophy begins with recognizing her grounding in the spiritual nature of the natural world. For
Williams, the material world of nature and the intangible domain of spirit
are not isolated from each other. "To be in relation to everything around us,
above us, below us, earth, sky, bones, blood, flesh," she writes, "is to see the
world whole, even holy" (2001, 104). Williams specifies in *Refuge* two very
particular seminal influences that form the bedrock of her cosmology: the
world of nature, specifically the birds to which her grandmother introduced
her, and the Church of Jesus Christ of Latter-day Saints in which she was
reared. In her first chapter she describes how the two were, for her, inseparable: "I was raised to believe in a spirit world, that life exists before the earth
and will continue to exist afterward, that each human being, bird, and bul-
rush, along with all other life forms had a spirit life before it came to dwell
physically on the earth" (14). Williams, it turns out, is quite comfortable with
the concept that all living things are part matter, part spirit.

Williams's allegiance to understanding both the natural and the spiritual
has not wavered over the years. She describes childhood camping trips with
her family and birding forays with her grandmother as times that established
those deepest kinds of connections: "Our attachment to the land was our attachment to each other" (15). She records how beliefs in the spiritual essence
of nature "made sense to a child," and her subsequent assessment reveals the
extent to which the two worlds, material and spiritual, merged for her from
earliest experiential memory. She writes: "And if the natural world was as-
signed spiritual values, then those days spent in wildness were sacred. We
learned at an early age that God can be found wherever you are, especially
outside" (14). From her earliest consciousness, then, interactions with the
natural world included a dimension for Williams that was divine. She was,
we could say, schooled in the spiritual by the natural and vice versa.

During her academic years, comprehending the spiritual was as much a
part of Williams's scientific inquiry as was understanding the material. This
she makes clear when describing the studies that led to her work as a natural
historian: "Perhaps my original impulse to pursue an understanding of biology and the ecological relationships that bind us together as living organisms," she explains, "was my desire to come that much closer to an understanding of God" (Williams, Smart, and Smith 1998, 214). Her early writings
also confirm that her view of the natural world has always included an attention to the concept of the sacred place. "We are a spiritual people," she

writes when associating Mormons and Navajo in *Pieces of White Shell.* "We believe in a power that moves us, directs us, cares for us. . . . The Navajo have their sacred mountains and we have our sacred groves and temples," referring to prominent Mormon sanctuaries (3). She characterizes *Pieces* as an offering of "the Navajo voice, of my voice, and the voice of the land that moves us" (8). The sense of sacrosanct place provides another form of binding that Williams sees in the relationship between humans and the environment.

In her more recent 1998 essay in *New Genesis: A Mormon Reader on Land and Community,* Williams states that she believes that "the earth is holy . . . created out of an intelligence we may only begin to glimpse through the lenses of science" (Williams, Smart, and Smith 1998, 214). Thus, even as Williams's writings have revealed her dedication to scientific accuracy, they have concurrently respected a mystery that cannot be traced through scientific inquiry. Williams makes much of the fact that Latter-day Saint "sacred texts were housed and hidden in the earth . . . pulled out of the side of a mountain," here referring to church founder Joseph Smith's claim that while praying for guidance in the woods near his home, he was divinely directed to unearth the buried golden plates inscribed with the Book of Mormon, the seminal sacred text of the church (2000, 23).[1] Williams clearly states in *Leap* that Smith is the prophet who taught her to go to nature with her questions: "Hieronymus Bosch invited me to seek. Joseph Smith taught me to seek truth in a grove of trees" (264).

Williams's ongoing search for spiritual understanding in her interactions with the natural world echoes the doctrine from her Latter-day Saint background that humans are not the only entities on earth with a spirit. The prophet Joseph Smith, reporting a revelation from Jesus Christ, wrote, "All things unto me are spiritual" (*Doctrine and Covenants* 1986, 29:34), and that is explained further elsewhere. In *The Pearl of Great Price* it is stated, "For I, the Lord God, created all things of which I have spoken, spiritually, before they were naturally upon the face of the earth"; "And out of the ground made I, the Lord God, to grow every tree, naturally, that is pleasant to the sight of man; and man could behold it. And it became also a living soul. For it was spiritual in the day that I created it" (Moses 3:5 and 3:9). When asking for clarification of John's biblical prophecies in Revelations, specifically concerning the four beasts mentioned in the sixth verse of chapter 4 in Revelations, Joseph Smith records in *Doctrine and Covenants* that the Lord explained they were representative of "beasts, and of creeping things, and of the fowls of the air; that which is spiritual being in the likeness of that which is temporal; and that which is temporal in the likeness of that which is spiritual; the spirit of man in the likeness of his person, as also the spirit of the beast, and every other creature which God has created" (77:2). From her earliest understandings, then, Williams has seen a merging of the physical and the spiritual. To be "fully present" in the natural world, as she describes of her experience in the Serengeti, includes not only an awareness via the senses—"native intelligence"—but also respect and humility that allow responsiveness to a "source of power" deriving from "worship" (1994, 4–12).

UNITED NOT DIVIDED

Williams is far from alone as an environmental writer in challenging the dualism between the physical and the spiritual postulated by Greek philosophers such as Anaxagoras and Plato that continues to influence Western culture and religion. Separating matter and spirit is more than a philosophically divisive exercise. For Williams and others, it is a false divide with real consequences, namely, the degradation of the environment. "Loving the land," she writes, is "[h]onoring its mysteries. Acknowledging, embracing the spirit of place" (1994, 84).

President of the Church of Jesus Christ of Latter-day Saints Gordon B. Hinckley speaks of the natural world in different words but also directs attention to its spirit. "The earth in its pristine beauty," he says, "is an expression of the nature of its Creator" (2000, 93). His statement implies the intrinsic value of nature and indicates that it teaches humans about—even is—the nature of God. Key, of course, is the Latter-day Saint principle that humans are able to sense that nature through the spirit, and discerning the spirit includes a physical awareness, a corroboration by the body.[2] Latter-day Saints view spirit as inseparable from matter because they understand it to *be* matter: "There is no such thing as immaterial matter," *Doctrine and Covenants* states. "All spirit is matter, but it is more fine or pure, and can only be discerned by purer eyes" (131:7).

Williams's writings indicate that she persistently seeks discernment with "purer eyes." Through sensory stimuli she expands her understanding of the natural world, recognizing that she is also expanding her understanding of what is more refined than tangible matter. "The body does not lie," she said in a recent interview. "Therefore, if we write out of the body we are writing out of the truth of our lives. This creates a language that is organic and whole. Original. We listen to what is coursing through our veins, what is held within our hearts, what is registered in our bones. Call it cellular knowledge. Something akin to instinct. . . . The body carries the physical reality of our spirits like a river" (2002, 17). Williams's search for the sacred via the body and the senses is undergirded by the unity implied in Mormon doctrine between the material and immaterial: "the spirit *and* the body are the soul" (*Doctrine and Covenants* 1986, 88:5; italics mine).

The opportunity to sense with a physical body is important in a Latter-day Saint framework because, significantly, it can lead to spiritual experiences. There is, of course, a moral edge to that combination. Noted Mormon historian and scholar Hugh W. Nibley has pointed out that the "body and mind—the temporal and the spiritual—are inseparable, and to corrupt the one is to corrupt the other. Inevitably our surroundings become a faithful reflection of our mentality and vice versa" (1994, 55). With the disconnection between the physical and the spiritual being one of Williams's key criticisms of contemporary culture, uniting them has become one of her aims. She, too, feels the division but seeks reunion, as works like *Desert Quartet* attest. Such claims as "there is no partition between my body and the body of the Earth" are often prelude to what Williams recognizes as a concurrent interplay of a life force, "the weathering of our spirit" (10–11).

Earth As Home for All Beings

The tenth Article of Faith of the Church of Jesus Christ of Latter-day Saints states: "We believe . . . that the earth will be renewed and receive its paradisiacal glory." At that time, the *Doctrine and Covenants* states, "the enmity of man, and the enmity of beasts, yea, the enmity of all flesh, shall cease from before my face" (101:26). That will be the day when the earth "shall be quickened," "shall be sanctified," for it "abideth the law of a celestial kingdom" (88:26, 25). To Latter-day Saints, then, this planet is humans' home and not merely for mortality; in addition, the earth is home to all, not merely people.

How individuals view this sphere and behave in it, therefore, carries eternal ramifications for Latter-day Saints. Referring to what Latter-day Saints learn in a sacred temple rite, a ritual in which Williams has participated, Mormon geologist Donald L. Gibbon points out that "the first half of the LDS endowment ceremony, where the Creation of the world is so beautifully depicted, confirms that the gospel enjoins total respect for the material earth and all its inhabitants" (Williams, Smart, and Smith 1988, 132). Consideration for the world and the living things that inhabit it, in other words, is one measure of human spirituality.

Williams returns to the original meaning of animal, "'endowed with mind and spirit'" (1984, 101), suggesting further kinship between humans and creatures. A story is told of the first prophet of the church, a man who viewed animals in this light. When seeing those he was with "about to kill three rattlesnakes at their campsite," Joseph Smith said, "[l]et them alone—don't hurt them! How will the serpent ever lose its venom, while the servants of God possess the same disposition, and continue to make war upon it? Men must become harmless before the brute creation, and when men lose their vicious dispositions and cease to destroy the animal race, the lion and the lamb can dwell together, and the sucking child can play with the serpent in safety" (Ludlow 1992, 15). Joseph Smith was not alone among Mormon leaders who perceive shortcomings in regard to treatment of companions in the natural world. Other leaders of the church have counseled against hunting for sport or in excess of need. Joseph F. Smith, an early-twentieth-century prophet, was known frequently to say, "Take not away the life you cannot give, for all things have an equal right to live" (1939, 371–72). The aspiration is to live with a celestial rather than terrestrial perspective.

Mormons are taught that "replenishing" is one means by which humans can treat this earth as an eternal home. The charge from God for human beings "to multiply and replenish the earth" has most commonly been interpreted in terms of our species, but Joseph Fielding Smith, Latter-day Saint prophet in the 1970s, returns to the original Hebrew of Genesis 1 and cites our obligation to assist *all* species to flourish (1954–1956, 1:94). This concept of the human race "replenishing" Brigham Young likewise understood in reference to "all forms of life" and our role in "multiplying those organisms of plants and animals God has designed shall dwell upon it [the earth]" (Nibley 1978, 87). Quoting Brigham Young, Nibley asserts, "This earth is the home he [God] has prepared for us and we are to prepare ourselves and our habitations for the celestial glory" (1994, 27).

It may surprise some to learn that, despite her critiques of the Mormon Church, Williams holds a good deal of optimism concerning its core "environmental" beliefs. "Maybe I am in denial," Williams has said,

> but I don't believe there is an antagonism in the Church toward environmentalists. If we read Genesis about the power and beauty of Creation, if we read about the obligation and responsibility of stewardship toward the land, if we think about what community really means in the broadest sense—I think you can find all these ideas and tenets, if you will, rooted deeply within the principles of the gospel.
>
> True, there may be individuals within the Church who do not respond to ecological concerns or who may view environmentalists with suspicion of one

kind or another. I certainly have encountered that kind of hostility. But that belongs to the realm of politics, not religion. (2002, 17)

Williams writes of "an ideal world, a world we might well inhabit one day," characterizing it with echoes of the Latter-day Saint celestial vision of this earth. She describes it as a time when we would no longer have to "designate" wilderness because we will have "learned what it means to be 'good stewards,' to see the larger community as an embrace of all species." Extending Aldo Leopold's concept of a land ethic, Williams envisions a time when humankind's morals will have evolved to the point that "our compassion for all manner of life" will be "responsive and whole" (2001, 18). Her writings appeal to readers to begin that evolutionary process now.

Stewardship: Spiritual Community in Training

When envisioning her "Home Stand Act of 1994," one that Williams saw initiating a community of vigilance and care toward the lands we inhabit, she turned to the Latter-day Saint women's organization, known as the Relief Society, as a model (1994, 135). She describes what "a constant source of comfort" were the two Relief Society sisters "'called' to watch over" her family (136). Former General Relief Society first counselor Chieko N. Okazaki defines the organization in this way: "Our real job is relationships" (1993, 13). Okazaki is speaking here of relationships person to person, but that is only the beginning in building a community in the larger sense that Williams intimates in her "Home Stand" vision. Regarding the earth community, Mormons view themselves in the role of stewards, responsible for what is God's. Although the notion of stewardship is not exclusive to Latter-day Saints, it is central to the operation of Mormon society. Furthermore, Christian stewardship has become a concept maligned in the twentieth century, so examining it assists in understanding Williams's perception of human and natural interaction.[3]

From the earliest days of the church, Latter-day Saints have felt the accountability that accompanies stewardship. Historian Thomas G. Alexander explains attitudes of nineteenth-century Mormons as they lived and built and grew together: "Strongly communitarian, Mormons . . . understood that Christ would not return to clean up the mess unmindful people make of the earth. Human beings had the responsibility to care for God's creation themselves" (Williams, Smart, and Smith 1998, 209).

Describing ancestors who fled religious persecution and who were compelled to move in order to find freedom to practice their beliefs, Williams implies a spiritual parallel to her move from Salt Lake City to southern Utah. "They gathered in the belief of an integrated life," she writes, "where nature, culture, religion, and civic responsibility were woven in the context of family and community" (2001, 129). Williams's move was to an area that seems particularly mindful, "a local community . . . struggling to 'create a society to match the scenery'" (15).

Noting that self-sufficiency, order, and frugality governed the designs of the isolated towns built by the Mormon pioneers, geographer and environmental designer Richard V. Francaviglia concludes that survival still pervades as a governing principle in Mormon interactions with the land (1978, 105, 161). Wanting to avoid further persecution, "Mormons purposely moved into rugged areas secluded from Gentile intrusions," Francaviglia explains. "The theme is biblical, a chosen but persecuted people fleeing to the wilderness and building a kingdom" (82). Because "there is no effective separation of religious and temporal matters" (88), there is a sense of divine mandate, even obligation, to make the desert "blossom as a rose" (Isa. 35:1), which, often in the case of the arid Great Basin land, means managing the landscape in order to survive. As recorded in many accounts in *Women's Voices: An Untold History of the Latter-day Saints, 1830–1900,* early Mormon communities in the Utah territory imaged themselves as "holy nations," striving toward "United Order" (see Godfrey, Godfrey, and Derr 1982).[4] With all members having specific duties and all roles considered vital in order for the community to succeed, the organization of the church can be seen as an effort to achieve unity.

Williams's concept of an erotics of place is driven by this desire to foster "a participatory relationship with the land" (2001, 16). In *Desert Quartet,* she asserts, "But I believe our desire to share is more potent and trustworthy than our desire to be alone" (7). The pull toward community is strong in this writer who treasures solitude, and she acknowledges: "I have inherited a belief in community, the promise that a gathering of the spirit can both create and change culture" (2001, 129). In the kinship Williams feels with the land, her Latter-day Saint heritage again contributed to the responsibility that she manifests in her communal efforts of writing and action.

In some detail in *Refuge,* Williams describes how in the mid-1850s, then apostle, later prophet, Lorenzo Snow originated a "community based on an ecological model," in which "[e]ach person" operates "within their own 'ecological niche,' strengthening and sustaining the overall structure or 'ecosystem'" (100). Williams also describes Brigham Young as the leader who brought the Latter-day Saints to Utah with "not only a religion and a life but a land ethic"; she quotes Young, confirming the reverence Latter-day Saints should hold for the earth: "Here are the stupendous works of the God of Nature, though all do not appreciate His wisdom as manifested in his works" (2001, 74). Ron Molen, a contemporary Latter-day Saint architect who designs for sustainability, explains in more detail that "Brigham Young had a clear concept of how the Great Basin should be developed. Based on Joseph Smith's model, the self-sufficient Mormon village was replicated over and over again . . . a community of communities. Each village controlled its own water, food, and fuel resources, and population did not exceed the carrying capacity of the surrounding land" (Williams, Smart, and Smith 1998, 43). Sustainability was the Mormon vision, and Williams clearly absorbed such mind-sets and models.

Latter-day scriptures state that "the beasts of the field and the fowls of the air, and that which cometh of the earth, is ordained for the use of man for food and for raiment, and that he might have in abundance" (*Doctrine and Covenants* 1986, 49:19). But Mormon sacred writings also emphasize that humans are to live, in current terminology, in a socially just manner and a sustainable way:

> But it is not given that one man should possess that which is above another, wherefore the world lieth in sin.
>
> And wo be unto man that sheddeth blood or that wasteth flesh and hath no need. (49:20–21)

Concerning the concept of stewardship, historian Erich Robert Paul concludes his study *Science, Religion, and Mormon Cosmology* observing that "Mormonism has historically deferred to the view that nature is not an object to manipulate and exploit but an entity to understand and revere." He continues, explaining that Latter-day Saints have not rejected realism; they have "drawn deeply from . . . the view that humans are caretakers of Nature" (1992, 233).

The tension in Williams's response to the concept of caretaker derives primarily from her discomfort with the hierarchical order implied in stewardship. Her environmental philosophy has inclined toward Native American understandings of human and nature. This she clearly establishes in *Pieces of White Shell* when she writes, "Navajo stories have been my guides across the desert" (3), noting how they became models "for ecological thought," providing "a balanced structure to live in" (105). Quoting Gladys Reichard's study of Navajo religion, Williams specifically cites the "Navajo Way" as "a design in harmony, a striving for rapport between man and every phase of nature" (3). Power *over* nature is not "the Way."

Position and power, however, are not ambitions set forth in Latter-day Saint theology; indeed, both are set forth as traps to avoid. "The goal of mortality is to overcome such 'carnal' tendencies as unrighteous dominion and to strive for oneness in relationships with others and with God," Jolene Edmunds Rockwood writes from the perspective of a Latter-day Saint with a master's degree from Harvard Divinity School (Beecher 1987, 27). There is no place for pride or importance, which church leaders constantly caution against. In a November 2000 address to all members of the church, Apostle Neal A. Maxwell said, "craving power and the spotlight sucks out the spiritual oxygen" (2000, 35).

How various stewardships have been translated socially and culturally among Mormons is something that Williams criticizes, urging them to develop more informed understandings of their responsibility to the earth. Williams along with the other editors of New Genesis suggest that the reality of how progress is construed by individuals too often focuses on temporal interpretations (viii–ix).

"When we conceived of this idea," Williams explains about the New Genesis anthology,

> Bill Smart and Gibbs Smith [coeditors] and I wanted to dispel the stereotype that only Democrats and non-Mormons cared about the environment. We didn't believe that. We wanted to bring together a diverse group of LDS people who love the land. We wanted to show that this is a bipartisan issue that transcends party lines. And we wanted to ask the question, How has the natural world influenced your testimony of the gospel and, conversely, how has the gospel influenced your view of nature? (18)

Leaders of the church have spoken of a relationship with the land in language indicating concern. Prior president of the church Spencer W. Kimball expressed alarm in his bicentennial address: "I have the feeling that the good earth can hardly bear our presence upon it," pointing out that leaders of the church "constantly cry out against that which is intolerable in the sight of the Lord: against pollution of mind, body, and our surroundings" (1976, 4). Neal A. Maxwell wrote in 1970 that our culture's concern with "developing a more harmonious relationship with nature by abiding by its physical laws is timely and legitimate. When we interrupt or destroy the larger ecology of man's relationship to God and to his fellowmen, we are violating transcendental laws that are as immutable and as inevitable as those breached laws of nature for which we are now beginning to pay a terrible price."[5] With deteriorating conditions of the land as well as increasing awareness of humans' role in its degradation, more Latter-day Saints are realizing that the way of discharging stewardship needs to change. Williams is at the forefront of that awareness.

In Williams's search for wisdom, she most noticeably cites thinkers and writers canonized in the nature-writing tradition, but seeded through her works we find Williams describing her defense of the land as "spiritual" (2001, 17). "If it is possible to hear the voice of an artifact," Williams has stated, "I heard many songs" (1984, 14). Because her story undoubtedly flows in more than one direction, Williams sees with an outlook toward the natural world that she derived from Mormon understandings of an earth community. Terry Tempest Williams holds out hope, anticipating a time foreseen in Latter-day Saint scripture, when "the earth shall be like as it was in the days before it was divided" when "in the barren deserts there shall come forth pools of living water" (*Doctrine and Covenants* 1986, 133:24, 29).

Notes

1. The four standard works considered as scripture in the Church of Jesus Christ of Latter-day Saints are the Bible, *The Book of Mormon, The Doctrine and Covenants of the Church of Jesus Christ of Latter-day Saints,* and *The Pearl of Great Price. The Book of Mormon,* whose subtitle is "Another Testament of Jesus Christ," explains in its introduction that it contains a "record of God's dealings with the ancient inhabitants of the Americas," primarily from 600 B.C. to A.D. 421, that were "written on gold plates" and "quoted and abridged by a prophet-historian named Mormon." The plates were buried by the last of those prophets. Joseph Smith was led to them, then translated the plates "by the gift and power of God" (*Book of Mormon* 1986, introduction). *The Doctrine and Covenants* "contains selections from the revelations given to Joseph Smith and his successors in the Presidency of the Church" (McConkie 1993, 206). *The Pearl of Great Price* includes certain "revelations, translations, and narrations" from Joseph Smith (563). It contains the Book of Moses, received by revelation; the Book of Abraham, translated from "Egyptian papyri that came into the hands of Joseph Smith in 1835" (*Pearl of Great Price* 1986, introductory note); an extract of Joseph Smith's translation of Matthew; excerpts from Joseph Smith's history; and the church's "Articles of Faith."

2. *Doctrine and Covenants* 9:8 is one scriptural explanation of the role of feelings in discerning spiritual matters: "But, behold, I say unto you, that you must study it out in your mind; then you must ask me if it be right, and if it is right I will cause that your bosom shall burn within you; therefore, you shall feel that it is right."

3. Max Oelschlaeger's 1994 *Caring for Creation: An Ecumenical Approach to the Environmental Crisis* is a thorough ecophilosophical treatise on the subject and provides a good overview of the arguments.

4. The establishment of the "United Order" was a move in the direction of a society in which all shared equally and an attempt to progress toward voluntary attitudes

of cooperation (England 1980, 221). Apostle and church scholar Bruce R. McConkie explains the United Order in a way that clarifies its distinction from a communal system: "In order to live the law of consecration, the early saints in this dispensation set up the United Order as the legal organization to receive consecrations, convey stewardships back to donors, and to regulate the storehouses containing surplus properties" (1993, 813). Joseph Smith was guided to establish this new order of society in the 1830s through revelation, stating, "[L]et every man deal honestly, and be alike among this people, and receive alike, that ye may be one," with the subsequent prompt received later that same year that suggested the difficulties in carrying it out: "[I]n your temporal things, you shall be equal, and this not grudgingly" (*Doctrine and Covenants* 51:9 and 70:14). The goal, of course, was to live as Jesus lived. Numerous attempts to live the United Order, however, failed, with Mormons placing "the blame for such failures on themselves—as not having reached the degree of moral development necessary" (England 1980, 213). Progressing toward a Zion society, though, remains a Latter-day Saint ambition. Wallace Stegner observes, "The United Order sleeps yet as a dream of the future in many a Mormon mind" (1970, 224), and Latter-day prophets suggest why; this is, according to prophet Joseph Smith, "the model upon which all human society would be organized when the Savior returned" (Arrington, Fox, and May 1976, 2).

5. Quoted by James B. Mayfield in his essay "Poverty, Population, and Environmental Ruin" in Williams, Smart, and Smith 1998, 62.

Works Cited

Allister, Mark. 2001. *Refiguring the Map of Sorrow: Nature Writing and Autobiography.* Charlottesville: University Press of Virginia.

Arrington, Leonard J. 1986. *Brigham Young: American Moses.* Urbana: University of Illinois Press.

Arrington, Leonard J., Feramorz Y. Fox, and Dean L. May. 1976. *Building the City of God: Community and Cooperation among the Mormons.* Salt Lake City: Deseret Book.

Beecher, Maureen Ursenbach, and Lavina Fielding Anderson. 1992. *Sisters in Spirit: Mormon Women in Historical and Cultural Perspective.* Urbana: University of Illinois Press.

The Book of Mormon: Another Testament of Jesus Christ. 1986. Rev. ed. Salt Lake City: Church of Jesus Christ of Latter-day Saints.

The Doctrine and Covenants of the Church of Jesus Christ of Latter-day Saints. 1986. Rev. ed. Salt Lake City: Church of Jesus Christ of Latter-day Saints.

England, Eugene. 1980. *Brother Brigham.* Salt Lake City: Bookcraft.

Francaviglia, Richard V. 1978. *The Mormon Landscape: Existence, Creation, and Perception of a Unique Image in the American West.* New York: AMS Press.

Glotfelty, Cheryll. 1996. "Flooding the Boundaries of Form: Terry Tempest Williams's Ecofeminist *Unnatural History.*" In *Change in the American West: Exploring the*

Human Dimension, edited by Stephen Tchudi, 158–67. Reno: University of Nevada Press.

Godfrey, Kenneth W., Audrey M. Godfrey, and Jill Mulvay Derr, eds. 1982. *Women's Voices: An Untold History of the Latter-day Saints, 1830–1900.* Salt Lake City: Deseret Book.

Hinckley, Gordon B. 2000. *Standing for Something: Ten Neglected Virtues That Will Heal Our Hearts and Homes.* New York: Times Books.

The Holy Bible. 1986. Authorized King James Version with explanatory notes and cross-references to the standard works of the Church of Jesus Christ of Latter-day Saints. Salt Lake City: Church of Jesus Christ of Latter-day Saints.

Journal of Discourses of President Brigham Young, His Counselors, and Other Church Leaders. 1854–1886. 26 vols. Liverpool: Latter-day Saints Book Depot.

Kimball, Spencer W. 1976. "The False Gods We Worship." *Ensign* (June):4–6.

Ludlow, Daniel H., ed. 1992. *The Church and Society.* Salt Lake City: Deseret Book.

Maxwell, Neal A. 2000. "The Tugs and Pulls of the World." *Ensign* (November):35–37.

McConkie, Bruce R. 1993. *Mormon Doctrine.* 2d ed. Salt Lake City: Bookcraft.

Nibley, Hugh W. 1978. *Nibley on the Timely and the Timeless: Classic Essays of Hugh W. Nibley.* Provo: Brigham Young University, Religious Studies Center.

———. 1994. *Brother Brigham Challenges the Saints.* Edited by Don E. Norton and Shirley S. Ricks. Vol. 13 of *The Collected Works of Hugh Nibley.* Salt Lake City and Provo: Deseret Book and Foundation for Ancient Research and Mormon Studies.

Oelschlaeger, Max. 1994. *Caring for Creation: An Ecumenical Approach to the Environmental Crisis.* New Haven: Yale University Press.

Okazaki, Chieko N. 1993. *Cat's Cradle.* Salt Lake City: Bookcraft.

Paul, Erich Robert. 1992. *Science, Religion, and Mormon Cosmology.* Urbana: University of Illinois Press.

The Pearl of Great Price. 1986. Rev. ed. Salt Lake City: Church of Jesus Christ of Latter-day Saints.

Ross-Bryant, Lynn. 1997. "The Self in Nature: Four American Autobiographies." *Soundings* 80:83–104.

Smith, Joseph F. 1939. *Gospel Doctrine.* Edited by John A. Widtsoe et al. Salt Lake City: Deseret Book.

Smith, Joseph Fielding. 1954–1956. *Doctrines of Salvation.* Compiled by Bruce R. McConkie. 3 vols. Salt Lake City: Bookcraft.

Stegner, Wallace. 1970. *Mormon Country.* 1942. Reprint, Lincoln: University of Nebraska Press.

White, Lynn, Jr. 1967. "The Historical Roots of Our Ecological Crisis." *Science* 155:1203–7.

Williams, Terry Tempest. 1984. *Pieces of White Shell: A Journey to Navajoland.* Albuquerque: University of New Mexico Press.

———. 1989. *Coyote's Canyon.* Salt Lake City: Gibbs-Smith.

———. 1991. *Refuge: An Unnatural History of Family and Place.* New York: Pantheon Books.

————. 1994. *An Unspoken Hunger: Stories from the Field.* New York: Pantheon Books.

————. 1995. *Desert Quartet: An Erotic Landscape.* New York: Pantheon Books.

————. 1997. Introduction to *The Land of Little Rain,* by Mary Austin. New York: Penguin.

————. 2000. *Leap.* New York: Pantheon Books.

————. 2001. *Red: Passion and Patience in the Desert.* New York: Pantheon Books.

————. 2002. Interview by Jana Bouck Remy. *Irreantum: Exploring Mormon Literature* (Association for Mormon Letters) (summer):14–22.

Williams, Terry Tempest, William B. Smart, and Gibbs M. Smith, eds. 1998. *New Genesis: A Mormon Reader on Land and Community.* Salt Lake City: Gibbs-Smith.

LISA DIEDRICH

∾

"A New Thought in Familiar Country"

WILLIAMS'S WITNESSING ETHICS

Terry Tempest Williams's memoir *Refuge: An Unnatural History of Family and Place* opens with a poem from Mary Oliver's book *Dream Work*. The poem, "Wild Geese," begins by telling its reader what one doesn't have to be or do:

> You do not have to be good.
> You do not have to walk on your knees
> for a hundred miles through the desert, repenting.
> You only have to let the soft animal of your body
> love what it loves.
>
> (1991, ix)

In *Refuge*, Williams offers a narrative that, like Oliver's poem, opposes the dogma of goodness and repentance with the capacity of the body to love what it loves. For Williams and the rest of us, however, this is no easy task. It requires transformation, and, as Williams learns, this transformation is both a personal and a political process.

Oliver's poem continues with a call for stories; in particular, she calls for stories of despair: "Tell me about despair, yours, and I will tell you mine" (ix). *Refuge* is a work that pays attention to despair, both by telling of it and by listening for it. But, as Oliver notes, even as we tell of despair, "Meanwhile the world goes on." Although we may attempt through narrative to wrest control over an experience of despair, that experience always exceeds our capacity to control it in and through language. There is always a "meanwhile" to the stories we tell, and it is to the meanwhile that we must direct our attention despite, or perhaps because of, our despair. In this essay, I consider the forms of attention that Williams practices in order to tell her stories of loss. Williams bears witness to the transformation of both her internal and her external landscapes, and only through the endless task of witnessing can she begin to see, as Oliver's poem suggests, the world that offers itself to her imagination and to hear the calls of the wild geese, "over and over announcing [her] place in the family of things." What must one do to come to know one's place in the family of things? And how does this knowledge help us to encounter the stories of despair that others may tell? *Refuge* teaches us a witnessing ethics with which we—the readers—might share the difficult task Williams has set for herself: to see and hear otherwise.

Before turning to the specific ways that Williams witnesses despair in and through *Refuge,* I want to begin my analysis of Williams's witnessing ethics by discussing briefly the work of feminist philosopher Kelly Oliver on the relationship between witnessing and subjectivity. In her most recent work, Oliver has developed a theory of subjectivity that does not posit recognition as the basis for subjectivity. According to Oliver, theories of subjectivity based on recognition require an other who is either objectified or abjected, and, as such, these theories fail to account for the "subject position of the othered" (2000, 32). In order to account for the subject position of the othered, Oliver argues for a subjectivity that emerges out of the process of witnessing, and she describes this process as an endless task. As Oliver notes in *Witnessing: Beyond Recognition,* the word *witnessing* has a double meaning: it means both "eyewitness testimony based on first-hand knowledge . . . and bearing witness to something beyond recognition that can't be seen" (2001, 16). The practice of witnessing, then, requires that we cultivate our "response-ability" to those things that we both see and don't see, that we both hear and don't hear, and that we both know and don't know. For Oliver, "[t]o serve subjectivity, and therefore humanity, we must be vigilant in our attempts to continually open and reopen the possibility of response" (19). This openness to the possibility of response is a means by which we might, as Mary Oliver calls for in her poem, let the body love what it loves.

In her philosophical investigations into the practice of witnessing, Kelly Oliver is concerned with the possibilities engendered in "working-through the trauma of oppression necessary to personal and political transformation" (85). How does one become a responsible witness in Oliver's terms, and what kinds of personal and political transformations are enacted by this sort of witnessing? Drawing on the psychoanalytic work of Shoshana Felman and Dori Laub on Holocaust testimony, Oliver is concerned less with the historical accuracy of testimony than with the possibility that the "performance of testimony says more than the witness knows" (16). Such a revelation of more than the witness knows is demonstrated in Williams's testimony to the flooding of the bird refuge and to the death of her mother in *Refuge*. However, as I will show, Williams, as naturalist and daughter, at times resists this "paradox between the necessity and impossibility of testimony," which Oliver calls the "paradox of the eyewitness" (86). Williams, as writer, performs this paradox in and through her text.

The Necessity of Testimony

Williams tells at least two histories in *Refuge:* she tells the history of a particular place (the land around the Great Salt Lake in Utah) and the history of a particular Mormon family (the Tempest and Dixon clans) with deep roots in this place. Although she is trained as a naturalist, and has been an avid birder since childhood, Williams discovers that there are some things that, even with this particular training, she cannot anticipate or prepare for. Thus, while she infuses her work with a naturalist's eye for the details of the land and the birds that inhabit it, she simultaneously discovers that this scientific knowledge that allows her to count and catalog birds in the Bear River Migratory Bird Refuge is not enough knowledge in the face of what she does not know: about the progress of the rise of the Great Salt Lake and about the progress of the rise of the tumor in her mother's body. In order to tell this story, Williams will have to be more than a naturalist and write more than a natural history. For this is also, as her subtitle suggests, an unnatural history; it is an unnatural history of the human impact on the natural world when humans have forgotten "their place in the family of things." To tell this story and to find refuge in the telling, therefore, she will have to "confront what [she does] not know" (4) and create a path for herself and others, not only through her eyewitness accounts of the changes in the landscape and the changes in her mother's body, but also through her witnessing to something impossible to fully account for: the devastation of the bird refuge and the death of her mother. In order to tell this story, therefore, Williams must be not only a naturalist, but also a poet and activist; she must describe what she sees as well as what she can only begin to imagine and, through "language and action," imagine into being.[1] In Williams's narrative of despair, "the unseen in vision and the unspoken in speech," in Oliver's formulation, emerges; *Refuge*, in other words, is a testimony to that which is beyond what we can easily see or say (Oliver 2001, 2).

At the outset of her story, Williams believes refuge is found in that which is familiar to us, in that which we recognize and know. Early on, she establishes for her reader what makes the bird refuge such a source of comfort for her:

> The Bird Refuge has remained a constant. It is a landscape so familiar to me, there have been times I have felt a species long before I saw it. The long-billed curlews that foraged the grasslands seven miles outside the Refuge were trustworthy. I can count on them year after year. And when six whimbrels joined them—whimbrel entered my mind as an idea. Before I ever saw them mingling with curlews, I recognized them as a new thought in familiar country. (21)

Although Williams states explicitly here that the bird refuge is for her a constant, something trustworthy and recognizable, at the same time and paradoxically, she reveals that the refuge represents more than the possibility of constancy and familiarity. The bird refuge is also a place in which a new thought might come into being. The history Williams must tell here is not only a history of the familiar, but also a history in which new thoughts emerge. Williams must be a witness, then, to the familiar landscape as well as to the landscape transformed by new thoughts.

Immediately following the above paragraph, Williams writes, "The birds and I share a natural history. It is a matter of rootedness, of living inside a place for so long that the mind and the imagination fuse" (21). Although she will remain rooted to this place and to her family, Williams will learn in the course of the events described in *Refuge* that nothing is constant, not the bird refuge, not the landscape of the natural world nor the landscape of one's body, not one's family history nor one's natural history. What Williams discovers, in fact, is that the only constant in life is change, and the change brought by death and devastation will have to enter Williams's mind as a new thought, and this new thought, as we shall see, will transform her notion of rootedness.

At the same time as her own scientific knowledge will prove not to be quite enough to meet the demands of her loss of familiarity with her place in the world, the scientific knowledge more generally available to meet the challenge of the Great Salt Lake's rise and her mother's cancer will also be found lacking. In *Refuge*, Williams chronicles the engineering battle against the Great Salt Lake's inexorable rise, as well as the medical battle against her mother's cancer. Both of these battles ultimately do very little to repair the changes in the environment around the Great Salt Lake and in her mother's body, and they threaten to do more damage than good. And both reveal the human arrogance behind the belief that nature and the body can be, indeed must be, dominated at all costs by human intervention. By approaching the changes in the Great Salt Lake and the changes in Diane Dixon Tempest's body as enemies to be conquered, we do not cultivate our response-ability; rather, we simply identify an other that must be eradicated at all costs. And yet, as Williams comes to understand, that other is a part of us: indeed, it may even be our refuge.

How, then, do we respond differently to bodily and environmental changes, even devastating ones such as those Williams and her family must respond to? Williams first catalogs the alternatives that the state of Utah considers in order "to control the lake" (58). All of these proposals require great feats of engineering and will cost anywhere from $3 million to $250 million. As Williams notes ironically, "Evidently, to do nothing is not an option" (61). Because the powers that be in the state of Utah perceive the rise of the Great Salt Lake as a threat against which a battle must be waged, their response-ability to the changes in the lake is severely limited. How might the state of Utah respond if it didn't perceive the rising Great Salt Lake as a threat that must be stopped? This is the new thought that Williams believes we must at least consider, along with, or instead of, the old thought of doing battle with the lake. This might require rethinking the boundaries between the natural world and the so-called civilized world. The new thought might involve considering the possibility that these boundaries are not as fixed as they seem, and that there may be benefits in their breach. The transformation of one of Salt Lake City's main thoroughfares into a river after City Creek overflows its banks is an example of the possibilities in adaptation and innovation—in thinking otherwise—that Williams favors over entrenchment in a war against nature (46).

In the case of her mother's cancer, Williams wants to do away with the military metaphors that require one to lay siege to one's body in order to defeat the cancer that is, in this view, in the body but not of it. Williams wonders if the notion of responding to cancer with aggression is "counterproductive to healing" (43). In her important works on illness and metaphor, Susan Sontag seeks to eliminate all metaphorical thinking in relation to illness, and in doing so attempts to detach moral meanings from medical diagnoses. By comparing the representations of tuberculosis in the nineteenth century and the representations of cancer in the twentieth century, Sontag suggests that diseases whose etiologies are unknown are most likely to be metaphorized in both medical and popular understandings. In the nineteenth century, according to Sontag, TB was a disease that was romanticized;

it was represented as not so much a debilitating disease, which it clearly was, but as an opportunity for "spiritual refinement" and "expanded consciousness." Unlike TB, Sontag asserts, cancer has never been romanticized, nor has it been aestheticized. In the twentieth-century representation of cancer, the disease becomes not a reflection of the sufferer's spiritual refinement, but, instead, a reflection of the sufferer's allegedly repressed character. Cancer does not expand consciousness, but obliterates it. Sontag, therefore, wants to show that these metaphors—both the good nineteenth-century TB metaphors and the bad twentieth-century cancer metaphors—are damaging for those persons who are suffering from the actual diseases, which in and of themselves, she insists, do not have moral meanings. Thus, Sontag is impatient with the need to make illness meaningful, even, or especially, by attributing to the experience of illness the impetus to change one's life, that is, to make it meaningful in ways it wasn't before.

Unlike Sontag, Williams does not attempt to eliminate all metaphors with which to describe the experience of cancer because certain metaphors have ethical uses, especially in the hands of a poet. Rather, Williams is interested in transforming the metaphors available to us to describe the experience of illness and its treatments. "How can we rethink cancer?" Williams asks, and she begins to answer this question not by attempting to describe cancer without making use of metaphor, but by attempting to describe cancer otherwise, as a new thought in the familiar country of one's body (43).

The new thought Williams offers about cancer is that it might be understood metaphorically as a creative process rather than simply as a destructive process that must itself be destroyed. This requires viewing the cancerous tumor not "as foreign, something outside ourselves," but as "our own creation" (44). Although this view of cancer as our own creation risks establishing a causal relationship between having cancer and having a personality prone to cancer, I do not believe Williams wants to make such a simplistic link between cancer and certain personality types.[2] Rather, what she seems to want to do is to reassert the creative agency of the person with cancer. She notes, therefore, that creative ideas, not unlike cancer, "emerge slowly, quietly, invisibly at first. They are most often abnormal thoughts, thoughts that disrupt the quotidian, the accustomed. They divide and multiply, become invasive. With time, they congeal, consolidate, and make themselves conscious. An idea surfaces and demands total attention. I take it from my body and give it away." Although I suspect Sontag would find such a metaphor problematic because it implies cancer be viewed as an opportunity that might be taken (and in this formulation it is a slippery slope from the "might" to the "must"), Williams's metaphor seems useful to me in that it attempts to break down the dichotomy between one's self and one's cancer that often leads to the use of aggressive medico-military tactics against the cancer. Moreover, Williams's metaphor also seems to call for a witnessing ethics: we must be attentive to that which disrupts the quotidian and the familiar, and respond not by seeking to destroy these abnormal thoughts, but by working through them so that they might be given away, passed on, and witnessed anew.

The Impossibility of Testimony

We might ask, though, if cancer is really like the creative process for Williams's mother. One of the things that Williams must witness in *Refuge* is her own failure to know precisely what cancer is like for her mother. *Refuge* gives us most clearly what her mother's cancer is like *for Williams herself,* but it can give us only glimpses of what cancer is like for her mother. This difficulty that *Refuge* performs exemplifies what Kelly Oliver means by the "paradox of the eyewitness," that it is both necessary and impossible for Williams to tell of her mother's dying. The ethical challenge for Williams as well as for us—as readers and as secondary witnesses—is not only to tell our story of despair but also to listen to the stories of others; that is, as Arthur W. Frank understands it, "narrative ethics takes place in telling and listening" (1995, 163). What is demanded of the readers of narratives of despair like *Refuge* is a "new kind of listening, the witnessing, precisely, of *impossibility*" (Caruth 1995, 10).

Diane Dixon Tempest does attempt to explain to Williams what this cancer is for her.[3] She tells her that it is like the Tolstoy story "God Sees the Truth, but Waits" in which a man is wrongly accused of murder and spends the rest of his life in a prison camp in Siberia. When the real murderer comes forward, and the man is given the opportunity to free himself, he chooses to stay on in the camp. When he makes this choice to stay in Siberia, as Williams's mother explains the story to her, "[h]is longing for home leaves him and he dies" (93). "Each of us must face our own Siberia," she tells her daughter. "We must come to peace within our isolation. No one can rescue us. My cancer is my Siberia." Dying is not familiar country for any of us, and perhaps it is in our attempts to make it an experience that is familiar and comfortable that dying becomes unbearable. Only in giving up her longing for her dying to be something she already knows or thinks she knows can Williams's mother come to terms with the loneliness of dying. But it is important to keep in mind that, in attempting to explain to her daughter what she is experiencing as she dies, Tempest must make use of metaphor.[4] For Williams's mother, cancer is not Siberia itself, but like the experience she imagines Siberia to be. Or, more to the point, her cancer is like Tolstoy's story about Siberia, which means, in a sense, it both is and isn't like the creative process for her.

In his essay on AIDS diaries and the literal and figurative death of the author, Ross Chambers describes witnessing as a mediating practice of mourning (1998). To witness to death is to carry the message deferred by death forward. In her work, Williams reveals the means by which she acts as a relay, as Chambers puts it, for her mother's words, and perhaps these words and this knowledge are the gift that her mother gives to Williams and to the reader of *Refuge.* This gift is also, however, that which Williams appears least capable of receiving. In some respects, if she had fully and effortlessly accepted her mother's isolation in the face of her cancer, we would not have the gift of *Refuge.* The knowledge that her mother has to offer Williams, and through Williams to the reader of *Refuge,* disrupts that which Williams is accustomed to: that is, her mother's Siberia becomes a new thought in the familiar country of one family's history in and of the Utah desert. In articulating what she knows and doesn't know, Williams acts as witness in both senses of the word as theorized by Oliver: she gives evidence of what her mother says about her own experience of cancer, and she reveals as well that there is more to her mother's experience of cancer than she (Williams) can fully know or bear witness to.

Williams vigilantly struggles to hear what her mother has to tell her about living with and dying of cancer. In her vigilance, she makes use of various techniques of witnessing learned from both the harsh desert landscape, which teaches "quietude and attention" (148), and from the magnificence and variety of the birds surrounding her, which teach Williams how to look and to listen closely (149). She listens for "other languages spoken by wind, water, and wings," and she communes with other lives present to her in this landscape. These other lives are often other than human—for example, "avocets, stilts, and stones" (29)—or that which remains of humans who lived long ago (including the Anasazi and Fremont) but still survive in the artifacts that have their own voice, if only we can learn to hear that voice. Birds are magical not just because they are beautiful creatures, but also because they "bridge cultures and continents with their wings . . . [and] they mediate between heaven and earth" (18). Quietude and attention, bridging and mediation: these are the tools Williams must use to witness this story of despair.

For Williams, the desert is not a barren land but is brimming with life for those who take the time to really look.

It is this inability to pay attention to the landscape, to witness something that is difficult to see, that informs, for Williams, Karl Momen's art installation in the desert titled *Metaphor*. According to Williams, "This was the work of a European architect who saw the West Desert as 'a large white canvas with nothing on it.' This was his attempt 'to put something out there to break the monotony.'" Alluding to another man-made structure tested in the desert because there was supposedly nothing there, Williams notes that "[w]ith the light of morning, [Momen's installation] cast a shadow across the salt flats like a mushroom cloud" (127).

It is in fact an actual mushroom cloud, not a metaphorical one, that casts its shadow over the story told in *Refuge* and over the tenuous idea of refuge itself. *Refuge* is punctuated by glimpses of knowledge received only in flashes, and Williams must be a witness to these flashes even without fully knowing what they mean in the moment of their emergence. In attempting to capture in language our usual relationship to change, which is, in a sense, a relationship to new knowledge, Williams describes "a sense of something tenuous": "These moments of peripheral perceptions are short, sharp flashes of insight we tend to discount like seeing the movement of an animal from the corner of our eye. We turn and there is nothing there. They are strong and subtle impressions we allow to slip away" (24). The form of witnessing that Williams practices in *Refuge,* therefore, is not just a matter of looking directly at something; rather, it requires that she sometimes glance out of the corner of her eye in order that the subtle impressions don't slip away entirely under her full gaze. This relates, I think, to what Slavoj Zizek, in his work on Jacques Lacan and popular culture, describes as Lacan's "metaphor of anamorphosis." According to Zizek, this phenomenon occurs when a detail of a picture viewed in a straightforward manner is blurred and unintelligible, but when the same picture is looked at awry or at an angle, it becomes a clear and distinguishable shape. It is precisely by "looking awry" that we might catch a glimpse of what Lacan calls "the real," which in Lacan's formulation is the traumatic event that defies symbolization (Zizek 1991, 11). In order to see something beyond the familiar, one must attempt to glimpse the traces of that which one tends to discount. Again, it is a matter not only of bearing witness to what one sees and recognizes, but also of bearing witness to what one misses seeing, or sees and doesn't see at the same time.

Williams, in fact, is haunted by a recurring dream in which she sees a "flash of light in the night in the desert." When she describes this recurring dream to her father after her mother's death, she explains that "this image had so permeated my being that I could not venture South without seeing it again, on the horizon, illuminating buttes and mesas" (282–83). What she learns from her father is that this image is not, or not only, a dream image, it is an image from her past, a remembered image. It is not simply something she has imagined seeing, but something she has seen, and yet not fully known. Her father tells her that she saw the "flash of light in the night in the desert" when she was a young child, and that the flash was a mushroom cloud from the testing of an atomic bomb in the southwestern desert on September 7, 1957. From her father, she will come to know something about the flash that she keeps seeing in her dreams, but the flash she keeps seeing will also represent something she cannot see: the deadly effects of the atomic bomb tests, many of which still remain latent and not fully known even after some thirty years. Williams and her family are "downwinders," and their exposure to radiation from atomic bomb tests in the 1950s has left permanent traces in their bodies and in their family history.

Even after seven female members of her family have died of cancer, Williams cannot know who or when cancer will strike next in her family. What she can do—and what it seems she must do—is witness to the lives of the women in her family who have not survived, and she does so as a writer and, eventually, also as an antinuclear activist. The irony of Williams's testimony is that of the many deaths she must record and work through in *Refuge,* one of them may be her own. In *Refuge,* then, she is not only a witness to the many past deaths that she has seen and known, but she is also a witness to cancer deaths in the future, including perhaps her own, that she cannot fully know from her present vantage point. The ethics of attention that Williams practices in *Refuge,* therefore, is both past and future directed.

Writing Death

I want to turn now to Williams's attempt to witness and capture in writing her mother's death before concluding with an analysis of Williams's emerging politicization as she comes to discover the reasons her family is a "clan of one-breasted women," as the final chapter in *Refuge* describes them. On January 16, 1987, Diane Dixon Tempest dies of ovarian cancer. Williams records the events of this day in what appears in the text as a separate journal entry written three days later. In the text, this rendering of death is in a slightly different typeface than the rest of the book, and it is the only piece of the story that is told by Williams in journal form. It is as if Williams wants to highlight that this event must be recorded in a different form than the rest of the story. And although it is on the one hand intimately connected with everything Williams must tell in *Refuge,* on the other hand it is also somehow not just one more aspect of a larger story, but something impossible to seamlessly integrate into the rest of the story. In fact, as Williams presents it, the story of her mother's death is both an interruption and a continuation of the larger story Williams tells in *Refuge.*

The scene of death as Williams presents it[5] begins with dissension within the family. In a rage over his helplessness in the face of his wife's dying, Williams's father angrily banishes her and her brother from his home after a particularly fraught moment dealing with a malfunction in Diane's morphine drip. Williams admits that she understands her father's rage but cannot immediately forgive him for his selfish behavior. She acknowledges that this is not the ending that she had imagined: "For years, I have imagined being by Mother's side at the moment of her death. I have to let that go—she has taught me there is no one moment of death. It is a process. Besides, she—" (228). Williams doesn't finish this thought, and we are left to wonder what else her mother has taught her daughter about death. We might recall Tempest's comparison of her cancer to the isolation of Siberia, and wonder if this thought that has been left unsaid has something to do with that sense of isolation. As it is, however, what seems important in this unfinished sentence is the performance in the text of a thought that is unsayable. The chasm signaled by the unfinished sentence that begins with "Besides, she—" represents all that is lost in Diane Dixon Tempest's dying.

Williams's journal entry begins with the call from her father that interrupted her attempts to come to terms with a different version of her mother's death than she had imagined. Her father apologizes for his behavior the preceding night and admits that he "cannot save Diane from death or shelter you from seeing it." In relinquishing his desire to be alone with Diane in her last moments, Williams's father must also relinquish his desire to control his wife's dying by controlling who is there to see it. When Williams arrives, she immediately sees something of what her father has wanted to prevent her from seeing: "Walking into her room, I could see death was imminent, and I was surprised to see the physical changes from the night before. Her color had changed—especially around the mouth and nose. Her face was waxen. Her feet were cold. It was as though dying moves from your toes upward" (229). The family is gathered around Diane, and although she is unable to participate in the talk and "even laughter" that goes on around her, Williams notes, "I never doubted her presence" (230). The family takes turns attending to her; they hold her hands, rub her forehead, and moisten her mouth.

As more time passes, however, Williams's father begins to get nervous that his wife "could go on for a few more days, that [the family] had kept vigil too many times." Williams realizes that her father "both wanted to be there when she died and yet he didn't. He was afraid he would not be able to survive it" (230). But also, perhaps, he was afraid *because he would survive it;* he was afraid not only because his wife would die, but also because he would go on living. In her work on trauma, Caruth asserts that trauma "is not simply an effect of destruction but also, fundamentally, an enigma of survival" (1996, 58). Trauma, according to Caruth, is not simply a "crisis of death," but a "crisis of life" as well (7). Williams's father may well wonder why his wife and not he must suffer an early death from cancer. Both, after all, were exposed to radiation from the nuclear tests in the desert, but it seems the traces of that deadly flash of light linger in this family in one gender and not the other. The final words that Williams records between her father and her mother sound like a final wish that he might not have to be there—in every sense of the word—when she dies: "Diane, you may outlast me yet" (230).

Williams's father does leave the house, and, perhaps unconsciously, he relinquishes what will be seen and known about his wife's death to his writer daughter. Williams finds herself alone with her mother, and at that moment, in her rendering of this event, she begins to help her mother to die: "Our eyes met. Death eyes. I looked into them, eyes wide with knowledge, unblinking, objective eyes. Eyes detached from the soul. Eyes turned inward. I moved from the chaise across the room and sat cross-legged on the bed next to her. I took her right hand in mine and whispered, 'Okay, Mother, let's do it'" (230). Williams begins to mirror her mother's breaths, and as they breathe together she notes that they "became one." According to Williams, by breathing with her mother and telling her to "let go," she is midwife to her mother's dying. The rest of the family begins to return to the room and can see that, finally, Diane Dixon Tempest is going to die. Williams describes her mother's last moments as "a crescendo of movement, like walking up a pyramid of light. And it is sexual, the concentration of love, of being fully present. Pure feeling. Pure color. I can feel her spirit rising through the top of her head." She notes as well that her mother's "eyes focus on mine with total joy—a fullness that transcends words" (231). The culminating moment of this perfect death occurs when her father arrives home just in time for his wife to meet his eyes one last time and smile before she dies. What he sees, in the end, according to Williams, is a good, peaceful death.

Williams's rendering of her mother's death is consoling to those in the family who must go on living. However, at the center of this scene is not the dying mother, but the daughter as midwife to her mother's dying and to the story of her mother's dying. Although Williams assures us that her mother left this world with only joy, we do not have her mother's version of her own death to challenge or correct Williams's version. In Williams's consoling version, she refuses the possibility that, in witnessing this traumatic event, she cannot know her mother's experience of it, nor can she break through her mother's isolation and be there with her in her Siberia. What is missing from Williams's account is that which is beyond consolation, an experience that might exceed her control over the story of it. I do not mean to imply that there is a better version of her mother's death than Williams offers, only that Williams's response-ability seems limited by her need to tell a story that offers consolation to herself, to her family, and to her reader. This is a moment in which Williams appears all-knowing and all-seeing, but this official version of her mother's death as full of joy, peace, and even a tinge of romance feels somehow forced to me. The performance of Williams's testimony, however, says more than she knows: it tells her reader about her need for control of her mother's dying through the story of her dying, and about her need to give something to her mother in the end, to be for her mother the refuge that her mother had been for her. It tells us, finally, about the impossibility of the living to bear witness to the absolute aloneness of the dying.

In this narrative of the death of Williams's mother, "the saying," in Oliver's formulation, "challenges the said," and, in doing so, it "*enacts* the impossibility of really ever *having said*" (2001, 87–88): in this particular case, Williams enacts the impossibility of really having said what her mother experiences in dying. In his insightful reading of Williams with and against Annie Dillard, John Tallmadge describes *Refuge* as enacting a "heroics of witness," as Williams "moves through suffering into a new mode of being" (1998, 206). In my reading of *Refuge,* I want to adapt Tallmadge's formulation somewhat, and emphasize not Williams's *heroics,* but her *vigilance,* in witnessing. *Vigilance* is a word that Kelly Oliver returns to again and again in her efforts to describe the process of witnessing and its ethical implications. Although I think it is perhaps true that at times Williams wants to be a heroic witness, what seems most striking to me are the moments when she fails to be heroic, but nonetheless continues to be vigilant. To be vigilant, as Oliver explains, is to be "wakeful and watchful, . . . on the alert, attentively or closely observant" (2001, 134). According to Oliver, vigilance is necessary in order to listen for "the performance beyond meaning and recognition" (133), and it is also necessary to keep open the possibility of further witnessing. As I have noted, Williams's text also implicates the reader in the process of witnessing; the reader, like Williams, is another relay who must carry forward the message deferred by the many deaths that *Refuge* tells.

WRITING MILITANCY *AND* MOURNING

Refuge does not end with the death of Williams's mother, however, nor does it end with the passage through the rituals with which the family mourns its loss. The beautiful death scene in which the entire immediate family surrounds Diane Dixon Tempest's body immediately after her death and celebrates and grieves her passing is replaced by a scene that is clearly beyond Williams's control (231). At the mortuary, her mother's body has become "a carapace, naked, cold, and stiff, on a stainless steel table." Worse even than this sight of her mother's body, is the sight of her mother's face painted orange. Williams asks that the makeup be removed, but is told that doing so will bruise the skin tissues of her mother's face. Williams is adamant, and the mortician eventually gives her a "rag drenched in turpentine" with which she spends an hour wiping her mother's face clean. But when she returns the next morning for the funeral, the morticians have again painted her mother's face orange. Williams is "enraged at our inability to let the dead be dead," and she weeps "over the hollowness of our rituals" (235). The face paint screens death from the eyes of the living, revealing a dread of death and a failure to accept the changes death brings as an essential part of living. The mortician's attempt to hide death underneath a layer of makeup is yet another example of the human need to dominate and defeat that which it does not fully understand: nature, the body, and now death.

Williams substitutes these hollow rituals with a mourning ritual of her own. In keeping with her new knowledge that refuge can be found not only in that which is familiar but also in that which disrupts the familiar, or, in Oliver's terms, that which is "beyond recognition," Williams is able to mourn the loss of her mother not in the place she knows best, but in another place, a place that she does not know very well. She goes to Mexico to celebrate *el Día de los Muertos* among strangers. In a church in the village of Tepotzlán, Williams listens to the prayers offered to the dead, and "slowly [her] individual sorrow was absorbed into a sea of collective tears" (277). She watches as the living become, for a time, the dead, and she listens to the stories of the dead told through the living. In this distant place, in an unfamiliar language, Williams recognizes not the precise meaning of the words, but something beyond an understanding born out of the familiar: "Their stories were not so unlike my own. It was the reverberation of tone I recognized, like a piece of music you return to again and again that awakens the soul. The voices of my Dead came back to me" (278). The performance of these testimonies of the dead say more than the words themselves say. Williams works through her mother's dying in a strange place, in the company of strangers, and in a language she does not know. In this ritual she opens and reopens herself to the possibility of response, and through her openness to that which is unfamiliar, she undergoes a personal transformation within a social space that does not seek to screen death from life.

She returns to the Great Salt Lake to complete her mourning ritual by sprinkling petals from a marigold she has brought back from Mexico into the lake that has finally, seemingly on its own accord, stopped its rise. And yet, what *Refuge* ends with is not mourning but militancy. In an epilogue to the story of personal transformation that *Refuge* tells, Williams signals not the end of the process of personal transformation, but the beginning of the process of political transformation in general and antinuclear activism in particular. "The Clan of One-Breasted Women" stands apart from the rest of the book as the only chapter whose title is not the name of a bird and does not include the current lake level that has linked the telling of Williams's personal narrative of despair to the changes in the landscape as signified in the "shorthand of lake levels" (7). Williams begins her epilogue by offering a part of her family history that has been, up until this point, only hinted at:

> My mother, my grandmother, and six aunts have all had mastectomies. Seven are dead. The two who survive have just completed rounds of chemotherapy and radiation.
>
> I've had my own problems: two biopsies for breast cancer and a small tumor between my ribs diagnosed as a "borderline malignancy." (281)

The somewhat oblique earlier references to the nuclear tests conducted by the U.S. government in the southwestern desert become explicit in the epilogue. At this point in the story, Williams begins to view her mother's dying not only in terms of personal loss, but also in terms of political outrage at the silence and accommodation surrounding a particular period of American history when "we bombed Utah" (203), and nothing was allowed to interfere with this series of tests, including concerns about public health.

For Williams, the movement from accommodation to politicization is a movement against Mormon teachings and even against the stoicism of the women in her family, most of whom have not survived despite their stoicism. She recalls a conversation between her mother and grandmother, which she accidentally overheard when she picked up the telephone on February 17, 1971, the eve of her mother's first surgery for cancer. Her mother asks her grandmother what she could expect from cancer, and her grandmother, who has had a similar experience, tells her, "Diane, it is one of the most spiritual experiences you will ever encounter" (282). The conversation that she chanced to overhear says more to her now than it did then. That conversation tells her after so many years and so many deaths that, although cancer may well be a spiritual experience that links the women in her family, it is also an experience that they didn't have to have and that must not simply be accommodated through spiritualization. Williams realizes that these cancers must also be confronted through politicization. In the end, then, both politicization *and* spiritualization, both militancy *and* mourning, must become part of the witnessing ethics that *Refuge* performs.

I take the phrase "militancy and mourning" from Douglas Crimp's well-known essay on the gay community's response to the AIDS crisis. I have intentionally reversed the order of the words in the title of Crimp's essay to highlight the somewhat different trajectory that Williams describes in *Refuge.* In his essay, Crimp is concerned not by the lack of politicized response to AIDS, but rather with the fact that, for many gay men facing AIDS, mourning had become a process that was not respected, but viewed with suspicion (1989, 5). Crimp wonders what might be some of the "unconscious effects" of replacing mourning with militancy (9). He encourages his fellow AIDS activists to "fight the unspeakable violence we incur from the society in which we find ourselves," but also to acknowledge the "psychic mechanisms that make us a part of this society," and that include, in the case of gay men who are HIV positive and those who are not, "our terror, our grief, and our profound sadness" (18). In using this piece as a framework through which to read *Refuge,* I mean to highlight the ways that illnesses, such as AIDS and cancer (particularly cancer caused by radiation from nuclear tests conducted by the U.S. government), require both affective and effective responses, that is, responses that are attentive both to the rhetoric and practices of politics as well as to the poetics and practices of suffering.

The refuge that Williams eventually finds is not only in her relationships to family and place, but also in something less tangible, but no less essential: the power to think otherwise, to challenge those in authority, and to vigilantly practice a witnessing ethics that incorporates militancy and mourning. Williams admits there is much she does not know and cannot prove about the deaths of her mother, grandmothers, and aunts. And she acknowledges as well that "[t]he more I learn about what it means to be a 'down-winder,' the more questions I drown in." But it isn't only the questions or the not knowing that she must confront, but "blind obedience": "What I do know, however, is that as a Mormon woman of the fifth generation of Latter-day Saints, I must question everything, even if it means losing my faith, even if it means becoming a member of a border tribe among my own people. Tolerating blind obedience in the name of patriotism or religion ultimately takes our lives" (286). What Williams has learned in the course of *Refuge* is what Mary Oliver's poem pointed toward at its outset. Her witnessing ethics is not about being good or falling to her knees in the face of the powerful institutions of religion and nation, but about questioning everything. As a member of her newly born border tribe, Williams will perform rituals not, or not only, of mourning, but of militancy. *Refuge* ends with her arrest, along with a group of women, "for trespassing on military lands" (289). When an officer discovers a pen and pad of paper tucked in her boot, she tells the officer that they are "weapons" (290). She has used these weapons to write of mourning the deaths of her mother and grandmother, but her witnessing does not end there. In fact, as the mourning becomes militancy, her witnessing to her mother's death becomes only the beginning of this story of transformation.

Notes

1. Audre Lorde, another poet-activist, calls for "the transformation of silence into language and action" (1984, 42).

2. The idea of a "cancer personality" is one of the things that Sontag seeks to challenge in her work. For further opposition to the idea of the "cancer personality," see also Lorde 1980 and Stacey 1997.

3. This is Diane Dixon Tempest's second cancer. In 1971, she had breast cancer, from which she recovered fully. Williams acknowledges that the family had not really been there for her the first time. She notes, "Twelve years ago, we had been too young to see beyond our own pain; children of four, eight, twelve, and fifteen. Dad was thirty-seven, in shock from the thought of losing his wife. We did not do well. She did. Things were different now. We would do it together. We made promises that we would be here for her this time, that she would not have to carry us" (28). In *Refuge*, Williams shows the family pulling together to support their wife and mother, but she also reveals occasions where it is still impossible for them to see beyond their own pain. I will show the ways that, in her account of her mother's actual death, Williams takes very seriously the notion that they (she and her mother in particular) "would do it together" and her need to carry her mother through the difficulty of dying.

4. This is what Sontag seems to lose sight of in her work: that patients themselves

make use of certain metaphors in order to make their experience of cancer communicable to others, and thus, on some levels, more under control.

5. Although it may seem awkward to continually remind my reader that Williams is *representing* her mother's death and that we are not getting death unmediated, the question of how we represent death is crucial to me. Williams's representation of her mother's death, as I will show, performs a particular function for her and her family.

Works Cited

Caruth, Cathy. 1995. *Trauma: Explorations in Memory*. Baltimore: Johns Hopkins University Press.

———. 1996. *Unclaimed Experience: Trauma, Narrative, and History*. Baltimore: Johns Hopkins University Press.

Chambers, Ross. 1998. *Facing It: AIDS Diaries and the Death of the Author*. Ann Arbor: University of Michigan Press.

Crimp, Douglas. 1989. "Mourning and Militancy." *October* 51:3–18.

Felman, Shoshana, and Dori Laub. 1992. *Testimony: Crises of Witnessing in Literature, Psychoanalysis, and History*. New York: Routledge.

Frank, Arthur W. 1995. *The Wounded Storyteller: Body, Illness, and Ethics*. Chicago: University of Chicago Press.

Lorde, Audre. 1980. *The Cancer Journals*. San Francisco: Aunt Lute.

———. 1984. *Sister Outsider: Essays and Speeches*. Trumansburg, N.Y.: Crossing Press.

Oliver, Kelly. 2000. "Beyond Recognition: Witnessing Ethics." *Philosophy Today* (spring):31–42.

———. 2001. *Witnessing: Beyond Recognition*. Minneapolis: University of Minnesota Press.

Sontag, Susan. 1978. *Illness As Metaphor*. New York: Farrar, Straus, and Giroux.

———. 1988. *AIDS and Its Metaphors*. London: Penguin Books.

Stacey, Jackie. 1997. *Teratologies: A Cultural Study of Cancer*. New York and London: Routledge.

Tallmadge, John. 1998. "Beyond the Excursion: Initiatory Themes in Annie Dillard and Terry Tempest Williams." In *Reading the Earth: New Directions in the Study of Literature and the Environment,* edited by Michael P. Branch, Rochelle Johnson, Daniel Patterson, and Scott Slovic, 197–207. Moscow: University of Idaho Press.

Williams, Terry Tempest. 1991. *Refuge: An Unnatural History of Family and Place*. New York: Pantheon Books.

Zizek, Slavoj. 1991. *Looking Awry: An Introduction to Jacques Lacan through Popular Culture*. Cambridge: MIT Press.

TINA RICHARDSON

ᴓ

Corporeal Testimony

COUNTING THE BODIES IN *REFUGE:*
AN UNNATURAL HISTORY OF FAMILY AND PLACE

> What qualifies as bodies that matter, ways of living that count as "life,"
> lives worth protecting, lives worth saving, lives worth grieving?
> —Judith Butler, *Bodies That Matter*

Forty-five thousand American women will die of breast cancer this year (Gould 1996). The following year that number will most likely increase. Acceptable levels of carcinogenic contamination and exposure are established by determining the amount toxic to a 150-pound male body (Finucane and Slovic 1999). In a society that refuses to acknowledge the not-so-hidden costs of toxic polluting practices, this standard for determining "safe" levels of toxic emission (as if such a thing exists) reflects the privilege of one group while ignoring a mounting body count of those whose embodied lives locate them outside the gendered pale of privilege and protection.[1]

In an attempt to cope with the horrific consequences of breast cancer, women, who, prior to their diagnosis or the diagnosis of someone close to them, had never thought of themselves as writers, have created a vast library of breast cancer narratives. In *A Darker Ribbon: Breast Cancer, Women, and Their Doctors in the Twentieth Century* (1999), a very important social history of breast cancer, author Ellen Leopold maps some of the literary territory of this literature. According to Leopold, the two emerging genres of breast cancer literature, personal narratives and self-help manuals, "share one critical attribute: a complete disregard for the determining influences of society and culture" (4). Taking this observation one step further in a specific discussion of personal narratives Leopold continues, they "have been more acceptable, not just because they provide immediate comfort to the newly diagnosed woman but also because they pose no challenge to the status quo" (4–5). Although this may be true of much breast cancer literature, it is certainly not true of Terry Tempest Williams's *Refuge* (1991), a text that, because of its sustained rhetorical engagement with breast cancer as a social justice, and even an environmental justice, issue, certainly belongs within this genre. That difference is significant and one of the most important contributions the book makes as either nature writing (where it is most commonly considered) or breast cancer literature.

Williams unfolds the drama of her narrative in the complete title of the book: *Refuge: An Unnatural History of Family and Place.* Using the familiar literary conventions of natural history discourses to discuss the flooding of the Great Salt Lake and the consequential loss of the Bear River Migratory Bird Refuge, Williams critically examines an unnatural phenomenon—the high occurrence of cancer, particularly breast cancer, within her family, community, and, by implication, our world. Weaving her observations of the natural world into a thought-provoking tapestry of social commentary emerging from the deeply personal experience of her mother's death from ovarian cancer, Williams uses personal narrative to create a unique space from which to investigate the various ways patriarchal ideology and its practices are inscribed on the bodies of women.

Unlike what Leopold accurately identifies in many other breast cancer narratives as an absent challenge to the status quo, *Refuge* unravels the threads of cultural practice that form our social fabric to reveal the naturalized power structures that ensure social privilege through such determining factors as race, gender, and economic status. In Williams's narrative, the commonly occurring mutilations of women's bodies and the increasing loss of women's lives testify to a careless disregard for the environment and a willful ignorance of the interconnectedness of natural systems. Williams presents her critique through an examination of the material connection between aboveground nuclear testing and breast cancer. "I cannot prove that my mother, Diane Dixon Tempest, or my grandmothers, Lettie Romney Dixon and Kathryn Blackett Tempest, along with my aunts developed cancer from nuclear fallout in Utah. But I can't prove they didn't" (286). Upon whose shoulders should the burden of proof fall: those who are responsible for the creation and maintenance of polluting industries and practices and, within our economic structure, profit from them, or those who are made to suffer, even die, from the unexamined consequences of the production of such contamination? In writing *Refuge,* Williams not only asks this question: she also answers it.

As a nature writer, Williams applies her skills of observation to create narratives that, with accuracy and insight, bring to presence the natural world; in *Refuge,* she applies those same skills of observation, with equal accuracy and insight, to bring to presence crimes perpetrated against an unaware citizenry. Firsthand observations are the stock-in-trade of nature writers. In writing *Refuge,* Williams adheres to the conventions of the genre within which she has established her writing career.[2] In structure, methodology, application, and, to a certain extent, content, this is nature writing, yet throughout the narrative Williams includes observations connecting breast cancer and environmental contamination. By adding the epilogue, "The Clan of One-Breasted Women," Williams clearly articulates the project of her book. Her strategy reflects emphasis, reiteration, and importance. The final image Williams leaves with her readers is that of a woman (de)formed as a consequence of culturally sanctioned practices. Her narrative is an attempt to (re)form the way such practices are viewed. In this way, Williams is engaged in a cultural critique—unfortunately, one that is too often ignored in the scholarship surrounding the book.

Williams's inquiry originates with the U.S. government's practice of aboveground nuclear testing at the Nevada Test Site between January 27, 1951, and July 11, 1962. Using this as the historical moment that informs the cultural critique of the narrative, Williams's text is thoughtfully constructed to function upon a number of levels as acts of subtle subversion—her words serve as chisels upon the monolith of patriarchal social organization. In this way, the narrative reveals connections between male power (represented as male genitalia); male privilege, perspective, and arrogance; the practice of colonization; and the production and use of nuclear weapons.

Penning these connections, Williams relates a visit she and her mother make to the "newly erected 'Tree of Utah.'" She observes that "the man-made tree rose from the salt flats like a small phallus dwarfed by the open space that surrounded it." They are stunned by the ignorance of an artist who considered the desert empty, monotonous space. "With the light of morning," Williams writes, "it cast a shadow across the salt flats like a mushroom cloud" (127).

Through this series of observations, Williams points out that a male, possessive gaze results in an absurd erection of artifice into a natural landscape, an act reflecting a lack of knowledge, understanding, and appreciation of that which is being altered. This ignorance of the natural world results in destructive practices. The shadow the tree casts represents aboveground atomic testing in the Nevada desert and the exposure of unaware citizens to nuclear radiation. Investigating the high cost of living near nuclear reactors, in his book *The Enemy Within,* scientist Jay Gould also discusses the high cost of living downwind of the Nevada Test Site: "[W]omen living in about 1,300 'nuclear' counties (located within 100 miles of a reactor and most directly exposed to man-made ionizing radiation) are at the greatest risk of dying of breast cancer. The largest source of such radiation since 1945 has been fallout from U.S./U.S.S.R. above-ground nuclear weapons testing" (1996, 16–17).

Building this critique through her own firsthand observations, Williams articulates what Biddy Martin and Chandra Mohanty have identified as "the underside of [paternal] protection" (1986, 204), revealed here through military "defense" practices. Late in the narrative, Williams reinforces her position by including a conversation with her father; however, in doing so, she raises additional issues: "A little over a year after Mother's death, Dad and I were having dinner together. He had just returned from St. George, where the Tempest Company was completing the gas lines that would service southern Utah" (282). Through the inclusion of this statement, Williams points out one of the tensions between the woman she has become (a liberal environmentalist) and the position she was born into (the privileged daughter of a white, upper-middle-class family). She also points to the exploitation of the environment for economic gain and her own complicity in that process. Writing her position as her father's daughter into the narrative, Williams acknowledges the economic advantages that position has provided her and the means by which those advantages were (and are) obtained. As the conversation continues in the narrative, what gets articulated is "her difference from her father [and] her rejection of his positions" (Martin and Mohanty 1986, 203). "Over dessert I shared a recurring dream of mine. I told my father that for years, as long as I could remember, I saw this flash of light in the night in the desert" (282). His reply is as shocking to Williams's readers as it is to Williams herself: she did see the bomb, the cloud, "a common occurrence in the fifties" (283). The presence of Williams's father at this point in the narrative is no rhetorical accident. As a patriarchal authority figure, John Henry Tempest III lends credibility to Williams's observation by providing uncontestable corroboration for the historical event(s) at the core of her cultural critique; these observations are not the imaginings of a hysterical female. Because Williams's knowledge comes to her through a dream, or, if you will, an alternative way of knowing, her father's presence as a "legitimate" witness is even more necessary. It is also relevant that this conversation is the final revelation in the book before Williams begins the epilogue. The proximity of these two rhetorical events within the narrative demands that readers examine the relationship between military defense practices and breast cancer.

In order to prepare readers to accept these connections, Williams first develops connections between the natural world and women's bodies. In a passage that has been read by some as "essentialist," Williams illustrates her ability to indict powerful cultural practices by reclaiming the female body and its reflection in nature by rejecting definitions emerging from a male gaze and supplying an alternate vision. The move illustrates the objectives that accompany a male gaze: dominance, possession, exploitation, colonization. An essentialist reading of the passage, advanced by both male and female literary critics, illustrates how deeply such objectives are etched upon the collective cultural consciousness of our society. Scientist and social theorist Donna Haraway states that "[f]eminists have to insist on a better account of the world" (1991, 187). In writing *Refuge*, Williams provides one:

> There are dunes beyond Fish Springs. Secrets hidden from interstate travelers. They are the armatures of animals. Wind swirls around the sand and ribs appear. There is musculature in dunes.
>
> And they are female. Sensuous curves—the small of a woman's back. Breasts. Buttocks. Hips and pelvis. They are the natural shape of the earth. (109)

In her work, Haraway "argue[s] for a doctrine and practice of objectivity that privileges contestation, deconstruction, passionate construction, webbed connections, and hope for transformation of systems of knowledge and ways of seeing" (1991, 191–92). In the above passage, Williams transforms a foundational system of knowledge by offering a new creation story. In contrast to the biblical narrative of Genesis, Williams's (re)vision has no man from whom God takes a rib to form woman, nor does she provide a God; instead, ribs appear from the earth through natural forces, and around these female ribs "there is musculature." It is precisely that musculature that is missing from a woman's body after a radical mastectomy.

In *Patient No More: The Politics of Breast Cancer*, Sharon Batt states that radical mastectomies were "the standard operation for breast cancer throughout North America and enjoyed this privileged status until the 1970s" (1994, 58). Williams has seen a woman's body that is natural as well as degrees of the unnatural. By looking at nature, Williams points to what is natural—musculature and curves—and juxtaposes it against the female bodies she has known all her life:

> As a child, I was aware that my grandmother, Lettie, had only one breast. It was not a shocking sight. It was her body.
> . . . Seeing Mother's scar did not surprise me either. It was not radical like

her mother's. Her skin was stretched smooth and taut across her chest, with the muscles intact. (97–98)

Williams's discernment of the shape of women's bodies in nature is not essentialist, a mere equating of a heterosexual signifier of womanhood to the moving shapes of the land. Instead, it is what Haraway describes as "politics and epistemologies of location [and] positioning, where partiality and not universality is the condition for being heard" (1991, 195). Williams's position, the partiality of her perspective, points to one crime after another perpetrated upon female bodies: from an imposed valuation of worth to the cause of breast cancer and the inscription of its treatment. Williams points to what is lost from women's bodies by showing what is present in the dunes of the desert and asking readers to acknowledge the connection. Batt provides another discussion of that loss:

> The super-radical mastectomy, commonly known as the Halsted, was introduced in the U.S. in the 1890s by William Halsted, a prominent professor of surgery at Johns Hopkins University. Halsted began his incision at the shoulder and removed not just the breast but the muscles of the chest wall, lymph glands, and all the fat under the skin. The Halsted leaves the woman with a sunken chest, restricted movement on one side of her body and, frequently, a painful chronic condition called 'milk arm,' caused when lymph fluid fails to circulate properly and accumulates in the arms. Capacity to breastfeed and derive sexual pleasure are, of course, lost from that side of the body. (1994, 58)

For nearly a century in the history of breast cancer treatment, these were acceptable losses: losses not only of flesh, but also of erotic pleasure, identity, and belonging. According to George Crile Jr.—a surgical oncologist who came out in strong opposition to this procedure in the 1960s—"Halsted's radical mastectomy seems to have been designed to inflict the maximal possible deformity, disfiguration, and disability" (1973, 38). Granting that the surgeons performing these operations were motivated by a desire to save lives, one wonders at the lack of motivation to discover and implement alternative procedures. The scientific reasoning that supported the Halsted procedure was disproved in multiple international studies many years prior to a change in practice in the United States.[3]

Williams takes up the issue of breast cancer treatment metaphorically in her discussion of the proposed pumping project to halt the flooding of the Great Salt Lake. She describes the proposal as invasive, scientifically ungrounded, and ultimately ridiculous: it comes with a huge price tag. In the hands of patriarchal power structures, the echo of sameness in the treatment of women and the environment is deafening.

Ultimately, between the generations of her grandmother and mother, the Halsted procedure was (thankfully) buried. But Batt illustrates what was at stake: "[F]or women . . . the Halsted dramatically illustrates the folly of trusting too much in authority" (1994, 68). Male-led governments, male health professionals, male spiritual leaders, male-embodied military and industrial apparatuses all claim a paternal care and objectivity while simultaneously poisoning and mutilating the bodies of women and refusing to consider alternatives or alternative perspectives. On this issue, Williams affirms her need to question everything, arguing, "Tolerating blind obedience in the name of patriotism or religion ultimately takes our lives. . . . [T]he price of obedience is too high" (286). Gould's position is equally clear: "[T]he true health effects of ingesting man-made fission products have been withheld from the public for nearly half a century. . . . [I]t has become a matter of life and death for all of us—breast cancer victims particularly—to learn all we can about how ingested fission products do their damage, and how we can protect ourselves. To do this we must first learn how officials lie to us" (1996, 28–29). That American citizens are being lied to is not in question. What occurred, and continues to occur, simply needs to be revealed, and, perhaps, most important, believed.

To illustrate the often futile search for hidden truths, Williams shares the story of Blackie, her mother's childhood dog. Run over by a car and killed, Blackie was buried before Williams's mother had a chance to say good-bye. The story relates her mother's need (as a child) to see and touch his buried body: "I remember sneaking out of the house in my nightgown, trying to find the place where they had buried my black lab. I found the disturbed soil, knelt on the damp grass and began digging with my bare hands to uncover him. I wanted to see his broken body. I wanted to cradle his bones and see for myself that he was dead. I wanted to cry over the death of my dog. But the hole was too deep and I never found him" (154). By including this story, Williams illustrates that her mother was never able to dig deep enough to find the buried evidence: in writing *Refuge,* Williams does. She digs deep into the complex connections between women's cancers and cultural practice. As readers, we bear the responsibility to dig deep within ourselves to understand those connections. We must examine the control of knowledge by interests of power that her testimony uncovers by viewing it from a different perspective. We must also be prepared to accept the insights her narrative reveals.

In typical minimalist fashion, Williams clearly names cancer as a metaphor for patriarchal power systems. She uses the abject experience of her grandmother giving birth to a tumor to name patriarchy as a disease within humanity manifesting itself in individual bodies:

> "She had felt labor pains all night long," my cousin Lynne explained. "And then in the middle of the night, she gave birth to a tumor. She reached into the toilet bowl, pulled out the bloody mass and set it in the sink. She walked into the kitchen, opened the cupboard, returned with a plastic bag, and placed the tumor inside it, ziplocked it shut, put it in the refrigerator and went back to sleep. The next morning Mimi called the doctor." (244–45)

Later, when Williams discusses these events with her grandmother, Mimi tells her: "I let go of my conditioning. . . . [W]hen I looked into the water closet and saw what my body had expelled, the first thought that came to my mind was 'Finally, I am rid of the orthodoxy.' My advice to you, dear, is to do it consciously" (246). If what Mimi is rid of is orthodoxy and if what she expelled is a cancerous tumor, then orthodoxy is cancer, a cultural disease just like its physical manifestation destroying bodies—both material and political— from the inside out. Williams's inclusion of Mimi's experience suggests *we* must let go of our cultural conditioning, the socially constructed ways of being and knowing we unconsciously perform and practice in our everyday lives. Rather than accepting this imposed construction of our world and internalizing its poison, Mimi asks us to abort it consciously: she asks us to abort patriarchal social dominance and its value of power and profit over life.

Williams's presentations of bodies reveal the "secrets hidden from [the] interstate travelers" (109) of life. She digs deep into the social construction of American society to expose the connections between patriarchal power systems and the multilayered exploitation, abuse, and neglect of both women and the environment and the connection between the two.

Through her firsthand observations of family and place, *Refuge* becomes a field guide to cancer, complete with unforgettable images of radical mastectomies, mastectomies, biopsies, tumors, and, ultimately, dead bodies. As readers of her nature writing, we enter an implicit contract to trust her observations of the natural world. If we trust her observations as she notes the level of the lake and the habits of birds, and if she presents alongside those observations others that note the practices of our culture and their consequences, then have we not also entered an implicit contract to trust those observations as well? If we do trust her observational skills when applied to both nature and culture equally, then why do those observations regarding the natural world achieve prominence (in conversation and criticism) while her observations regarding social structures and practices are only (at best) superficially acknowledged? What elements of cultural conditioning are in operation during our reading of *Refuge*? In part, readers are led to understand *Refuge* through the literary categories in which Williams's book is located: most commonly, "Women's Studies" or "Nature Writing." This categorization artificially imposes restrictions regarding who will constitute the audience of the book and limits the impact of the critique in which Williams is engaged. As important as it may be to read *Refuge* with a copy of the *North American Field Guide to Birds* by your side (as one of my colleagues has suggested),[4] it is equally—or even more—important to have a material understanding of the environmental justice and public health issues Williams's narrative inserts into environmental discourse.

In the time it has taken to read this essay, two women have died of breast cancer and eight have been newly diagnosed with the disease.[5] To disclose the hidden costs of toxic, polluting practices, I am suggesting we take a particular type of nature writing seriously—nature writing that challenges the genre and disrupts its conventions by engaging in a gendered cultural critique of human interaction with the environment and the heavy toll we are all forced to pay as consequence: there is a body count.

Notes

1. Obviously, children of both sexes are also at risk within this formulation.

2. Although I disagree with her conclusion, Cheryll Glotfelty provides a solid discussion of Williams's use of nature writing conventions in her article "Flooding the Boundaries of Form: Terry Tempest Williams's Ecofeminist *Unnatural History*," in *Change in the American West: Exploring the Human Dimension*, edited by Stephen Tchudi (Reno: University of Nevada Press, 1996), 158–67.

3. See Batt 1994 for a further discussion of these studies.

4. Laird Christenson, "Reading and Writing the Bioregion" (paper presented at the Taking Nature Seriously Conference, Eugene, Oreg., February 2001).

5. This year, breast cancer will be newly diagnosed every three minutes, and a woman will die from breast cancer every twelve minutes. Statistics from the Women's Action Coalition's booklet, *The Facts about Women* (New York: New Press, 1993).

Works Cited

Batt, Sharon. 1994. *Patient No More: The Politics of Breast Cancer.* Charlottetown, Canada: Gynergy Books.

Butler, Judith. 1991. *Bodies That Matter.* New York: Routledge.

Crile, George. 1973. *What Every Woman Should Know about the Breast Cancer Controversy.* New York: Macmillan.

Finucane, Melissa, and Paul Slovic. 1999. "Risk and the White Male: A Perspective on Perspectives." Decision Research Report no. 98–11. Decision Research, 1201 Oak Street, Eugene, Oreg., 97401.

Gould, Jay M., with members of the Radiation and Public Health Project: Ernest J. Sternglass, Joseph J. Mangano, and William McDonnell. 1996. *The Enemy Within: The High Cost of Living near Nuclear Reactors: Breast Cancer, AIDS, Low Birthweights, and Other Radiation-Induced Immune Deficiency Effects.* New York: Four Walls Eight Windows.

Haraway, Donna J. 1991. "Situated Knowledges: The Science Question in Feminism and the Privilege of Partial Perspective." In *Simians, Cyborgs, and Women: The Reinvention of Nature,* 183–201. New York: Routledge.

Leopold, Ellen. 1999. *A Darker Ribbon: Breast Cancer, Women, and Their Doctors in the Twentieth Century.* Boston: Beacon Press.

Martin, Biddy, and Chandra Mohanty. 1986. "Feminist Politics: What's Home Got to Do with It?" In *Feminist Studies: Critical Studies,* 191–212. Bloomington: Indiana University Press.

Williams, Terry Tempest. 1991. *Refuge: An Unnatural History of Family and Place.* New York: Pantheon Books.

KARL ZUELKE

༄

The Ecopolitical Space of *Refuge*

In her definition of ecocriticism, Cheryll Glotfelty notes that literary criticism, in general, examines the relations among writers, text, and the world, and that "the world" in most literary theory is synonymous with society—the social sphere. But ecocriticism "expands the notion of 'the world' to include the entire ecosphere" (1996, xix). In terms set down by the political philosopher Hannah Arendt, writers and critics concerned with human ecology endeavor to reintegrate the ecosphere into the "political space," or polity, that characterizes much of the social sphere. While there has been movement recently to establish a philosophical foundation that provides for the rights of nature, Western society, on the whole, does not conceive of nature as a political entity, and this has had far-reaching consequences. Terry Tempest Williams examines some of these consequences in an intriguing way in *Refuge: An Unnatural History of Family and Place.*

Hannah Arendt's thinking may seem an unusual vantage from which to discuss *Refuge*. Arendt devoted most of her energy to an understanding of human politics in an attempt to come to terms with the frightening actualities of the twentieth century. *Refuge*, in its celebration of family and the natural world, is deeply life-affirming; Arendt, by contrast, was compelled by some of the horrors of twentieth-century history, especially the Holocaust, to examine what might be termed extreme "life-denying" events to which, she admits, "we cannot reconcile ourselves" (1994, 14). But I believe that Arendt's philosophy is relevant to an understanding of *Refuge* in two important ways. Most important is that her concept of the political space, and the consequences of exclusion from the political space, has profound ecological implications, once we take the step of recognizing the natural world as having "personhood" with a voice that merits political recognition. The other important aspect of Arendtian philosophy is the resonance of her ideas on identity with feminism and ecology.

The recognition of nature's personhood and speaking presence is characteristic of humankind's original stance toward nature, but it is a conception that would appear absurd to conventional Western thinking. A number of contemporary writers are engaged in a tradition that acknowledges nature as an entity, however. In *The Spell of the Sensuous*, for example, David Abram examines the "psychological latency" (1996, 193) of the enveloping landscape, and he points out numerous residual linguistic cues embedded in our language that show how Western peoples once communicated with the speaking presence of an inspirited nature in ways that mirror the awareness of indigenous peoples. From a less theoretical standpoint, Barry Lopez writes that our obligation, when confronted with an unfamiliar landscape, is to be alert for that moment "when something sacred reveals itself within the mundane, and you know the land knows you are there" (1986, 228).

Refuge clearly develops this awareness of nature's person, coming as it does from a writer for whom birds and landscape assume a defining importance. "The birds and I share a natural history," Williams writes. "It is a matter of rootedness, of living inside a place for so long that the mind and imagination fuse" (1991, 21). The fusing of mind, imagination, and landscape is pushed in the text to a point that allows a direct declaration: "I am desert. I am mountains. I am Great Salt Lake. There are other languages being spoken by wind, water, and wings. There are other lives to consider: avocets, stilts, and stones" (29). The fusing of the speaking presence of the author with the surrounding landscape confers upon the landscape attributes of the speaking person, which, in this passage, is immediately confirmed by the recognition of languages being spoken by wind, water, and wings. Nature's person is established because it speaks. It follows that nature's speaking presence merits membership identity in a political realm, what we might term an "ecopolitical space."

Refuge is deeply concerned with nature's inclusion in the political realm, but the role of women in the political is also very much at issue in Williams's text. The implications of the concept of political space for feminism seem clear, in that women have historically been excluded from full participation in the political. In order to justify this, women have often been labeled en masse by patriarchal forces—as less intelligent, as essentially closer to nature—in ways that parallel race-thinking, class-thinking, and other means of stereotyping groups of people.

Interestingly, Arendt herself was impatient with the feminism that arose during her lifetime, dismissing it as "merely another (mass) movement or ideology. She believed strongly that feminism's concerns with gender identity, sexuality, and the body were politically inappropriate" (Honig 1995, 1). Arendt was excoriated by early feminists for this reason, most famously by Adrienne Rich who called Arendt's *Human Condition* "a lofty and crippled book" that embodied "the tragedy of a female mind nourished on male ideology" (1979, 211–12). Bonnie Honig notes, however, that feminism, and feminist response to Arendt, has changed. Shaped by new multicultural and postcolonial contexts, recent work challenges older, dichotomizing approaches to feminist theory.

Although a full discussion of feminist response to Arendt is beyond the scope of this essay, it is important to note that the evolution of feminist theory over the past thirty years has enabled a new set of feminist engagements with Arendt's work that is quite different from its predecessors. Honig maintains that from recent feminist perspectives that "interrogate, politicize, and historicize—rather than simply redeploy—categories like 'woman,' 'identity,' or 'experience,' Arendt's hostility to feminism and her critical stance toward identitarian and essentialist definitions of 'woman' begin to look more like an advantage than a liability" (1995, 2). Feminists have developed a renewed engagement with Arendt's political philosophy based on more complex conceptions of gender and identity, and this in turn enables an application of Arendt's political philosophy to the ecofeminist *Refuge*, especially since Arendt's thinking about the formation of individual identity within political systems may help reconcile several reservations that some feminist critics hold toward *Refuge*.

Identity issues have caused some negative criticism to be leveled at *Refuge* due to its seemingly essentialist characteristics. *Refuge* is multifaceted and complex, part nature writing, part memoir of personal tragedy, but it is also a statement of the politics of ecological feminism positioned in reaction to the life-denying power of oppressive, patriarchal military, medical, and political systems. To this end, the text often expresses outrage, which is mostly directed at male-dominated political systems, and the rage is also sometimes directed toward men and male patterns of thinking. Because male-dominated systems are responsible for painful environmental depredations that the author feels intensely, the linking of a female-nature linkage against a male-culture linkage arises as a dominant motif, with women and nature linked in ways that sometimes seem essentialist.

Essentialism, according to Janice Birkeland, results from a patriarchal way of thinking that presupposes the legitimacy of constructs that separate nature from culture (1993, 22). Seeing it manifest in the text of *Refuge,* Cassandra Kircher criticizes the "confrontational, linear dichotomies" of *Refuge* that situate a female-nature linkage in opposition to the male-culture linkage. Kircher pronounces *Refuge* "slippery"—"so slippery that many readers, especially ecofeminists committed to exposing the negative implication of linking women with nature, may be tempted to dismiss the book" (1996, 111).

Williams's establishment of the person of nature takes place in a genderless context. But Williams also tells the reader at one point, "I want to see the lake as Woman, as myself, in her refusal to be tamed" (92). When the narrator invokes gender or compares the shapes of desert sand dunes to the female human body (109), any reader concerned with ecofeminist issues might reasonably find objections to Williams's essentialist connection of the female with nature.

In her discussion of Susan Griffin's *Woman and Nature,* another text criticized by some feminists for its essentialist tendencies, Elizabeth Carlassare asks if there might be a legitimate purpose in constructing a text that refers to essentialist tropes: "Can Griffin's text be interpreted as an instance of deploying essentialism strategically as a form of resistance? Furthermore, is it possible to read constructionism within Griffin's use of an 'essential' connection between women and nature?" (1994, 224).

The problem with essentialism, as Carlassare's questions of it imply, is that when it is conceived as being truly "essential"—that is, if its critics are "guilty of resorting to an essentialist notion of essentialism" (Carlassare 1994, 226)—its utility as a tool that perpetuates the superiority of culturally dominant groups becomes manifest, and questions arise regarding its political motives and the objectivity of claims supporting it. If, however, we regard essentialism as a deliberate strategy, a rhetorical stance arising from a specific situation, what we might term a "constructed essentialism," then the potential for "seizing and reconstructing the gender category 'woman' for the sake of empowering women" arises (Carlassare 1994, 225).

Essentialism should always be regarded as a cultural construct that serves a specific agenda. Were Williams's essentialist tendencies to be read as an unconscious internalization of the patriarchal dominant paradigm's misogynist conception of women, then *Refuge* might be deservedly criticized for unwittingly perpetuating stereotypes that function to marginalize women. If, on the other hand, her essentialist strategy is read as a self-conscious rhetorical ploy with the political objective of reimagining the categories of "woman" and "nature" in order to subvert the dominant patriarchal culture's demeaning notions of them, then the criticism of essentialism based on the idea that it is truly essential doesn't apply. Women are connected to nature not on the basis of shared characteristics but on the grounds of their analogous position in regards to patriarchal power. A constructed essentialism serves only to underscore the similarities, and the connection of women to nature becomes potentially empowering, especially in light of some of the catastrophic failures of patriarchy to which *Refuge* also calls attention.

Karla Armbruster raises the same point about the analogous positions of women and nature in her discussion of *Refuge*. Position, Armbruster maintains (as opposed to essence), takes on significance in the text. Williams tells the reader that the events of her mother's death and the flooding of the bird refuge put her into "retreat"—in other words, her identity in connection with nature had been at least partially forced upon her by events that prompted an emotional separation from the cultural and political realm. As Armbruster maintains, "In representing her own relationship to nature as constructed, shifting, and variegated, Williams foregrounds a poststructuralist sense of subjectivity that incorporates yet goes beyond simple essentialism" (1995, 213).

Hannah Arendt proposes an understanding of identity that is also distinctly poststructuralist in character because it is so inextricably linked to relationships with others. According to Arendt, the identity we put forth, which leads to the relationships we form, depends on the characteristics of "speech" and "action," which, she maintains, "are the modes in which human beings appear to each other, not indeed as physical objects, but *qua* men" (1958, 176). Arendt also maintains that life without speech and action is not possible; it "is literally dead to the world" (176). Thus, she sees *word* and *deed* as the means whereby "we insert ourselves into the human world, and this insertion is like a second birth, in which we confirm and take upon ourselves the naked fact of our original physical appearance" (176–77).

There arises as a component of the human condition an emergent mode of being, then, that defines us as human and that is as necessary to our overall being as the facts of our bodies. It is an extension of our physical body but also a transcendence of it. We enter into it as if by a "second birth," and it is within this secondary realm that we function as humans. It is here that we assert our identity through the formation of stories, manifestations of the combination of word and deed—action disclosed through speech. This secondary realm of being, unlike the primary physical, however, is not fixed. Identity, which can be established only within it, is also never fixed. "The manifestations of who the speaker and doer unexchangeably is, though it is plainly visible, retain a curious intangibility that confounds all efforts towards unequivocal verbal expression," Arendt explains (1958, 181). As a result, "The realm of human affairs, strictly speaking, consists of the web of human relationships which exists wherever men live together" (184).

John McGowan succinctly condenses Arendt's ideas on identity: "Identity is not something one possesses inherently, internally, or essentially as an individual entity. In fact, it is probably wrong to think of identity as the kind of thing that can be possessed. One doesn't so much *have* an identity as *discover* an identity when it manifests itself in various interactions with others" (1998, 22). Identity, then, is never fixed and never isolated, having meaning only within the greater contextual structure of relationships, affecting the relationship web and simultaneously being affected by it.

Arendt considers the realm of human identity as a transcendence of the physical world of the natural, which is represented by the fact of our bodies as mere "physical objects." From this standpoint, she is admittedly not in the camp of contemporary, ecologically aware philosophy. Arendt's attitude toward the human-nature relationship is conventional. For her, the realm of the human is dependent upon but superior to the natural. Her understanding of identity is anything but conventional, however, and it happens to resonate with ecology in that it is founded on an awareness not of essence but of relationships. Arendt herself considered identity a strictly human phenomenon, the thing that most definitively makes us human, which is to say, that which is beyond the merely natural.

For Williams, the identity that she constructs in the text indeed comes from her interactions with other persons. These persons, as we have seen, are not only human. They include the nonhuman persons of landscape and its creatures, and her interactions with them take place on the emergent plane of existence that, to Arendt, exists only in connection with the human realm, but that to Williams's understanding is also characteristic of nature.

She uses this identity as part of a two-pronged strategy, to connect with nature and simultaneously to reconnect with and subvert male-dominated political structures. She manages the latter because a key aspect of Williams's stance in *Refuge* is that she maintains an awareness of the legitimacy of her role as a speaking political presence, even if at times it is forced to be an underground, subversive presence. "A museum is a good place to be quietly subversive on behalf of the land," she writes. "I close my door and begin to plot my strategy" (44). When asked, when she is arrested in an act of civil disobedience, what the pen and pad of paper tucked in her boot are, she responds, "weapons" (290), an utterance that underscores the mode of her resistance to the patriarchal forces prompting her arrest.

Williams maintains from the beginning that "this story is my return" (4).

Though she returns armed with the weapons of language, her reasserted presence is less confrontational than it might seem. Her return is to the world of the political, but she comes back changed by new sets of relationships forged while in retreat, including the landscape and its nonhuman persons, but also, interestingly, imagined persons of past Native American cultures and even, at one point, with the spirits of dead persons. Her stories aren't weapons in the conventional sense, meant for attack. They are language-based representations of her deeds, which will affect the polity of which she is a part from the inside. Though her rhetoric often seems confrontational, she returns with an overall understanding that her participation in a polity is a more effective way of changing it than to attack it, and she understands that the writer of stories asserts an especially effective political participation. The fact that she writes is more important than her rhetoric.

The existence of a polity to which Williams can return finally matters even more than her identity because identity is meaningless outside of the relational context of the polis. In her recognition of the critical importance of a polis, Williams shares much with Hannah Arendt. Arendt insisted that it is free participation in the polis that gives life meaning. "It was the polis," she writes, in response to a quotation from Sophocles' *Oedipus at Colonus,* "the space of men's free deeds and living words, which could endow life with splendor" (1963, 285).[1]

Arendt understood that suffering and loss are aspects of the human condition that we must bear, but she felt that free political interaction could make the human condition not only bearable, but splendid as well. For Central European Jews like Arendt, the ordinary suffering inherent in the human condition swelled to inconceivably monstrous proportions in the twentieth century, and while Arendt managed, after great hardship, to escape the Holocaust herself, it haunted her thinking. Once the horrific details of European genocide became clear to the world, Arendt's stunned response was that *"This ought not to have happened"* (1994, 14). She then bent her considerable intellect toward an attempt to explain why indeed it did happen. In the resulting text, *The Origins of Totalitarianism,* she proposes that the political and social nightmares of the twentieth century were the end result of a long-developing historical process that created mass groups of "stateless" people who were not afforded protection by any nation. Even in the case of the Jews at the hands of the Nazis, Arendt notes:

> The Nazis started their extermination of the Jews by first depriving them of all legal status (the status of second class citizenship) and cutting them off from

the world of the living by herding them into ghettoes and concentration camps; and before they set the gas chambers into motion they had carefully tested the ground and found out to their satisfaction that no country would claim these people. The point is that a condition of complete rightlessness was created before their right to live was challenged. (1948, 296)

The process of the ultimate dehumanization of genocide begins by the creation of masses of "placeless" persons. Place becomes crucial in Arendt's thinking, both literally and metaphorically:

> The fundamental deprivation of human rights is manifested first and above all in the deprivation of a place in the world which makes opinions significant and actions effective. Something much more fundamental than freedom or justice, which are the rights of citizens, is at stake when belonging to the community into which one is born is no longer a matter of course and not belonging no longer a matter of choice, or when one is placed in a situation where, unless he commits a crime, his treatment by others does not depend on what he does or does not do. This extremity, and nothing else, is the situation of people deprived of human rights. They are deprived, not of the right to freedom, but of the right to action; not of the right to think whatever they please, but of the right to opinion. (296)

Persons included in any political community are afforded protection by it and are empowered by it to act and speak freely—within its confines. Arendt theorizes that persons are not innately born free in the political world as it has evolved; freedom is contextually endowed by membership in a polity, and polity must exist in a place. European Jews were stripped of membership in any state by a totalitarian political system. The result, writes John Mc-Gowan, is that, "[b]y placing certain persons outside the boundaries of any state, by stripping them of citizenship in any polity, totalitarianism creates persons upon whom it can unleash the most fearsome terror" (1998, 6).

It is necessary to make the point that patriarchal governmental and political institutions of the United States, and, locally, of Utah, which *Refuge* criticizes explicitly and implicitly, are not totalitarian systems by Arendt's measure, and I do not believe that Williams would see them in that light, either. Totalitarianism represents the apotheosis of mass movements, with race-thinking (which evolves into outright racism), imperialism, and nationalism figuring in a process that leads eventually to totalitarianism, a complete eradication of individual rights and identity, enforced by terror. Arendt was, of course, horrified by the realities of totalitarianism, and this led her to suspicion of any kind of mass movement, because mass movements and mass thinking are what lead to totalitarianism. She implicates the rise of bureaucracy, nationalism, and the bourgeois obsession with the accumulation of capital as among the instrumental mass forces that diminish the vitality of political spaces. In order for relationships of any kind to have real meaning for Arendt, they must be local, and the political spaces they create will of necessity cherish the diversity of individuals. Mass movements tend to homogenize groups and to undermine the individuality that a polity encourages—bureaucracy, for example, diminishes plurality by substituting varied interpersonal relationships with a simplistic relationship to the machinery of the state.

Mass totalitarianism itself is not actually a "political" system by Arendt's definition; it is, rather, the opposite of the political. Politics, for Arendt, depends on plurality and on involvement by individuals in a variety of relationships—familial, work, citizenship, the relationship with the self that we call thought. Identity for Arendt is fluid, and it is determined in context by relationships. In contrast, Arendt writes, "Totalitarian movements are organizations of atomized, isolated individuals" (1948, 323). As McGowan notes, "[T]he world is diminished when this full plurality of relationships is truncated. Arendt means this quite literally; reality shrinks where plurality is scaled back. Totalitarianism offers the most extreme case of such diminishment. . . . But totalitarianism is only one example of working against plurality" (1998, 23).

The establishment of utterly totalitarian states, especially in Russia and Germany, compelled Arendt to search for an explanation of what had been unprecedented, but her explanation of the history that led to their establishment traces a long developmental process that progressively withered the established polities of Europe. Other ways of working against plurality are more at issue in *Refuge,* so I will leave considerations of totalitarianism behind, acknowledging that they were what gave rise initially to Hannah Arendt's thinking about the nature of human politics. But clearly, Terry Tempest Williams sees influences that, even if they are less than fully totalitarian, nevertheless work to threaten the pluralistic polities that give her life meaning and that threaten to diminish the reality of a life lived in connection with nature's places.

As the natural world literally shrinks away by actions that stem from our inability to acknowledge nature's person, the reality in which we exist as humans literally shrinks as well. These actions are responsible for catastrophic environmental degradation, and ultimately, Williams makes clear, they are directly responsible for the loss of her mother. In Arendtian terms, they threaten us as physical beings and as human beings.

The results of the lack of open political membership for women and the land are made explicit in the final chapter of *Refuge*, "The Clan of the One-Breasted Women," when it becomes apparent that the cancers that killed Williams's mother and grandmother may very well have been caused by nuclear weapons testing conducted in the Nevada desert in the 1950s. It appears more than merely tragic coincidence that ovarian cancer and breast cancer—diseases that prey on women—are the means by which a "most fearsome terror" is unleashed on an unsuspecting populace. Women and nature, for Williams, thus appear to be connected on political rather than essentialist grounds in that they are both excluded from a viable political space that should have protected them.

Early in *Refuge*, Williams makes this position clear when she relates a conversation with a friend: "We spoke of rage. Of women and landscape. How our bodies and the bodies of earth have been mined" (10). The connection of women and landscape here seems indeed to be on the basis of victim status, a result of the loss of political participation influencing the forces that "mine" women and landscapes. Williams's anger is the land's anger, her pain is the land's pain, and her political return, through her presence as activist and writer, comes with her representing the land as a participating, speaking presence.

Given the state of our presence on earth, nearly all ecological writing has a political subtext. Unchecked economic and political systems behave toward the earth in ways that mirror how totalitarian systems have behaved toward disfranchised peoples—which is to say that persons outside of the political community are not afforded protection from terror and murder, and the earth, which by definition in a patriarchal understanding of humans and nature is "extrapolitical," or not capable of meriting a political voice, is also open to fearsome abuse. American society, then, though not totalitarian toward its people, behaves in totalitarian ways toward a disfranchised, displaced nature.

This is ultimately self-destructive, and in bringing these attitudes to light, Williams acts with the well-being of her entire political community in mind. As John Tallmadge proclaims, "Hers is a 'heroics of witness'" (1998, 205). With her return, she transforms her political space by extending it outward over the landscape, making it into an ecopolitical space. She takes advantage of the participation in culture that is embodied by the language of the text as a means of effecting change in that culture, which will open the way to fuller participation in cultural and political systems by both women and nonhuman entities. The "voices" of birds and the landscape will then be represented in the polis, and they in turn will contribute to a literally expanded reality. As Williams tells us, "My refuge exists in my capacity to love" (178). Refuge comes not in retreat, but in full engagement with the web of relationships.

Note

1. Arendt translates Sophocles: "Not to be born prevails over all meaning uttered in words; by far the second-best for life, once it has appeared, is to go as swiftly as possible whence it came." This quote from Theseus is uttered as commentary on Oedipus's life in banishment from the Athenian polis.

Works Cited

Abram, David. 1996. *The Spell of the Sensuous.* New York: Vintage Books.

Arendt, Hannah. 1948. *The Origins of Totalitarianism.* San Diego: Harcourt Brace.

———. 1958. *The Human Condition.* Chicago: University of Chicago Press.

———. 1963. *On Revolution.* New York: Viking.

———. 1994. *Essays in Understanding, 1930–1954.* Edited by Jerome Kohn. New York: Harcourt Brace.

Armbruster, Karla. 1995. "Rewriting a Genealogy with the Earth: Women and Nature in the Works of Terry Tempest Williams." *Southwestern American Literature* 21:209–20.

Birkeland, Janice. 1993. "Ecofeminism: Linking Theory and Practice." In *Ecofeminism: Women, Animals, Nature,* edited by Greta Gaard, 13–59. Philadelphia: Temple University Press.

Carlassare, Elizabeth. 1994. "Essentialism in Ecofeminist Discourse." In *Key Concepts in Critical Theory: Ecology,* edited by Carolyn Merchant, 220–34. Atlantic Highlands, N.J.: Humanities Press.

Glotfelty, Cheryll. 1996. "Introduction: Literary Studies in an Age of Environmental Crisis." In *The Ecocriticism Reader,* edited by Cheryll Glotfelty and Harold Fromm, xv–xxxvii. Athens: University of Georgia Press.

Honig, Bonnie. 1995. "Introduction: The Arendt Question in Feminism." In *Feminist Interpretations of Hannah Arendt,* edited by Bonnie Honig, 1–16. University Park: Pennsylvania State University Press.

Kircher, Cassandra. 1996. "Rethinking Dichotomies in Terry Tempest Williams's *Refuge.*" *ISLE* 3:95–113.

Lopez, Barry. 1986. *Arctic Dreams: Imagination and Desire in a Northern Landscape.* New York: Scribner's.

McGowan, John. 1998. *Hannah Arendt: An Introduction.* Minneapolis: University of Minnesota Press.

Rich, Adrienne. 1979. *On Lies, Secrets, and Silence: Selected Prose, 1966–1978.* New York: Norton.

Tallmadge, John. 1998. "Beyond the Excursion: Initiatory Themes in Annie Dillard and Terry Tempest Williams." In *Reading the Earth: New Directions in the Study of Literature and the Environment,* edited by Michael P. Branch, Rochelle Johnson, Daniel Patterson, and Scott Slovic, 197–207. Moscow: University of Idaho Press.

Williams, Terry Tempest. 1991. *Refuge: An Unnatural History of Family and Place.* New York: Pantheon Books.

SELECT BIBLIOGRAPHY

Books by Terry Tempest Williams

The Secret Language of Snow. 1984. Coauthored by Ted Major. Illustrated by Jennifer Dewey. San Francisco: Sierra Club Books.

Pieces of White Shell: A Journey to Navajoland. 1984. Albuquerque: University of New Mexico Press.

Between Cattails. 1985. Illustrated by Peter Parnall. New York: Charles Scribner's Sons.

Coyote's Canyon. 1989. Photographs by John Telford. Salt Lake City: Peregrine-Smith Books.

Earthly Messengers. 1989. Salt Lake City: Western Slope Press.

Refuge: An Unnatural History of Family and Place. 1991. New York: Pantheon Books.

An Unspoken Hunger: Stories from the Field. 1994. New York: Pantheon Books.

Desert Quartet: An Erotic Landscape. 1995. New York: Pantheon Books.

Leap. 2000. New York: Pantheon Books.

Red: Passion and Patience in the Desert. 2001. New York: Pantheon Books.

Patriotism and the American Land. 2002. Coauthored by Richard Nelson and Barry Lopez. Great Barrington, Mass.: Orion Society.

Books Edited by Terry Tempest Williams

Great and Peculiar Beauty: A Utah Centennial Reader. 1995. Edited with Thomas J. Lyon. Salt Lake City: Gibbs-Smith.

Testimony: Writers in Defense of the Wilderness. 1996. Compiled with Stephen Trimble. Minneapolis: Milkweed Editions.

New Genesis: A Mormon Reader on Land and Community. 1998. Edited with William B. Smart and Gibbs M. Smith. Salt Lake City: Gibbs-Smith.

Scholarly Work on Terry Tempest Williams

Allister, Mark. 2001. "An Unnatural History Made Natural: Terry Tempest Williams's *Refuge.*" In *Refiguring the Map of Sorrow: Nature Writing and Autobiography,* 58–80. Charlottesville: University Press of Virginia.

Armbruster, Karla. 1995. "Rewriting a Genealogy with the Earth: Women and Nature in the Works of Terry Tempest Williams." *Southwestern American Literature* 21:209–20.

Glotfelty, Cheryll. 1996. "Flooding the Boundaries of Form: Terry Tempest Williams's Ecofeminist *Unnatural History.*" In *Change in the American West: Exploring the Human Dimension,* edited by Stephen Tchudi, 158–67. Reno: University of Nevada Press.

Kircher, Cassandra. 1996. "Rethinking Dichotomies in Terry Tempest Williams's *Refuge.*" *ISLE: Interdisciplinary Studies in Literature and Environment* 3:97–113.

Libby, Brooke. 2000. "Nature Writing as *Refuge:* Autobiography in the Natural World." In *Reading under the Sign of Nature: New Essays in Ecocriticism,* edited by John Tallmadge and Henry Harrington, 251–64. Salt Lake City: University of Utah Press.

Mitchell, Charles. 2003. "Reclaiming the Sacred Landscape: Terry Tempest Williams, Kathleen Norris, and the Other Nature Writing." *Women's Studies* 32:169–81.

Petersen, Boyd. 2002. "Landscapes of Seduction: Terry Tempest Williams's *Desert Quartet* and the Biblical Song of Songs." *ISLE: Interdisciplinary Studies in Literature and Environment* 9:91–104.

Ross-Bryant, Lynn. 1997. "The Self in Nature: Four American Autobiographies." *Soundings* 80:83–104.

Schauffler, F. Marina. 2003. *Turning to Earth: Stories of Ecological Conversion.* Charlottesville: University Press of Virginia.

Schmidt, Maia Saj. 1998. "Literary Testimonies of Illness and the Reshaping of Social Memory." *A/B: Auto/Biography Studies* 13:71–91.

Tallmadge, John. 1998. "Beyond the Excursion: Initiatory Themes in Annie Dillard and Terry Tempest Williams." In *Reading the Earth: New Directions in the Study of Literature and the Environment,* edited by Michael P. Branch et al., 197–207. Moscow: University of Idaho Press.

Whitt, Jan. 2002. "'The Sorcery of Literature': Terry Tempest Williams and Her Stories of the West." *Journal of the West* 41:83–89.

Yuki, Masami. 1998. "Narrating the Invisible Landscape: Terry Tempest Williams's Erotic Correspondence to Nature." *Studies in American Literature* 34:79–97.

CONTRIBUTORS

KATHERINE R. CHANDLER is Assistant Professor of English at St. Mary's College of Maryland. An originating member of the college's interdisciplinary environmental studies program, she teaches courses in nature writing in addition to composition and literature. She has published in *Philological Quarterly* and *English Language Notes,* but her scholarly interests have shifted to spirit, place, and healing, with publications on Terry Tempest Williams, teaching outdoors, and Linda Hogan.

LISA DIEDRICH received her Ph.D. in women's studies from Emory University and is currently a lecturer in women's studies at the State University of New York at Stony Brook. Her research and teaching focus on bioethics, disability studies, and autobiography.

ELIZABETH DODD is Professor of English at Kansas State University, where she teaches literature and creative writing. She is the author of two collections of poetry, *Like Memory, Caverns* and *Archetypal Light;* a critical study of twentieth-century women poets, *The Veiled Mirror and the Woman Poet;* and *Prospect,* a collection of essays.

LISA EASTMOND is the director of the Utah Valley State College Writing Center. She edits for an environmental journal, *Borrowed Earth,* at Brigham Young University where she is completing an M.A. in rhetoric, focusing on the rhetorical power of landscape and story. She is dedicated not only to writing but also to the Utah landscapes that she calls home. She volunteers at organizations such as the Southern Utah Wilderness Alliance and spends much of her free time up in the canyons near her home.

MELISSA A. GOLDTHWAITE received both her M.F.A. in creative writing and her Ph.D. in rhetoric and composition from The Ohio State University. She is Assistant Professor of English at Saint Joseph's University, where she teaches courses in rhetoric, composition, nature writing, poetry, and creative non-fiction. Her essays and poems have appeared in a number of books and journals, and she is coauthor of *The St. Martin's Guide to Teaching Writing,* 5th ed.

NATHANIEL I. HART is Professor of English Emeritus at the University of Minnesota at Morris, where he has taught English and American literature and served as head of the Division of the Humanities. His conference papers and publications include discussions of Victorian and twentieth-century English poetry, Native American literature, scholarly editing, and the teaching of English.

RICHARD HUNT is a graduate of the Program in Literature and Environment at the University of Nevada at Reno. He currently lives in Iowa, where besides teaching writing courses at Kirkwood Community College, he is working on a collection of place-based essays and continuing his study of the intersections of faith and science in American nature writing. Between books, he plays his guitar and mandolin as often as possible.

ROBERT MILTNER is Assistant Professor of English at Kent State University, Stark Campus, in Canton, Ohio, where he teaches composition, literature, and creative writing. His essays, poems, and stories have been published in many journals, and he is the author of five chapbooks of poetry: *The Seamless Serial Hour, On the Off-Ramp, Four Crows on a Phone Line, A Box of Light: Prose Poems,* and *Against the Simple,* winner of a Wick chapbook award. He is also the author of two artists' books: *Ghost of a Chance* with waterless lithographer Wendy Collin Sorin, and a forthcoming collection of microfictions, *Jealous Light,* with letterpress printer and bookbinder Keith Berger.

MARY NEWELL has a master's degree in English literature from Columbia University as well as a master's in biobehavioral studies from Teachers' College, Columbia University. She is a doctoral candidate at Fordham University in English literature, with a focus on ecocriticism. Newell has taught at Marymount College, Queens College, and Westchester Community College. She presented "The Nectar of Experience: Emily Dickinson's Bee Poems" on an ecofeminist panel at the Northeast MLA conference, 2002.

SHARON A. REYNOLDS completed an M.A. in American literature at San Diego State University and an M.F.A. in creative writing from Vermont College in Montpelier after twenty-one years as a career naval officer. Currently, she is an adjunct faculty member in the English Department at Palomar College, in San Marcos, California. She also conducts independent seminars and private consulting on writing.

TINA RICHARDSON has recently completed graduate studies at the University of Oregon in both English and women's studies. Her research focuses on the intersection of literature and the environment, with particular interest in environmental justice as illuminated by feminist theory and perspectives. Recently, her research has become increasingly focused on breast cancer as an environmental justice issue, as her contribution to this collection illustrates.

JEANNETTE E. RILEY is Assistant Professor of women's studies and English at UMass Dartmouth. Much of her work focuses on contemporary women writers and feminist theory, with a special interest in ecofeminism and writers Terry Tempest Williams, Gretel Erhlich, North T. Cairn, and Mary Oliver. In addition to teaching courses in women's studies and contemporary American literature, Riley has published works on Irish poet Eavan Boland and Adrienne Rich and presented papers on Barbara Kingsolver, Elizabeth Bishop, and Toni Morrison at national conferences.

MAUREEN K. SCHIRACK graduated from Kent State University and is currently working on her master's in English literature at the University of Akron. She lives in Canton, Ohio, with her husband and three daughters. In her spare time she writes poetry.

BART H. WELLING is a Ph.D. candidate in English at the University of Virginia. His dissertation, "Inescapable Earth: William Faulkner, Yoknapatawpha, and the Book of Nature," approaches Faulkner's modernist vision of the natural world from a hybrid ecocritical–textual studies perspective, exploring Faulkner's place in an understudied American tradition of self-referential landscape writing. Bart and his wife, Elizabeth, have three children.

MASAMI RAKER YUKI is Associate Professor of English at Kanazawa University in Japan. She is the author of several articles on American and Japanese environmental literature and soundscape. A Japanese translator of American nature writing, literary criticism, and ecocriticism and theory, Yuki cotranslated Terry Tempest Williams's *Desert Quartet*. She is currently working on a book that examines soundscapes in contemporary American and Japanese environmental literature.

KARL ZUELKE studied biology and English literature at the University of Cincinnati and received an M.F.A. from Indiana University in fiction writing. He recently completed his doctoral dissertation at the University of Cincinnati, a multidisciplinary examination of the ways that writers in a number of genres, including science writing and postmodern fiction, represent the natural world. He lives in the Cincinnati area with his wife and son.

INDEX